NEW
american
plays
1

NEW american plays 1

STARTING MONDAY
Anne Commire
YANKEE DAWG YOU DIE
Philip Kan Gotanda
THE BUG
Richard Strand
INTERROGATING THE NUDE
Doug Wright

with an introduction by Peter Filichia

HEINEMANN  Portsmouth, NH

Heinemann Educational Books, Inc.
361 Hanover Street
Portsmouth, NH 03801-3959
Offices and agents throughout the world

Library of Congress Cataloging-in-Publication Data

New American plays/with an introduction by Peter Filichia.
    p.   cm.
   Contents: 1. Starting Monday / Anne Commire. Yankee dawg you die / Philip Kan Gotanda. The bug / Richard Strand. Interrogating the nude / Doug Wright—2. Judevine / David Budbill. Daytrips / Jo Carson. Pill Hill / Samuel L. Kelley. Away alone / Janet Noble.
   ISBN 0-435-08604-9 (1).— ISBN 0-435-08605-7 (2)
   1. American drama—20th century. I. Filichia, Peter.
PS634.N364   1992
812'.5408—dc20   91—32100
                                               CIP

Series design and cover by Wladislaw Finne
Printed in the United States of America
92 93 94 95 96 10 9 8 7 6 5 4 3 2 1

contents

Welcome to a book of problems, struggles, and dilemmas—in short, *drama*. That means drama in both dictionary senses of the word: drama as in conflict, drama as in theatre.

It means you'll find some pertinent questions raised and answered in these four plays. Doug Wright's *Interrogating the Nude* wonders if it's a crime to try something artistically new, while Richard Strand's *The Bug* fears that we're fast losing our humanity in a computer age. As for that question that's plagued mankind since the dawn of time—will youth and old age ever come to terms?—that's what's on Philip Kan Gotanda's mind in *Yankee Dawg You Die*. The demands of friendship—and the willingness of some to do for their friends some very difficult tasks—is what's on Anne Commire's in *Starting Monday*.

Some of the plays play fast and loose with the unities of time, place and action, while others adhere to the preferences that Aristotle held dear. The playwrights have opted for approaches as varied as dadaism, crisp cosmopolitan dialogue, and plain ol' idiomatic conversation. Their characters argue, challenge, and try one-upsmanship; they express idealism, blatant human emotions, and wildly divergent points of view—all the ingredients, of course, that make for drama in each wonderful sense of the word.

STARTING MONDAY

Emily Dickinson once said, "We never know how tall we are till we are called to rise," and playwright Anne Commire proves it in *Starting Monday*. No, it's not a play about a diet, but on a much tougher subject—cancer and death. Not only does Commire make victim and caretaker rise to deal with the illness, but the playwright herself is also tall enough in the way she writes.

Commire has the fine sense of observation you'd expect

from a good writer; "Baby chicks peck 10,000 times to get outta the shell" is the type of information a real writer jots down and then puts to good use some day. But it's much harder for any writer to come up with the original observations; Commire's just fine there, too — like when she recalls a kid who used to give her the creeps: "I'd always get the same kind of ice cream she did, so she wouldn't ask for a lick." Add to these a very nice way with words (describing people who buss each other while leaning forward as giving the other "A-frame hugs") and you have a feeling early on that you're reading a genuinely gifted writer.

When you read her characters, you're sure of it. Commire orchestrates well the two smartly detailed opposites. She knows you can tell something about people when one will use a broken crayon and one won't; as Lynne says, "Some ride roller coasters; some wait below, holding the coats."

Still, as is the story of many opposites, the pair wind up becoming friends: Lynne likes "the kid" in Ellis, and Ellis needs "the mother" in Lynne — because Ellis isn't natively courageous in a play where she's going to need to be. Ellis, as would many of us awaiting a diagnosis, swears that if she's got cancer, she won't take chemotherapy, she just won't — until she actually hears the bad news. Then, as so many of us do, she immediately accepts the treatments, and enters the world where previously unknown and irrelevant medical terms are to be learned and understood. "You nodded like you know," Lynne says of her friend's seeming to understand what she'd just heard. "I nod well," Ellis admits.

Not that Ellis is all endearing answers. Commire's smart to make Ellis a director; that explains her great anxiety once the disease takes over, when she's not in control. "Demanding [that] I be rational is controlling," she accuses, eventually goading Lynne into confrontation — "We'd never be together if I weren't dying." The playwright doesn't pull her punches here, either: Ellis at one point claims to want Lynne out of her life, and Lynne is only too glad to leave. For a moment, anyway. She comes back. Good friends always do.

Commire shows a world unsympathetic to the disease, where cops still give tickets, where nuts-and-bolts issues of money and power of attorney must be discussed, where waiting two more minutes for a doctor is, pro rated, too much time for a terminally ill patient to give up. Yet she also shows the human ability to be optimistic: when Ellis's doctor is late in seeing her, Lynne gives the best possible interpretation; perhaps he's a better doctor for taking his time with others, maybe the one who's seeing many patients is doing a slapdash job. And when Lynne wonders, do you buy your friend with cancer the travel or the economy size toothpaste, we love her (and Ms. Commire) for buying the largest size possible.

Even the stage directions are entertainingly well written. For example, Commire says that Lynne, when administering a treatment to Ellis, "struggles with glove — [it's] like an udder gone wild." Reading stage directions may not seem like much of a thrill, but good writers who express themselves well in dialogue don't necessarily have the muse desert them when writing stage directions. And while it's one thing to see a stage full of medical equipment, it's profoundly another to read a playwright's long list of individual items that poignantly lets us know that Commire knows what she's writing about.

But even more touching: at the end of the first act, we see Lynne in a l-o-n-g scene of struggling to get everything right when administering the first home treatment to Ellis, every move carrying with it a myriad of germs, bubbles, clots, and booby traps; then, at the beginning of Act 2, some time later, we see Lynne, now proficient with all that had previously stymied her, managing to deliver this same treatment while barely giving it a thought.

At this point, some may be asking, why read a play replete with such unpleasant situations? No, it's not what Dietz and Schwartz meant when they wrote "That's Entertainment," but *Starting Monday* shows us how two human beings, victim and observer, coped with a debilitating illness — and we can use any advice we can get on that hard-to-prepare-for subject. Reading such a play, then, introduces us to the inevitable illnesses that, like it or not, will be coming in our lives — if not directly to us, then to others we know and care about.

It's moving, too, to discover a real hero, the type more increasingly seen: the friend who does what used to be done solely by the family. Lynne and Ellis weren't lovers, nor did they have to be for this level of commitment to occur. Commire shows us the great rewards in stretching the boundaries of friendship — and also reminds us not to put our lives on hold. "Starting Monday, I'll do it." Whatever plan or dream "it" is for any of us, we should start now, in case we don't have time to procrastinate.

YANKEE DAWG YOU DIE

The generational struggle between young and old is a time-honored theme in drama — so much so you may already be sighing because it's *too* time-honored and you're not in the mood to read another play about it. But don't despair, for here's a new slant from Philip Kan Gotanda, in *Yankee Dawg You Die*.

Victor is a late-middle-aged Oriental actor who has made a good career — and an even better living — playing stereotypic Orientals in Charlie Chan—like movies and Broadway's *Tea Cakes and Moon Songs*. "I have never turned down a role," he says proudly to young Bradley.

But Bradley doesn't see it Victor's way. He's an "Asian" actor who can't respect the *Flower Drum Song*—Starkist Tuna school of performing in which Victor participated and therefore condoned. With the rampant idealism that only youth can have (or afford), Bradley works at the Theatre Project of Asian America, and also recently appeared "in a Matthew Iwasaki film."

It takes a while before the two even call each other by their first names. Sure, Bradley has some condescending admiration for Victor; how else would he be able to recite the venerable actor's big scene — the one that got him an Academy Award nomination for Best Supporting Actor? And he'll even join Victor in a *Tea Cakes* musical number just for the fun of it.

But it's not long before he stops. It *is* degrading. It's not that Victor wasn't a good actor; it's that, according to Bradley, he didn't make good choices. Still, as Victor explains unapologetically, "Back then you did everything." Why should he apologize, he reasons; he once so impressed Anna Mae Wong and Sessue Hayakawa that they gave him a "standing o." What, he challenges, has Bradley accomplished? He calls Bradley's "real work" at the Theatre Project just "Amateur Hour" where performers are "scared of the outside world" (though he doesn't really feel that way; he knows what Bradley's talking about). Then he brands that "independent film," as the young actor calls it, "a low-budget movie." (Ah, but don't come down too hard on Bradley; what actor doesn't use euphemisms when describing what he's done?)

They also argue about drinking, smoking, exercising, and even nose jobs. They'll compare their agents (Victor is, ironically enough, represented by an Asian firm, while Bradley is a William Morris client). And as is of course the case with any play about performers, there's the standard one-upsmanship of actor versus actor that would erupt no matter to what race(s) the individuals belonged.

Bradley has the resistance to prejudice that only the next generation can have, because he didn't have to suffer the slings and arrows as directly as Victor did. But, credit where it's due, when he's tested professionally, he's true to himself, refusing to play a giggling Japanese in a commercial.

And he pays for it. The phone stops ringing, and the previously idealistic Bradley must come to terms with the ways of the world. Ironically enough, Victor, after years of doing and delivering exactly what was asked, now has the financial wherewithal and independence to act in what he wants. Does that make Victor correct to view the glass as half full? — "At least an Oriental was on screen acting." And does he really believe it? Or does he buy it because he must, for what would he think of himself if he entertained the other interpretation?

As in any good play, both characters are right — and

wrong. Bradley has the luxury (and lesser accomplishments) that those with youth and potential always have; Victor has the craft that's been developed through years of performances and experience, and has achieved the best possible career. The irony is that the two characters, heritage in common, are both on the same side: each bemoans roles he could have played that were portrayed by Caucasians but needn't have been; each must contend with the inevitable white man's confusion over things Chinese and Japanese.

And as in any *very* good play, each comes around to understand the other's point of view. Playwright Gotanda has seen to it that he's been fair to both, while also including some universal observations about the struggle of business versus art, and the need for legitimate heroes. The playwright of course still isn't satisfied with the system, but he wants us to know that through examining it he's found it a hard one and that for him to portray it any differently would be as false as an Oriental stereotype.

THE BUG

If you're chagrined at the prospects of merely reading and not seeing *The Bug*, be assuaged that if you were at a production of the play, you wouldn't for much of the night see most of the cast's faces, anyway. They're almost always behind computer terminals.

Except for Dennis.

In Stanley Kubrick's classic *2001: A Space Odyssey*, Hal the Computer wound up having more human emotions than the astronauts "he" served. Playwright Richard Strand apparently agrees—his play introduces us to a trio of people who have, for all intents and purposes, become machines by virtue of their rubber-stamp jobs (or whatever today's high-tech term for "rubber-stamp jobs" is) at Jericho, Inc.

But in walks Dennis, who is unwittingly about to fight the battle of Jericho. In this librarylike atmosphere where no one talks, Dennis is a contemporary Everyman (though he does have a bit of Inspector Clouseau in him), but his ordinariness makes him extraordinary in a world of computers.

Not that he remembers that. Why should he? All of us can often forget our human worth in an age of awfully smart machines. But Strand's here to remind us of the realities. Sure, Dennis's brain has atrophied a bit; why else would he ask so many times, no matter how reassured, that he not be transferred to St. Louis? But that does make him human after all — especially compared with the higher-ups at Jericho.

These include Linda, who points out the "good thing about red tape" and matter-of-factly says, after being nasty, "I don't want you to think I'm being rude" (for she's lost the ability to realize that indeed she has been); Kimberly, a worker who "goes by the numbers" and insists that an "efficient operation does not take shortcuts" (a claim that turns out to be quite ironic as the play unfolds); and David, the type who doesn't apologize for not having a sense of humor (he doesn't see it as a flaw), and, when a gun is pulled on him, is more worried about his computer terminal than his own life. "Don't shoot the computer," it seems, has replaced the ol' cry of "Don't shoot the piano player."

When the three suggest that Dennis go through channels, he's amenable enough — but even his compromising doesn't take him closer to getting what he wants. He's not afraid of appearing vulnerable, for he expects they'll be considerate (they're not), though he does have the fear we all have over losing our jobs and is careful not to complain in a company where the policy is "We don't complain." (The preferred euphemism is "report.") Yes, a newspaper help-wanted may have boasted of a "most exciting" job, but, as usual, it's one that often doesn't quite live up to the promise, not in an office where employees of course don't want to get involved and are always ready to call Security, and where one employee doesn't seem to have authority even to let someone walk onto the carpet; that must be left to her superior.

Nevertheless, Dennis soon finds himself on the carpet in more ways than one. He turns out to prize his humanity more than even he realizes. Once a report points out it's "unlikely he would be a serious threat," Dennis becomes more threatening; when the way he *dresses* is criticized, well, that and only that gets him to turn in his supervisor — who also turns out to be a bug in the computer. You've heard of inmates running the asylum? Here are computers running the company — until Dennis starts playing with his computer, and playing and playing. In the process, he discovers a bug peculiar to these machines: If Dennis had asked a person the constant questions he asked of the computer, the person would have gotten annoyed and Dennis would have been too embarrassed to continue asking. But a computer doesn't mind the questions Dennis asks of it, nor how often he asks them. And that bears the type of fruit that sends Dennis on an adventure. At first Strand is talking about a bug in the computer, but we soon see that the bug in the system is Dennis himself.

And because a playwright, not a computer, wrote this play, we know whose side he's on. Watching Strand — and Dennis — make "the machine people" become human is a treat, for up until that point, the cry "I'm only human" has had the emphasis placed on "only." Strand shows us what a great "only" that is.

INTERROGATING THE NUDE

In the time between the writing of *Interrogating the Nude* and the writing of this introduction, Art and Politics were waging war. It was Robert Mapplethorpe and his controversial photographs versus Jesse Helms, who decried The National Endowment for the Arts' funding the photographer's exhibitions.

How ironic, considering that *Interrogating the Nude* addresses similar issues. Doug Wright has chosen to write about Marcel Duchamp, who played havoc with the conventions of painting when he exhibited his *Nude Descending a Staircase* at the 1913 New York Armory Show. The cubist painting was judged a sensation by some, but more a "crime" by many traditionalists, for it didn't show the female form in the manner to which the art world had become accustomed. And so the Duchamp of Wright's play reacts to the traditionalists by essentially saying, if you claim that I "broke the laws" and you judge my painting a "crime," then I'll take responsibility for it.

The play, then, is hardly biography. Instead, this Duchamp shows up at a New York police station to confess his crime—of tearing apart a beautiful woman. Only trouble is, it takes a while for the Inspector to catch his meaning, just as it took some time for the public to catch up with Duchamp's painting. The Inspector calls Duchamp a monster (as did so many in the art world)—"Art and crime, they don't tango"—while being much more accommodating to a photographer named Man Ray, for "accuracy and detail—these are my interests."

Yes, the play also deals with the conflict between photography and painting. Ironically, it's the innovative painter who rails against the innovations of photography—that it "chops you up" and that even "in a photograph things aren't always what they seem." Photography's representative rebuts, "I don't invent pictures, I capture the truth.... Men test the limits of law every day to forward their careers: lawyers, bankers, politicians. Why should an artist behave differently?" Wright makes a case for and against photography's utter reality, giving both the assets and liabilities of the medium.

Wright gives us a metaphor while at the same time takes literally the charge of the "crime." (And isn't a marriage of metaphorical and literal what good avant-garde art should forge?) Moreover, in the spirit of the painter who eschewed conventions, Wright also made the adventurous stylistic decision to disregard naturalism, to disassemble and skewer the elements that make up his work. You may occasionally long for the conventional curves of an "ordinary," well-made play, but you may very well find yourself in admiration of Wright's staying true to the spirit of Duchamp's painting; indeed, he has succeeded in writing a literary equivalent of *Nude Descending a Staircase*.

Still, Wright knows there's more shape and structure to avant-garde pieces than meets the eye, and he fills his play with many prerequisites of more conventional drama, even including the Aristotlean unities of time, place, and action. "Try creating one thing without killing something else," his character says—but Wright takes it as a challenge and delivers.

So after all this, what does the play mean? Well, what did Duchamp have on his mind when alarming the art world? What was the meaning of the nude that was infamous for not being a nude at all? Some will say that Wright must mean that Duchamp's complaint was that his propelling the art world in new directions was ephemeral, quickly eclipsed by photography's technological advances. Others will insist that Wright means that painting can only portray the body while photography can be even more specific than painting, that it shows the mind, no, *invades* the mind. Add these to those who'll note that the artist must get into the mind of the other sex, and that he has the right to show things his figurative way as opposed to the photographer's literal way. But as poet John Ciardi said about yet another art form, *How Does a Poem Mean?* Wright has written a play, like Duchamp's painting, where you can choose your interpretation—which will be just fine with the playwright. As Duchamp says to the Inspector, "Fact or fiction—that's your department, not mine."

Of course, Wright is talking about himself, too, for he's written an unconventional, symbolic play. It's not what producers call "commercial"; don't look for *Interrogating the Nude* to overtake *Life with Father* as Broadway's longest-running play. What does it mean? That we want to know more about ourselves, so cubistic techniques could never be more popular than the specific realities of photography? That because art rejects naturalistic techniques, its models had to resort to photography? Reader's choice.

According to Wright, artists tell law and order what to do and how to behave. "I don't like it!" says the Inspector.

"It's not the way the world should be.... I shouldn't be listening to this pornography—I've got a wife and three kids at home." And though he wants to hear every detail, the Inspector is aware that "I can't put that in my report! I'd be discharged!" That's right; the nonartistic world can't; can artists still? You, the reader, today know better, for you now know the results of Mapplethorpe versus Helms.

anne commire
starting
monday

We met in May of 1978. We were attending the O'Neill Playwrights Conference.

Every year approximately fourteen plays and three teleplays are selected from over 1,500 submissions to be presented and honed during a month-long conference. In 1978 my play *Put Them All Together* was one of those chosen.

Based in New London, Connecticut, where the Long Island Sound meets the Atlantic Ocean, the O'Neill is a rural retreat for theatre professionals from all over the world. There are three theatres: a barn, a Greeklike amphitheater, and the "Instant" where plays compete with a magnificent copper beech tree for the audience's attention. All are filled with the echoes of many plays in their infancy: *Bent, Agnes of God, House of Blue Leaves*; the plays of August Wilson, Lee Blessing, John Patrick Shanley, Tom Babe.

Every summer, a flock of strolling players — actors, playwrights, directors — are sequestered in an airless dormitory, affectionately known as "the slammer." After four days of rehearsal, actors take to the stage and present each play — using minimal props and carrying the script. Big talents play big parts; big talents play bit parts. And leading it all: George White and Lloyd Richards — continually experimenting and enlarging. No pretention, no claims. Some of it works, some of it doesn't. No apologies.

I love the O'Neill. I love the mansion with its generous lawn sweeping down to the ocean. I love sitting on the sea porch at night as a New England fog rolls in, listening to the sound of the foghorn, the same foghorn that Eugene O'Neill used to such effect in *Long Day's Journey into Night*.

But before all this short-lived summer glory, the month of May brings on the infamous "*pre*conference." I have taken Valium only four times in my life — the four times I've had to read my plays at the preconference. In an ordeal known by playwright alumni as "the Rack," seventeen plays are read in three days to a casual audience of playwrights, directors, designers, administrators—all sitting or lounging on the floor, all wearing sunglasses or summer caps to hide their dozing eyes—while the drone of an outdoor lawnmower blends with the drone of the reader's voice. The only authors who benefit are actor-playwrights. Their eyes sparkle as they walk confidently to the podium: "I am going to read this play, and I have *every* part."

This is when you wish your two-hour play were a four-minute skit. This is when tomorrow's authors are making desperate cuts the night before. One playwright skipped that process. The play was six hours long. On Canadian history. After dinner. By 1:00 A.M. members of the audience were crawling out the back door, crawling up the steps, and crawling into bed.

The official reason given for this beneficent torture is that the director and set designer can clearly see the author's intention. But this ritual that smacks of de Sade has curious results. The neophyte playwrights band together with veteran playwrights to hear the horror stories of other preconferences: "What slot did you draw? After lunch? Don't be surprised if you hear a few snores. It's not your play; it's the tuna noodle casserole." Like boot camp or fraternity hazing, the playwrights come out of that weekend tightly knit.

The ploy is probably needed. Not known for their herd instincts, playwrights are people who hide in small rooms and periodically send out messages. Arriving in that first week in May, they tend to set themselves off from each other, standing like awkward teenagers around the grounds—some silent, some cynical, some intimidating, some meek, mostly strangers—sizing up their peers, amazed by their lack of stature.

The next day after breakfast brings the first session. Playwright #1 takes his seat in front of the group, clears his throat, and starts: "Act One, Scene One. Time: 1905. Place: Cincinnati...." You stare at him for two hours while he reads. You memorize his ears, the journey of his hairline, the shape of his nose, the twitching of his right eye. You hear his concerns, see his shyness. He is no longer intimidating. In fact, you decide that you like him. Second session; Playwright #2. You stare at her for two hours while she reads. You notice her socks, her hair, the mole on her cheek, the quiver in her voice. She is no longer intimidating. In fact, you decide that you like her. The bonding begins.

Now, seventeen playwrights who have been abruptly released from those small rooms for a thirty-six-hour party have a tendency to imbibe. That's why that particular May I went to the preconference with trepidation. The enjoyment of a "night on the town" can leave a hypo-glycemic with a debilitating hangover; about the only thing I can manage the "morning after" are old *Life* magazines and a few pathetic groans.

I'd been to the Playwrights Conference once before and I knew the score. I knew the first night there would be libations, so I brought my own. A large bottle of Martinelli's Sparkling Cider that came in a festive champagne bottle. We gathered. We heard the speeches of welcome. The wine was unveiled. But I remained seated on the floor with my Martinelli's by my side. As the party progressed and the pilgrims became happier, I chanced to look across the room. There, sitting on the floor, was a young woman, talking, laughing. I had met her earlier; she was there to direct the teleplays for the O'Neill. And by her side? A large bottle of Martinelli's Sparkling Cider. I stared at her Martinelli's, she stared at mine; kismet. Gravitating toward each other, we shared our fears of drinking, her fears of eating; she had recently lost weight and was down to a striking 114 pounds.

Later that evening, the revelers decided to continue the festivities at a local pub. Finding myself jammed around a crowded table — pitchers of beer to the right, pitchers of beer to the left — I turned to my Martinelli friend.

"Oh hell, let's have a drink. Want a drink?"

"No," she said. "And neither do you."

Seven hours later, as we stood next to each other in the breakfast line of the cafeteria, she turned to me.

"I'm going to have a donut. Want a donut?"

"No," I said. "And neither do you."

We were inseparable during the rest of the preconference, the rest of that year, and mentally inseparable the rest of her life.

In May of 1983 — five years from the day we met — I was once again due at the O'Neill preconference, but the night before found me living in a Santa Monica hospital room; the doctors were saying my Martinelli friend had two weeks to live. I called the O'Neill to see whether I could skip the preconference and still have my play presented that summer. They were kind, understanding, but the answer was a reluctant no. They had a rule, they said, each author had to read her play.

"Just come one night. Just read your play, and then go back."

When I returned to the room and told my friend, she was concerned.

"But you have to go," she urged. "You're going to need the O'Neill."

"No," I said. "I can't do that."

She died that night. I went to New London and read my script the following day.

For the next five years I worked on the play you are about to read — fearful that it might be dismissed as another disease of the week, fearful that it might be dismissed as a playwright's catharsis, fearful that it might be dismissed.

In May of 1988 — ten years from the day we met — I was again invited to the Playwrights Conference. I took my fourth Valium, sat down at the lectern, and read *Starting Monday*.

original productions

Starting Monday was first presented in Waterford, Connecticut, at the 1988 Eugene O'Neill National Playwrights Conference (with Linda Hunt, Deborah Hedwall,

Ellen Parker, Kaiulani Lee, Helen Stenborg, Kirk Jackson, Patrick Kerr, and Polly Draper; Amy Saltz directing). It was subsequently produced in Winterfest at the Yale Repertory Theatre with the following cast:

LYNNE	Sara Botsford
ELLIS	Leslie Lyles
GERMAN, AND OTHERS	C. Phillips Kaufman
DR. BENBERG, AND OTHERS	Charles Bartlett
HELEN	Sylvia Short
NURSE EATON	Mary Louise Wilson
TRISH	Rosalyn Coleman
FARMER'S WIFE, AND OTHERS	Babo Harrison
ORDERLIES	Jim MacLaren
	Michael W. McCarty

Director: Peter Mark Shifter
Dramaturg: Ernie Schier
Set designer: Sarah Lambert
Costume designer: Nephelie Andonyadis
Lighting designer: David Birn
Stage manager: Robin Rumpf
Production dramaturg: Steven S. Oxman
Artistic director: Lloyd Richards

It was first produced in New York at the WPA Theatre in March 1990 with the following cast:

LYNNE	Pamela Wiggins
ELLIS	Ellen Greene
GERMAN, AND OTHERS	Ilo Orleans
DR. BENBERG, AND OTHERS	David Manis
HELEN	Patricia O'Connell
NURSE EATON	Paddy Croft
TRISH	Pamela Tucker-White
FARMER'S WIFE, AND OTHERS	Susan Brenner

Director: Zina Jasper
Set designer: Edward T. Gianfrancesco

Costume designer: Mimi Maxmen
Lighting designer: Craig Evans
Sound design: Aural Fixation
Stage manager: Jana Llynn
Producer: Kyle Rennick

The following acknowledgment must appear on the first page of credit in all programs distributed in connection with performances of the play:

STARTING MONDAY WAS GIVEN A STAGED READING AT THE 1983 NATIONAL PLAYWRIGHTS CONFERENCE AT THE O'NEILL THEATRE CENTER.

FIRST PRODUCED IN "WINTERFEST" AT THE YALE REPERTORY THEATRE.

NEW YORK CITY PREMIERE PRESENTED BY THE WPA THEATRE IN MARCH 1990, KYLE RENNICK PRODUCER.

characters

LYNNE

MAN

ELLIS

JIM

ONE GERMAN

ANOTHER GERMAN

HELEN

NURSE

MALE NURSE

DOCTOR IN SURGERY GARB

TRISH

PATIENT IN WHEELCHAIR

NURSE EATON

MRS. KOENIG

DR. BENBERG

FARMER
FARMER'S WIFE
BLOOD NURSE
SKYCAP
LOS ANGELES COP
TECHNICIAN

production notes

The set should consist of three playing areas with levels or modules for sitting, lounging, and prop containment. The main focal area contains a bed, the headboard being an elective variable to suggest different locales. [In some productions a hospital bed has been used, disguised with mock headboards or cloth coverlets, until hospital scenes in Act 2. The bed might also be on a pivot to allow for quick position changes. It would also be helpful if upstage side of bed had compartments for cast-off props.] The bed will be underdressed with spreads and blankets. Thus, a change of scene can be accomplished with the removal of the top spread. Also, actresses may enter wrapped in the described bedding: messy sheets, quilts, etc. The bed is accompanied by a nondescript bedtable (upstage of it) and a chair. Headphones (no cords) have a permanent position on the bedpost. Playing area 2 contains a bench with upstage shelving to contain props. Playing area 3 is neutral.

Props should be representational, used only for the sake of definition or the comfort of actors. They should never be complete; that is, use preset drawings on sketch pads, mime crayons; use journal, mime pencil; use coffee mugs, mime liquid; use grocery bag, mime contents; use clipboards, mime paper; headphones, no cords. Lynne is the beast of burden: arranging scenery, carrying props on and off. Ellis wafts through Lynne's memory. If the amount of props become ludicrous, if Lynne looks like an overloaded pack horse, she should play this with the audience.

Similarly, costumes should be changed only to make a

point, not to suggest change of day. As much as the script and the director are limited to the use of props to keep the pace, ditto the costume designer. Since Lynne is narrating the story, she should have a base attire, changed only by the addition or subtraction of a blazer or sweater, etc.

It will be tempting to visit the local hospital for accuracy. Remember three things: (1) this play takes place in the early 1980s; (2) medical procedures vary with locale; (3) the medical ephemera need not be complete (i.e., representational ointment, no goop). The changing-of-the-dressing scene is by necessity abridged.

Because of the complexities of the play, stage directions should be followed, or at least read. In one production blackouts were inserted between each scene, adding thirty-five minutes to the playing time. There should be very few blackouts: the ends of Act 1 and Act 2; the ends of scenes one and two. Those first two "hangover" scenes should be treated as a prologue — with the second scene creating the illusion that it's about Lynne a year later, until Ellis pops up.

act 1

TIME & PLACE: *11:00* A.M.; *New York City.*

AT RISE: SOUND: *Guy Lombardo strains in with "Auld Lang Syne."*

Slatted light streams from the fourth-wall window illuminating the bed. A blanket covers the vitals of an over-thirty-five-year-old lump; a pillow covers its head. There is a phone on the bedtable; a man's shoe, sock, and shirt are on the floor. The phone rings, the lump extends an arm from the swaddling clothes in one-quarter time; picks up the phone slowly. As music fades, announcer blends in with: "1978! Happy New Year, everybody!"

LYNNE. (*Groans something resembling*) Hello ... (*Eyes like mail slots*) What time is it? What year? Don't tell me, I don't want to know; I feel awful. ... A party at Doubleday, but I left before nine. Why do I feel awful?

MAN. (*Singing "MacArthur Park" offstage, sort of*) "Someone left the cake out in the raaaain."

LYNNE. Mystery solved, I did it again.

MAN. "But I didn't want to take it. 'Cause it took so long to bake it ..."

LYNNE. I did it again.

MAN. (*Offstage*) "And I'll never find that recipe agaaaaaiiiinn. Ohhh, noooooooo."

LYNNE. In the bathroom, taking a shower ... Hmmmm? Wine, Drambuie, Creme de Menthe and, yes, I vomited. Let me check. (*Bends over side of bed; picks up size-84 shoe*) He's tall. (*Puts finger through hole in heel of sock*) Single. (*Picks up shirt*) No convention tag, that's a good sign. And I better not bend over anymore. (*Leans back hard; feels a bump. Finds a coin changer under pillow; stares at changer*) Oh, sweet Mother of Mary, it's a paperboy. ... I don't remember, I don't remember, I do remember. It's the taxi driver. I drove the cab, he rode in the back. Then we frolicked in Central Park. ... It was safe. It was safe, he had a gun. ... (*Beat*) Whaddya mean, why do I do it? I need a hug. (*Mutters*) Yah, well, needing sex seems more adult. (*Louder*) I said, "needing sex seems more adult." I gotta get off the phone, I'm out of cigarettes. Because, I can't talk without a cigarette. I'm not kidding, I can't. (*A dawning realization*) Oh God, I called Australia. I hope they weren't home.

MAN. (*Yells, offstage*) They were home!

LYNNE. They were home. Forgive me, I gotta get off the phone. (*Hangs up; crawls beneath sheets as lights fade out*)

MAN. (*Sings, offstage*) "Ohhhh, noooooooooo."

Guy Lombardo strains in with "Auld Lang Syne." Fadeup on same bed. Light streams from the fourth-wall window. A bedspread and sheet are carelessly covering the vitals of two lumps. The phone rings, a beefy male arm reaches out from the foot of the bed, blindly feeling for phone; the other lump extends a feminine arm. The fairer arm wins, taking the phone under cover. As music fades, announcer blends in with: "1979! Happy New Year, everybody!"

ELLIS. (*Moans*) Hello . . . (*Sits straight up; wearing her sheet*) Oh hi, Aunt Grace, Happy Ne . . . No, I'm awake. . . . Really. . . . Huh? (*Picks up train schedule from bedside table. Reads*) "The Shoreliner 9:15; arrives Barnegat Bay 11:05." What time is it? . . . You're right, I'm not on it. And you're all at the station? Oh hi, Mom, Happy N . . . I know, I'm not on it. What ti . . . Uh huh . . . What t . . . (*Quickly*) What time's dinner? Oy. (*Starts to get up*) Ham'll be fine . . . I'll talk to her when I get there, okay? . . . I didn't meet Guy Lombardo. I'll talk to her wh . . . Oh hi, Mrs. Kepler. . . . I didn't meet Guy Lombardo. We were shooting in Times Square, he was at the Waldorf. Could we t . . . Ham'll be fine. (*Goes to hang up*) I'll talk t . . . Right. (*Hangs up. Swaddles in sheet and trundles out*) Jim, wake up. Jim! (*Offstage*) Why do I smell donuts? (*Offstage*) There's not much in the fridge. I didn't expect company or I'd've stocked the larder. Anyway, help yourself, I'm on a diet. (*Returns to room partially dressed. Hurriedly puts on ring from bedside table*) Why do I smell donuts? (*Struggles with earring*) I don't have a hangover. (*Beat*) I'm manifesting a hangover to punish myself. (*One earring on*) Would you pick up my check when you get yours? Why do I taste donuts? (*Exits rapidly. Enters in fury, throws donut box on bed*) We ate donuts! (*Even louder*) Four weeks, four lousy pounds and we ate donuts! (*Sits on bed; attempts other earring*) Oh God, I can't afford people. I drink, I eat, I miss trains. Now I'm on sugar. (*Struggles with earring*) I'm not on sugar. It's within my power. (*Still struggling with earring*) "If a man is an inebriate, convince the wrongdoer there is no real pleasure in false appetite." (*Drops earring on floor*) Shit. (*Gets down on hands and knees looking under bed*) Shit! (*Slumps against side of bed*) Why do I have the feeling everything that happens today, and everybody I see, will punish me for being cranky?

Cross-fade as Ellis and Jim exit. Lynne walks casually into the neutral playing area with a bathroom scale under her arm like a notebook. She addresses audience.

LYNNE. For the record, we had loftier goals than that, we really did. (*Beat*) Every Monday, we'd embroider our brains with bumperstickers: "Happiness Is Being Good." Every Saturday, we'd end up with a hangover, a man over, and the early morning regrets. Did you know baby chicks peck 10,000 times to get outta the shell? Can anyone tell me why? (*Beat*) Some would argue, "You'll die if you stay in the shell." (*Sets down scale*) Well, that's what I'm here to tell ya. (*Ellis enters with journal; steps on scale, impervious to Lynne*)

ELLIS. (*To herself*) Four. I gained four. (*Steps off scale; sits on floor; writes in journal*) For breakfast: one egg, small juice. For lunch: Scotch Broth soup. (*Lynne picks up scale and exits. A confirmed soliloquizer — one-quarter to her journal, three-quarters to herself — Ellis speaks with energy and determination, laughing throughout. The more apocalyptic, the more she laughs. Even the derision lacks self-pity*) I got back from the Shore on Sunday, loaded down with New Year's resolutions: no eating, no drinking, go to gym, go to yoga. By Friday, I was sitting next to a buffet in Philadelphia, stuffing myself with stuffed grape leaves. I like sitting next to the food; gives me something to do with my hands. Saturday, we shot all day. For breakfast: one egg; small juice. For lunch: split pea soup. At dinner, my roast beef was an ounce over, but there wasn't much choice — or I didn't recognize the choice. Then I mini-binged on Melba Toast. I'd have gone to bed and avoided it if I hadn't been waiting for Glenn to call. (*Has stopped writing*) Sunday was wonderful. We were together the whole day. That evening, I had a cheeseburger, two glasses of wine, and a six-pack of cottage cheese. (*Writes*) On the train, I ate yogurt and stuffed in a Fresca. At home, things were frozen so I settled for crackers. It's lucky I got tired or I would have fried flour. I don't know what's bothering me. I don't want to cause trauma to Glenn's wife and children. I don't want to feel like a bad person again. I'd like to move someplace where I don't know anyone. Start all over. (*Laughs*) But then I'd just end up being me. And have to move again. I'm probably just angry because I gained four lousy pounds. (*Lights fade, along with voice*) Starting Monday, I'll go to gym, go to yoga, and follow my eating plan religiously whether I like myself or not. I may make exceptions for extenuating circumstances but I won't create the extenuating circumstances. I must control my compulsiveness. Signed Ellis Crowley. (*Beat*) I need to take a long cruise to Katmandu.

Blast of an ocean liner; sound of ship's orchestra wafting through the night playing German "oom-pa-pa" version of "Auld Lang Syne." Band member (offstage) yells above the music: "1980! Happy New Year, everybody!" Lights up on bench area as Lynne enters carrying sketch pads, knapsack, and a blanket. She sits on the bench that is now representing a deck chair, blankets her lap, and begins to sketch. One German and Another German enter, martinis in hand, wearing "1980" New Year's glitter hats. As they look over Lynne's shoulder, she sketches faster. Silence.

ONE GERMAN. Illustrahtor?
LYNNE. (*Smiles shyly*) Ja.
ONE GERMAN. Kinderbuchen?
LYNNE. Hm?
ANOTHER GERMAN. Kin-der-buch-en?
LYNNE. No Sprechen so hot.
ONE GERMAN. Sprechen Sie kein Deutsch?

LYNNE. Un poquito.

ANOTHER GERMAN. (*Laughs*) Un poquito. (*Germans cross out of light to boat railing, still laughing*)

LYNNE. Un poquito. Wonderful. (*To audience*) I was invited to a Book Fair in Bremerhaven. I decided to take a slow boat because I wanted to be alone. I also thought I'd straighten out my life: no drinking, no smoking. I'd been on that boat three days. Greek Line out of New York. Everyone spoke German. Boy, was I alone. (*Pulls blanket up tightly*) And riddled with insomnia. A direct result, I suppose of going to bed every night at eight. Can people die from lack of touch? (*Returns to sketching. Ellis enters upstage left, carrying knapsack; crosses to deck chair*)

ELLIS. Besetzt? [Occupied?]

LYNNE. (*Guesses*) Nein.

ELLIS. Danke. (*Sits on bench. Lynne burrows into sketching. Ellis points to Lynne's sketch book. Lynne burrows further*) Illustrahtor?

LYNNE. Ja.

ELLIS. Kinderbuchen?

LYNNE. Ja. Kinderbuchen. (*Both smile; awkward*)

ELLIS. Wo kommen Sie her? [Where are you from?]

LYNNE. Hm?

ELLIS. Wo kommen Sie her? Verstehen Sie?

LYNNE. Nein, verstehen Sie. Amerikaner.

ELLIS. Amerikaner?

LYNNE. Ja.

ELLIS. Amerikaner, allzu.

LYNNE. Amerikaner, allzu?

ELLIS. Ja.

LYNNE. Ja? Then why are we talking like this?

ELLIS. I don't know. (*Laughter from Germans; Another German mockingly mutters "Un Poquito." Ellis and Lynne gaze enviously at the Germans' drinks. Long silence*)

LYNNE. I want a drink so bad.

ELLIS. Have one.

LYNNE. No, thanks. I'd rather wake up alone tomorrow morning.

ELLIS. I know the feeling. (*They continue to stare at drinks. Long silence*)

LYNNE. I want a drink so bad.

ELLIS. I know the feeling. (*Both watch as Germans exit laughing. Long, uncomfortable, silence*)

LYNNE. Oh God, I know it's my turn but I'm lousy at small talk. Did you see tonight's movie?

ELLIS. I hate "Benjy" movies.

LYNNE. Did you see last night's movie?

ELLIS. (*Matter of fact, rapidly*) Benjy's gonna get lost, right? He's gonna get attacked by wolves and lay there, bleeding and whimpering—all alone—while people wander through the forest yelling, "Benjy, Benjy." Then he's gonna limp 4,000 miles, crossing freeways that look like the Indianapolis 500, until he gets home and everybody's so glad to see him, they cry. Why should I put myself through that?

LYNNE. (*Looks at Ellis, then looks directly at audience. Beat*) I should have known then, right? (*To Ellis*) Oh, hell, let's have a drink? Want a drink?

ELLIS. No. (*Beat*) And neither do you.

Lighting change. Sound: Guy Lombardo's "Happy Days Are Here Again" or Bette Midler blasts in: "But you've got to have friends./ The feeling's oh so strong./ You got to have friends/ To make that day last long." Sound of thunder; sound of rain. Lynne and Ellis on bench, huddled in blankets, sketch pads in laps, box of 48 Crayola's by Lynne's side. Both are coloring.

ELLIS. Pass the mauve magenta.

LYNNE. There's no such thing as mauve magenta.

ELLIS. Pity. What else ya got?

LYNNE. Maize. Thistle. Bittersweet.

ELLIS. Thistle.

LYNNE. (*Hands Ellis "thistle"; colors*) I'm so weak from lack of cigarettes, I can hardly color.

ELLIS. We can get a car when we dock at LeHavre. Cheap.

LYNNE. How cheap?

ELLIS. Doesn't have reverse; doesn't have a rear-view mirror.

LYNNE. Doesn't have reverse; doesn't need a rear-view mirror. You drive, okay?

ELLIS. Oh, c'mon. What are you afraid of?

LYNNE. People, life, parallel parking. When I grow up, I want to be like Mrs. Minnock [min-knock]: (*In harsh Brooklynese*) "Can we have more strudel over here, honey?" (*Beat*) She's getting to you, isn't she?

ELLIS. Not at all.

LYNNE. She got to you at breakfast.

ELLIS. Maybe to you; not to me.

LYNNE. Then why were you eating two donuts?

ELLIS. I wasn't eating two donuts.

LYNNE. You were, too. You had one in each hand.

ELLIS. I was?

LYNNE. Must be nice to be able to turn off your brain. I think about everything I ever did, and why I did it. Then, I analyze everybody else. (*Beat*) Have you noticed depression's easier to handle than euphoria?

ELLIS. (*Crosses a page out*) Yuck.

LYNNE. That's the fifth page you've started.

ELLIS. I'm into perfect. Pass the "burnt sienna." (*Lynne does*) It's broken.

LYNNE. Still colors.

ELLIS. (*Hands it back*) I don't want it. It's broken. (*Takes another crayon; back to coloring*) My world; I make the rules. (*Lynne checks Ellis for any sign of humor but Ellis proceeds to color, feverishly*)

LYNNE. I think we might be dealing with a serious character defect.

ELLIS. And plenty more where that came from.

Lighting change. Sound: "I've got some friends but they're gaw-awn./Someone came and took them away." Both rise and exit during music. Ellis enters downstage right, walking briskly. Lynne follows.

ELLIS. You like picnics?

LYNNE. I love picnics.

ELLIS. Good, we'll go on picnics. You like boardwalks?

LYNNE. I love boardwalks.

ELLIS. Good. We'll stroll boardwalks.

LYNNE. Boy, you walk fast.

ELLIS. Got to get to A-Deck before it closes. (*Sound: "And from the dusk 'til the daw-awn/ Here is where I'll stay . . ." Ellis enters*

downstage left, walks rapidly; Lynne follows) You like sailboats?
LYNNE. I love sailboats.
ELLIS. Good. We'll take your car to my sailboat.
LYNNE. Where's it moored?
ELLIS. Barnegat Bay, near my mother's. You like church?
LYNNE. It's been awhile.
ELLIS. On Sundays we can go to church. (*Hurries off stage right.
Sound: "'Cause you got to have fri-ends. La la, la la, la la la la."
Ellis enters downstage right; Lynne races in, just in time to speak
her line*) You like tilt-a-whirls?
LYNNE. I vomit on tilt-a-whirls.
ELLIS. Good. We'll ride separate tilt-a-whirls.
LYNNE. You like cats?
ELLIS. I hate cats.
LYNNE. You do?
ELLIS. (*Both stop in their tracks*) You don't?
LYNNE. No.
ELLIS. Actually, I like cats. Cats just don't like me.
LYNNE. How do you know?
ELLIS. I had a kitten once. It attacked my ankles.
LYNNE. Kittens do that.
ELLIS. (*Well, I'll be damned*) Oh. I thought it didn't like me.
(*Sound: Blast of ocean liner; runs to railing*) Land Ho!
LYNNE. (*Joins her; looks down*) Where are the drums? The canoes?
The brown-skinned Tahinis swimming to greet us?
ELLIS. This is Ireland.
LYNNE. Oh.
BOTH. (*Mutual bear hug*) Ireland!
LYNNE. There's a lot to be said for the buddy system.
ELLIS. True. If you're swimming and a shark comes along,
there's a fifty percent chance he'll eat your buddy.
LYNNE. (*Stops, looks directly at audience. Beat*) I should have
known then, right?
ELLIS. Ready to go?
LYNNE. But we just got here.
ELLIS. Got to get to C-Deck before it closes. (*Walks off downstage
right*)
LYNNE. (*Begins to follow Ellis out; then circles abruptly and returns to
face the audience*) I could show you more Hollywood vignettes:

the walk on the beach, the run in the sand, the bicycle built for two; but, suffice it to say, we became good friends. Probably because, through all our travels, we shared one basically profound belief: If we were taken hostage, no one . . . would negotiate. (*Shyly*) That was some hug, did you catch that hug? People of the same sex usually give A-frame hugs, sparing all vital parts. Or kisses that meet in the air. But that was *some* hug. (*Lights up on bed area. Ellis enters with quilt, covers bed, lies down, and begins to write a TV treatment in her journal*) I liked the kid in Ellis. The skater in search of a smooth sidewalk. I think mine suffered crib death. I've always been a bit stiff; afraid to be seen having fun. Some ride roller coasters, some wait below, holding the coats. Now, there's a T-shirt if I ever heard one. (*Crosses to bed area; sits on floor*) We got back from Europe on the 23rd and spent the next three weekends at her mother's apartment in Barnegat Bay. (*Pulls out scrapbook from underneath bed; opens it*) And I never did make it to Bremerhaven. (*Points in scrapbook*) Who's that?

ELLIS. Me. Galveston. When I was six.

LYNNE. Another Easter, another stunning dress. The only thing missing are the Mary Janes.

ELLIS. Mom said they were too much work. She'd have to keep Vaseline on them or they'd crack. (*Touches Lynne*) Listen. (*Reads*) "This nightime series will run the gamut of comedy, tragedy, et cetera." First episode: "Jennifer McCarthy looked in the mirror and declared herself fat." (*Shakes head; erases*) "Lindsay J. Lakin looked in the mirror and declared herself fat."

LYNNE. What happened to "eina kleina film direktor"?

ELLIS. You *write* "Rocky"; you *direct* "Rocky."

LYNNE. All these pictures. You're never smiling.

ELLIS. I'm not? (*Fascinated*) I'm not, am I? (*Beat*) I didn't speak 'til I was five.

LYNNE. Jesus, who were you mad at?

ELLIS. Mom says I was born angry.

HELEN. (*Enters in robe and slippers. She is small, thin, deeply tanned, and subject to outbursts of childlike wonder*) What do you kids want for Sunday dinner? Tuna noodle casserole or Malarkey stew? (*Flops prone at foot of bed*) I could make a quiche. What about meatloaf? With french fried onion rings . . .

LYNNE. I love meatloaf.

HELEN. I know, a pot roast! Now all I have to do is figure out breakfast. Sure hope you kids brought better weather this weekend. I feel so fat and swollen; I need some sun.

ELLIS. Mom's a firm believer: If you can't lose it, tan it.

HELEN. (*Jumps up; plops next to Ellis*) Oh, I love it when you're with Lynne! (*Smothers her with kisses*) Then you're in a good mood. Then I'm in a good mood.

LYNNE. (*Points to scrapbook*) Who's this?

ELLIS. Marlene Fronzak. She was voted Most Repulsive. You know the kind, all gums and teeth. I'd always get the same kind of ice cream she did, so she wouldn't ask for a lick. That's it! Marlene Fronzak looked in the mirror . . .

HELEN. (*Jumps up*) I know, croissants! With sweet creamery butter. That's it, croissants. (*Beat*) Or would you rather have bagels?

LYNNE. We'll have what you have.

HELEN. Me? (*Laughs*) You'd end up with half a grapefruit and dry "glutton" toast. Now all I have to do is figure out lunch. (*Exits; voice drifts off*) What sounds good? Soup? Sandwich? I could make egg salad. Better yet, hamburgers with thick melted cheese . . . (*A scrutable silence. Lynne studies Ellis*)

LYNNE. What are you thinking?

ELLIS. I don't know.

LYNNE. You really don't know, do you?

ELLIS. (*Leaps into lotus*) Let's meditate. Want to meditate? Concentrate on the mantra, exclude all thoughts.

LYNNE. What are you meditating?

ELLIS. I'm thinking about the Sara Lee Cheesecake I'm not going to eat.

LYNNE. That's not what you're thinking.

ELLIS. Then why don't you tell me? You always do.

LYNNE. You're angry.

ELLIS. No, I'm not.

LYNNE. You're furious.

ELLIS. She's always talking about food. Why should I be angry about that? (*Thinks about it; amazed*) You know, you're right. (*Furious*) Boy, am I pissed. (*Gets up*) I'm gonna get a donut. Want a donut?

LYNNE. No. (*Beat*) And neither do you.

Sound of congregation in full chorus: "Praise God, from Whom all Blessings Flow." They cross into area lighting; raise hymnals. Ellis sings; Lynne tears up. Ellis hands Lynne a Kleenex.

LYNNE. (*To audience*) One sang; the other was sobbing into her hymnal over lost youth. (*Closes hymnal; crosses to downstage apron as lights fade on Ellis*) I gotta tell ya, it was more than I could bear. All that clean living: the sky cobalt blue, the sun, cadmium #4, tiny little ions scrubbing my soul; no booze, no cigarettes, no taxi drivers; and, on top of all that, *church.* I gotta tell ya . . . (*Breathes in the sea air*) The sun felt wonderful, the heat felt wonderful, even the Jersey flies felt wonderful. (*Ellis enters, carrying a knapsack, sits on apron, downstage left. Sound of surf and gulls*) After church, we'd head for Island Beach — a long peninsula jutting into the Atlantic with mile after mile of sand. Ellis walked there in winter to sort things out. Her ritual became our ritual. We'd drive to the last parking bay, then walk the three miles to Barnaget Bay inlet, meeting no one. (*Crosses to Ellis*) We were quite a team, I was always concentrating on the path below; she was always looking ahead, on the way to getting there. I don't think either of us ever saw the view. And I, of course, preferred to follow, preferred any-one's destination to my own. (*Sits next to Ellis*) We'd sit on a large piece of driftwood, staring into the wind. We didn't talk much; we didn't need to. (*Lynne rummages through knap-sack; gets out baggie of trail mix*) Obviously, we'd become very close. (*Takes a piece out*) Probably, too close. (*Starts to put it in mouth*)

ELLIS. Oh, did I tell you? I'm moving to L.A.

LYNNE. Pardon me?

ELLIS. There's a possible shoot. Paramount. Not directing, but it'd be a foot in the door. (*Lynne returns piece to trail mix*) I feel so good about myself, lately. I've changed; I know I have, and if I don't move now, I never will. I won't allow any negative suggestion that failure is possible. Even if the Directors' Guild goes on strike. Starting Monday, I'll phone Roger Corman, Orion, revise my résumé, and just plain start over. (*Lynne has returned trail mix to knapsack; has pulled out address book and is thumbing through it*) You gonna call someone?

LYNNE. I just thought I'd read my address book. It's been a long time.

ELLIS. Who knows. I'll probably be making enough in a year to afford a house. Especially if I'm directing. I *will* be directing. (*Silence; gets up; brushes sand off skirt*) Ready to go?

LYNNE. Yep. (*Ellis crosses, turns to see if Lynne is behind her. No Lynne. Exits. Silence. Then to audience*) We'd made it through fifty-one days, but that's not a record. In August, 1837, Patricia Bingham of Bayonne, New Jersey, traveled with her friend, Cicely Tubb, for fifty-three days before they jumped into the Watanabe [Wa-tah-nah-bee] River. Their hands around each other's throats. (*Beat*) Actually, I like being alone. I think my mother left me a lot when I was little. I only want to be alone or with people I love. Everybody else feels like babysitters. (*Rises; dusts herself off*) It really is a lovely day. (*Points*) One of the last sailboats of autumn just entered Barnegat Bay.

Exits. Lighting change as phone rings once. Helen enters, sits on bench, sunbathing in sleeveless top. Another ring, lights up on Ellis pacing near bed with phone, speaks energetically. Helen listens as if in reverie.

ELLIS. Mom, L.A. is great! I'm directing a soap! Twice a week, an hour soap! (*Puts down phone; lifts up phone; phone rings once*) Mom, L.A. is great! I bought a house! It needs a little work, but I bought a house. (*Puts down phone; lifts up phone; phone rings once*) Mom, L.A. is great! I met a man! He needs a little work, but I met a man. (*Puts down phone; lifts up phone; phone rings once. Lights out on Helen; lights up on Lynne in neutral area — smoking a cigarette, sans phone*) Lynne, L.A. is great! I got a soap, I bought a house, I met a man. (*Laughs; reverses quilt for L.A. change*) Sometimes he becomes the enemy for liking me but he's terrific. So's the house. And I found a doctor who believes in allergy diets. And a psychiatrist, Ardis Baker — you know the one, on all the talk shows. She said she'd take me on but I'd have to be better in six months because she's got a new book and a national tour. So, I'll just skip my childhood and get to the good stuff. (*Lights out on Ellis*)

LYNNE. Signed Ellis Crowley. (*Lights up on bed area as Lynne crosses through*) Ellis leapt from platitude to platitude across a shallow brook — until she came to deep water. (*Sound: Guy Lombardo, "Auld Lang Syne."*) 1981. Happy New Year. (*Exits*)

Ellis crawls under L.A. quilt, grocery bag on floor, headphones on bedpost. Sun trying to peek through drawn shades. Writes in journal. Stops. Thinks aloud. Voice is a little less energetic.

ELLIS. I was sick again all weekend. There's a thousand things I should be doing, like working on this house. I thought I'd earn enough to fix it, but I got fired. Well, not fired. They didn't renew my contract. It felt like fired. It was fired. (*Beat*) I set out to prove I was a good director; all I proved was the need for perfection and two shows a week make you tired. And every month there'd be this pain. The crew'd have coffee breaks, I'd have vomit breaks. I didn't dare tell them. It's so hard for women to break into television, and cramps is such a lame excuse. Wednesday, I had spearmint tea, two Naprosyn, and an Alka Seltzer Plus. I'd like to call Lynne, but I don't dare. People get to know me, then walk away. Or did I walk away? (*Grabs stomach*) Maybe I'm just depressed about this hysterectomy business. I went to one of the best doctors in Beverly Hills five months ago. She said it was all in my head. Now, this doctor says fibroids. "My body and my brain are my servants not my master." (*Beat*) Thursday, I had three ounces of veal, four ounces of spinach, and a brief affair. Why does going to bed with someone you don't even care about hurt so much when they don't call after? I guess I feel he didn't respect me. I guess I didn't respect myself. I guess I don't trust men. (*Beat*) I'd like to call Lynne, but

I don't dare. When you start to depend on someone, you give away too much power. Mom is so needy — I don't want to be like that. You can't depend on anyone, ever. It's as simple as that. (*Laughs*) I guess I don't trust women. (*Beat*) Starting Monday, I'm going to run five miles around the lake whether I have cramps or not; mail ten résumés instead of five; call eight people instead of four; go to Paramount, go to Warner's. Signed Ellis Crowley. I can't keep calling Lynne. (*Puts on headphones from bedpost. Sound of "Fame" bumps in mid-tape: "Baby, look at me. . . ." Burrows under covers. Lynne enters on "I'll make you forget the rest," crosses to bed; lifts off headphones*)

LYNNE. Say anything you want, okay? Just don't be polite.

ELLIS. What are you doing here?

LYNNE. That's too polite.

ELLIS. What are you doing here, Fuckface?

LYNNE. (*To audience*) She didn't say that. And I didn't just show up. Truth be told: she started to phone — once in November, twice in December — laughing so high, I could hear the lows. (*To Ellis*) Jesus, this house is colder than Minnesota.

ELLIS. There's no heat.

LYNNE. (*Looks around*) Furniture?

ELLIS. (*Abrupt energy change*) One card table, one chair, one couch, one bed. But it really is a good investment. It's right near Carroll Avenue, where they have those large Victorian houses. Want to see? (*Walks a few feet, upstage left. Lynne follows*) Voila. Living room.

LYNNE. (*A pathetic "ooh"; a delayed*) Nice, really nice.

ELLIS. The speckled mirrors aren't staying.

LYNNE. What about the bamboo wallpaper?

ELLIS. Not staying. The fireplace, however, is. (*Walks upstage center; Lynne follows*) Kitchen avec pantry.

LYNNE. Nice. Really nice. (*Beat*) And blue. Really blue.

ELLIS. (*Walks upstage left; Lynne follows*) Bathroom.

LYNNE. Nice. Nice spirit. Where are the walls?

ELLIS. I tore them down. (*Walks a few feet, upstage right*) Den. (*Lynne emits an anemic "ah"; a delayed "ni . . ."; Ellis continues hastily to bed area*) My bedroom. (*Lynne looks in; silence*) I have to admit, it needs a little facelift. (*Lynne is stunned*) But it really is Victorian. (*Lynne is more than stunned*) Like Mrs. Sutphen's [Sut-fen]. Remember Mrs. Sutphen's ... (*Lynne wants to go home*) On the road to the shore ... (*Silence*) This house could look as nice. (*Silence*) Whaddya think?

LYNNE. Excuse me. (*Rushes to audience; words pour out*) How could I tell her it looked like a whorehouse? I was swallowing eight lines per: Den of what? Thieves? Opium? Needs a little facelift. Needs a little forklift. Who did the color scheme, Shanghai Lil? There were holes in every wall. I don't mean nailholes ... (*Holds out arms*) I mean holes. And her bedroom. Her bedroom. Was the ugliest color I'd ever seen. No wonder she was depressed. It looked like a whorehouse. (*Returns reluctantly. Both continue to gaze at room in silence. Finally*)

ELLIS. Whaddya think? Like the color? (*Silence*) I call it: Puke green. God, it's good to see you. (*Bear-hugs Lynne; Lynne looks at audience, pleased*)

LYNNE. What about upstairs?

ELLIS. (*Points to offstage steps*) Feel free.

LYNNE. Aren't you coming? (*Exits*)

ELLIS. I'd rather not. (*Ellis rushes to bedroom; gets grocery bag from side of bed; looks for hiding place. Yells as she goes*) I've been going to paint. But I'm terrified I'll choose the wrong color. Well, would I change in one year? The roof leaks, it's in the worst crime district in L.A., the back door's paper thin, and I'm still living out of suitcases.

LYNNE. (*Offstage*) Ellis! This *was* a whorehouse! There are nude women wallpapering the walls in every conceivable position. (*Hurries in, aghast; same voice pitch*) Some not so conceivable. This *was* a whorehouse!

ELLIS. Why do you think it was so cheap?

LYNNE. Doesn't it bother you?

ELLIS. Not if I don't think about it.

LYNNE. What's in the bag?

ELLIS. (*Rummages in grocery bag*) Sara Lee Danish, donuts assorted, Mint Milanos, and a Peter Paul Mounds.

LYNNE. (*Takes bag; rolls down top*) Look. Want to do something tomorrow? Scripps museum? Venice Beach? "Let's Make a Deal?" We could win a refrigerator or boat for your house.

ELLIS. I can't.

LYNNE. What about Friday?

ELLIS. I can't.

LYNNE. Booked, eh?

ELLIS. Sort of.

LYNNE. (*Goes to door*) Well, hey, I've kept you long enough. The house is wonderful, the windows are wonderful, the fireplace is wonderful, the vestibule's wonderful and I'm gonna keep invoking "wonderfuls" as I back out the door, hoping I can get out of here with my dignity intact and not all over your kitchen floor.

ELLIS. I'm glad you came.

LYNNE. Yah, same. (*Turns to exit*)

ELLIS. I have to go to the hospital tomorrow.

LYNNE. Who's sick?

ELLIS. Me. Hysterectomy. Just partial, nothing serious.

LYNNE. Who's taking you?

ELLIS. Me.

LYNNE. You're going alone?

ELLIS. Is that odd?

LYNNE. What time should I pick you up?

ELLIS. It's okay.

LYNNE. I know it's okay. What time should I pick you up?

ELLIS. Is ten too early?

LYNNE. Ten's just fine. (*Turns to go*)

ELLIS. Where you staying?

LYNNE. A motel on Sunset.

ELLIS. Want to stay here?

As lights fade, there is a swirl of activity. Nurse and Male Nurse enter and add white sheet to bedding, position chair away from the bed as Ellis gets into it. Doctor enters neutral area in surgery garb, stands with back to audience. Area lighting as Lynne approaches him and converses quietly. She addresses audience with no emotion.

LYNNE. He told me there were complications, the fibroids weren't fibroids. He told me she had cancer; he hoped it hadn't spread. (*Doctor exits*) That's all I remember. That and his pocket. To this day, I can remember ever detail of his pocket: light green institutional stitching, one thread hanging out. And a pen, a small black felt tip, a white dot on its crown. I remember wondering if the pocket would break my fall. It was the only thing to grab on to; except for the words hanging in the air. (*Crosses to "hospital" bed. Ellis is sleeping lightly. Ellis wakes, incapable of movement*) Hi.

ELLIS. Hi.

LYNNE. How you feeling?

ELLIS. Pummeled. I keep thinking I've done something wrong.

LYNNE. Your mother should be here any minute. Her plane got in at four.

ELLIS. I wish you hadn't done that.

LYNNE. My God, she had to know.

ELLIS. I really wish you hadn't done that.

LYNNE. Why?

HELEN. (*Crashes in, carrying suitcase*) I am so exhausted! (*Plops in chair*) I don't know why I'm so exhausted, but I am. I'm just exhausted!

ELLIS. (*Gently; unable to see her*) Mom.

HELEN. (*Staring at floor; trembling*) I feel so fat and swollen . . . could be the ham. I drank gallons of water all night last night; got up this morning and weighed five more pounds.

ELLIS. Mom.

HELEN. (*Relates to no one*) Either that or the diuretic. I should know better than to take a diuretic when I'm flying; but I took a diuretic. I am absolutely exhausted.

ELLIS. (*Softly; as to a child*) Would you like Lynne to take you to the house?

HELEN. Could she?

LYNNE. Now?

HELEN.(*Crosses to neutral area as voice drifts off in the dark*) If I could just get some potassium. That's all that's wrong: potassium. If I could just lie down. . . .

Cross-fade as Nurse enters and helps Ellis exit, striking sheet. Lynne walks into bench area, addressing audience.

LYNNE. She really did that; I didn't make it up. (*Admits reluc-

tantly) Okay, the Germans and the cruise I made up. But that's all I made up. She *really* did that. And I *really* judged her. By some vague motherhood measuring stick. She wasn't too strong in the best of times and now she was reeling. (*Lights up, neutral area. Helen is sitting on suitcase, staring at floor, despondent; Lynne grabs bucket from behind bench and crosses to her*) You take the bed, I'll take the couch. (*Beat*) I want to fix up her room. Paint, plug up the holes, get curtains. (*Beat*) What time do you want to go to the hospital in the morning?

HELEN. I just need a day or two to rest.

LYNNE. You're not going to the hospital?

HELEN. Just a day or two.

LYNNE. (*Gently*) You're burying her, you know. You've got the shovel and you're burying her.

HELEN. (*Becomes Lynne's child*) What do you want me to do?

LYNNE. Wanna grab a brush? (*Helen takes bucket; Lynne addresses audience*) By God, she did. And we painted four rooms. (*Helen dips brush into bucket, paints*) The biopsies were good news: the cancer hadn't spread. The doctors decided on an aggressive approach: chemo and radiation. I convinced Ellis that people with pets live longer. So she got a kitten, pronounced him "Holbein [Hole-bine]." Got a dog, pronounced her "Grace." Grace was part German shepherd, part timberwolf.

HELEN. (*Looks back at her handiwork*) Oh, she's gonna love this room.

LYNNE. (*To audience*) Neither of us had ever lived with anyone; so we both had a long way to go. Ellis had trouble if the shower curtain was left the wrong way. And I reflected her every mood. If she had a bad day, I had a bad day. I asked her once, in the middle of our weekly fight, what she was getting out of this. She said, "I'm no longer lonely."

HELEN. (*Stands up, stiff with arthritis*) She's gonna love this room.

LYNNE. We worked hard on the house: bought used furniture; scraped off nudes; I started a book; we didn't drink. Ellis sent out résumés; lost her hair; directed a sitcom; her hair grew back; we didn't drink. I loved her hair. (*Helen exits with suitcase and paint*) We became quite a family. Nestled in on Sunday mornings, reading *The New York Times*. I'd always wanted an "old shoe" relationship. You know like Dagwood and Blondie, reading newspapers in an overstuffed living room, twin floor lamps. We sort of had that. (*Beat*) I've always loved indiscriminately: men, women, families, dogs, Blackwing Pencils. I have sex with men; no love. Love with women; no sex. I don't think there's a name for me yet. (*Beat*) Two months later, her mother went home. Eight months later, I went home. And Ellis got a clean bill of health. (*Lights up on bench area, which is now a large waiting area in the hospital, Houston. Sound of TV-movie. Ellis enters, carrying a pen and her journal; sits on bench. Trish wheels in a Patient in Wheelchair, dazed and extremely thin, parks him/her nearby. Trish exits. Ellis and Patient in Wheelchair stare up at an unseen television screen*) Then one day in August an X ray resurfaced, filed away by mistake. They held it up so she could see the smudges on the lungs. They said to go to Houston. The cancer center there. They'd do more tests in Houston. Then tell us what was up. (*Joins Ellis. Sound fades down*)

ELLIS. Ask them how much longer.

LYNNE. But we just got here.

ELLIS. Our appointment was at eight, right? It's eight-o-two.

LYNNE. Shouldn't we give it a reasonable length of time?

ELLIS. Today, two minutes is reasonable. My world; I make the rules. I wish they'd turn off this movie.

LYNNE. What is it?

ELLIS. "Death Be Not Proud."

LYNNE. Jesus.

ELLIS. Can you change the channel? (*Beat*) Well?

LYNNE. (*Amazed. Looks around*) I can't just change the channel!

ELLIS. Why not?

LYNNE. *Everybody in this room* is watching it. (*Slumps. Nurse Eaton enters stage left, looks directly at Ellis, looks down at clipboard. Ellis braces*)

ELLIS. No chemo. I don't care what they say. If I've only got two years to live, I don't want to live it over a toilet bowl.

NURSE EATON. Mrs. Sternlicht. Mrs. Trudi Sternlicht.

ELLIS. (*Unbraces*) We're going to miss our plane.

LYNNE. It doesn't leave 'til four. We've got eight hours.

> *Sound out. Nurse Eaton exits, stage right. Lighting change to suggest passage of time. Ellis jots down notes in journal. Sound: Theme song from "The Young and the Restless." Sound fades out. Ellis itches ankle.*

ELLIS. Ask them how much longer.

LYNNE. I've asked a hundred times.

ELLIS. You afraid to ask?

LYNNE. Yes.

ELLIS. I'll ask. (*Nurse Eaton enters stage right and walks to Patient in Wheelchair. Ellis, sweetly*) Excuse me.

NURSE EATON. (*Merry singsong as she exits with Patient in Wheelchair, stage left*) Shouldn't be long.

ELLIS. I want to punish them. I really do. I won't tell them about anything that hurts.

LYNNE. Good, Ellis.

ELLIS. We're going to miss our plane.

LYNNE. It doesn't leave 'til four. We've got six hours.

> *Lighting change. Sound: "Like sands in the hour glass, so are the 'Days of Our Lives.'" Lynne exits. Ellis is writing in journal as Mrs. Koenig enters and sits next to her. Ellis looks up — too late to say anything. Sound fades as Lynne returns; stands next to Ellis.*

LYNNE. They say we're next.

ELLIS. Ask them what "next" means.

LYNNE. They're getting annoyed.

ELLIS. How annoyed?

LYNNE. Maybe not annoyed, maybe . . . remote.

ELLIS. Then why did you say, "annoyed?"

LYNNE. I got carried away.

TRISH. (*Enters stage right*) Mrs. Koenig [Kay-nig]. Mrs. Doris Koenig. (*Exits with Mrs. Koenig, stage left*)

ELLIS. But she just got here!

LYNNE. Maybe she's seeing a different doctor.

ELLIS. Maybe she's seeing a faster doctor.

LYNNE. (*Sits next to Ellis*) Maybe it's good yours is slow. Once you're in there, he might take his time.

ELLIS. I don't want him to take his time.

LYNNE. You want him to hurry?

ELLIS. (*Whispered frenzy*) I want you to stop being rational!
(*Lynne becomes riveted to TV, as Nurse Eaton enters stage left*)

NURSE EATON. Miss Howe. Miss Bobbie Howe. (*Exits stage
right*)

ELLIS. (*With urgency*) There's a scream coming up my throat.
(*Lynne looks around; embarrassed*) I'm not kidding, keep
talking. I'm not kidding, keep talking.

LYNNE. (*Talks fast*) Okay, I'm talking. Hear me, I'm talking.
Maybe they can't find your chart. Maybe they lost it;
maybe ...

ELLIS. You mean the doctor can't see me until they find my
chart!

LYNNE. I'm talking in "maybe's." I'm talking in "maybe's."
Lunch! We need lunch. How 'bout some hot chicken soup?
Peanut butter and jelly? Tuna on rye. I sound like your
mother. How 'bout a luscious grilled cheese?

ELLIS. We're going to miss our plane.

LYNNE. We'll get one tomorrow.

ELLIS. They're booked for tomorrow.

LYNNE. We'll get one on Sunday.

ELLIS. And spend the weekend in Houston?

LYNNE. We'll go to the Houston Zoo.

ELLIS. Swell. Two horses and a cow.

LYNNE. That's not fair, it's an international zoo.

ELLIS. Two llamas and a cow.

NURSE EATON. (*Enters stage left; exits stage right*) Mrs. McAllister.
Darlyne McAllister.

TRISH. (*Enters stage right; exits stage left*) Miss Jasper. Miss
Barbara Jasper.

ELLIS. I'm not kidding, keep talking. I'm not kidding, keep
talking.

LYNNE. We'll drive to Galveston.

ELLIS. Without a car?

LYNNE. We'll rent a car.

ELLIS. And where will we stay?

LYNNE. We'll rent a room. A beautiful room with a beautiful
view.

ELLIS. Of what? A beautiful oil rig.

LYNNE. We'll walk on the beach.

ELLIS. And wade in the oil.

LYNNE. We'll swim in the ocean.

ELLIS. It has men-of-war.

LYNNE. You said you liked Galveston!

ELLIS. I changed my mind.

LYNNE. You're sure you want me to keep talking?

ELLIS. When I'm upset, I hate small talk. It just makes me more upset.

LYNNE. (*Screams; or keels slowly off bench onto floor. Holds position for a beat; gets up, and sits back in bench. To audience*) That's what I wanted to do. ... This is what I did. (*Turns to Ellis*) Sure you don't want some lunch?

ELLIS. This is barbaric. (*Bolts off bench; exits stage right*)

LYNNE. (*Chases after her*) Ellis! Ellis!

ELLIS. (*Cross-fade as Ellis enters stage left; paces stage apron; Lynne joins her. Whispered fury*) You want me to be a good sport, don't you? They're gonna tell me how long I have to live and you want me to be a good sport. What if I decide not to get help, what if I decide to go home? No drugs, no treatments. And if I die in two years, I die.

LYNNE. Then I'll go with you. But I'll tell you something. You're going to sit in L.A. wanting to know. You will, Ellis. You'll spend every minute wanting to know. (*Beat*) You're right, the waiting sucks. It's crap, it's shit, it's every toilet term I can think of. But you can't control it. You can't control the waiting, you can't control the doctors, you can't control anything.

ELLIS. Then what do I do?

LYNNE. Hand it over.

ELLIS. To what?

LYNNE. Believe me, there's a metaphysical Tootsie Pop somewhere at the end of this.

ELLIS. You know what my biggest fear is? Honest to God, my biggest fear.

LYNNE. What?

ELLIS. That I'll cry when they tell me.

LYNNE. My God, don't you think they've seen tears?

NURSE EATON. (*Offstage*) Miss Crowley. Miss Ellis Crowley.

Cross-fade as both cross to neutral area, which is now the examination room. Nurse Eaton enters, sets down chair for Ellis. Ellis sits, takes out journal. Lynne addresses audience.

LYNNE. Her moment of truth turned into another twenty minutes. (*To herself*) I wonder if I should leave when the doctor comes? (*To Ellis*) You think I should leave?

ELLIS. We're going to miss our plane.

LYNNE. I know. (*Beat*) You think I should leave? (*Ellis braces as Trish and Dr. Benberg hurry in. They do not, however, hurry the interview; nor do they have southern accents. Benberg is wearing a large cowboy hat with what looks like a peacock feather*)

TRISH. Good morning.

ELLIS. Good afternoon.

TRISH. Whatever.

BENBERG. How you feeling? (*Peruses file*)

LYNNE. (*Steps out of scene; to audience*) This really happened; I didn't make it up. Okay, okay, the Germans and the cruise I made up. But this *really* happened. There was Cougar madness in Houston. The team was in contention for the NCAA [NC Double A] title and half the hospital was in cowboy clothes. T-shirts with Phi Gamma Slamma or Phi Slamma Jamma. This *really* happened. (*Beat*) But I don't think I want it to happen again. (*Takes off Benberg's hat*) Excuse me. (*Walks hat to wings; returns*)

BENBERG. How you feeling?

ELLIS. I have a sore throat. First time I've been sick in a year. (*Laughs*) If you don't count cancer.

BENBERG. (*To Trish*) I'm missing a scan. (*Trish exits*) I see you had adriamycin. (*Seems disappointed*) Kind of a conservative dose.

ELLIS. You going to increase it?

BENBERG. Can't. They gave you just enough to make you immune.

ELLIS. I see. (*Looks at journal. Throughout the following, her journal is her anchor*) What about nutrition?

BENBERG. Only for slow-growing cancers.

ELLIS. Mine's not so slow?

BENBERG. Not so slow.

ELLIS. (*Checks off list with pen*) Interferon? (*Benberg shakes head "no"; Ellis checks off list*) Thermal?

BENBERG. Your best bet's another form of chemo.

ELLIS. I thought adriamycin was the best.

BENBERG. It was.

ELLIS. I see. (*Tries to control voice*) What if I don't do anything? How long would I have?

BENBERG. (*Not harsh; straightforward*) Without treatment? Six months.

ELLIS. (*Beat*) With treatment?

BENBERG. Six months, maybe longer.

ELLIS. I see. (*Checks off list*) How much longer?

BENBERG. Less than 10% chance of complete remission for about two years.

ELLIS. I see. (*Checks off list*) Quality of life?

BENBERG. If all goes well, you'll only be sick the last month.

ELLIS. (*Looks at journal*) How will I die?

BENBERG. Malnutrition.

ELLIS. I see. (*Checks off list*) What would *you* do?

BENBERG. If it were my life? Take the chemo; go for the odds. (*Beat*) You'd be here two weeks. (*Hands blank paper to Ellis*) And you'd have to sign this consent form. (*While Ellis reads form, Trish enters with report and clipboard. Subtly but visibly thrown, she hands report to Benberg. Benberg reads it. He, too, reacts*)

ELLIS. It says one of the side effects is heart damage. (*Laughs*) I guess it doesn't matter.

BENBERG. (*Feels her shoulder*) There's another small tumor in your shoulder. Feel it?

ELLIS. Yes.

BENBERG. Good. We can watch the cancer's growth with it. There are two tumors on the liver, one on the vertebrae. Not good.

ELLIS. Can things be worse?

BENBERG. Three months worse.

ELLIS. I just lost three months?

BENBERG. Yes.

ELLIS. I see. (*They wait for decision. Ellis places a check in journal, laughs nervously*) Guess I'd better take the chemo.

BENBERG & TRISH. Good! (*Laconic tone changes to urgent and personable. He looks at Trish; she looks at clipboard*)

TRISH. EKG nine tomorrow. Subclavian at ten. The earliest I can get a cat scan is at Del Oro, a week from today.

ELLIS. A week? Eight weeks of quality time, three of them in Houston?

BENBERG. Could be worse, could be Lubbock. Can I see her tomorrow?

TRISH. You've got poor Mrs. Blane. What about tomorrow evening?

BENBERG. I've got poor Mr. Hoffman and poor Mr. Vogel.

TRISH. (*To Lynne and Ellis*) Don't worry, we'll fit you in. (*Benberg rushes out; Trish follows. Long silence*)

ELLIS. Malnutrition? (*Explodes into laughter*) Malnutrition! Did you get that statistic?

LYNNE. "Less than 10% chance of complete remission for about two years."

ELLIS. Can you tell me what it means?

LYNNE. I was going to ask you.

ELLIS. Hell, I don't know.

LYNNE. You nodded like you knew.

ELLIS. I nod well.

LYNNE. You didn't know and you didn't ask?

ELLIS. Well, would I change in two minutes? (*Roars; infectious; Lynne tries not to but then joins in*)

LYNNE. Maybe it means, "If you last two years, you're out of the woods."

ELLIS. Maybe it means, "There's less than 10% chance of lasting two years."

LYNNE. What about after two years?

ELLIS. (*Roars*) Then everybody's dead. (*Laughs; stops abruptly*) What's the date?

LYNNE. September 7th.

ELLIS. I'll be dead before Christmas. (*Flips pen in air; it sails behind her*) I'm going to die in three months and I don't even have a headache.

LYNNE. You have a sore throat. (*This sends both into high hysterics*)

ELLIS. (*Serious*) I feel like I'm on some kind of journey.

LYNNE. Can I come along?

ELLIS. What? Share my death? You're asking a lot. I never shared my life.

LYNNE. I don't know what to say.

ELLIS. How 'bout, "Bye, bye?" (*Roars*) Maybe I found my life's work. I die well. (*Roars*) Malnutrition!

Lights come up on bench area. Farmer and Farmer's Wife enter carrying chairs and subclavian kits — clear plastic buckets containing a t-tube, an alcohol prep pad, a tubex, a heparin needle, and an op-site bandage. They place pamphlets under chairs. Ellis gets up and crosses out of Lynne's light.

ELLIS. (*Sits on bench; laughs again*) Malnutrition?

LYNNE. (*Addresses audience as Nurse Eaton enters with a lectern or tray containing a catheter, hemostat, and heparin needle and stands opposite class*) The nurses were our lifeline. That one's name was Trish. There really was a Trish. (*Crosses stage*) When the nurses were good, they were very very good. And when they were bad ...

NURSE EATON. (*Booms loudly*) YOU ARE HERE (*Lynne rushes into scene, sliding timidly onto her bench seat*) because you've had a catheter inserted into your subclavian area.

FARMER. Subclavian?

FARMER'S WIFE. Shoulder.

FARMER. Oh.

NURSE EATON. Because chemotherapy weakens veins — the subclavian catheter is your best friend. To administer chemo, the technician need only insert the IV into the heparin cap ... (*Farmer raises hand*) I'll be happy to answers all questions at the end. (*Continues to demonstrate*) ... and the liquid courses through the catheter into the blood stream. It is imperative the tube be kept clean, the line kept from clogging. Before you leave Houston, your "significant other" must demonstrate his ability to maintain it.

ELLIS. You mean I won't be able to take care of this myself?

NURSE EATON. (*Laughs*) Hardly. (*Holds up heparin needle*) This is heparin solution. It is used daily to flush the catheter. (*Like Houdini; rapid speed*) Pick up your tubex. (*She holds it up. All scramble to find the newly named tubex*) Crack it ...

(*She does; they try*) ... insert the heparin needle and pull. (*Voila. Class has only just begun. Farmer raises hand*) It is imperative, I repeat, imperative to rid the heparin solution of air bubbles. (*Farmer's Wife raises hand*) If you do not, air will enter via the t-tube into the blood stream. You don't want air bubbles in your t-tube.

LYNNE. (*Raises hand, hesitantly*) Uh ... what's a t-tube?

NURSE EATON. (*Singsong*) Figure six, page four. Nor do you want water. Never — under any circumstances — get your catheter wet.

ELLIS. You mean I can't take a shower?

NURSE EATON. They didn't tell you?

ELLIS. No.

NURSE EATON. They should have. (*Holds needle up*) To eject the air bubble, hold the needle straight up and push the plunger.

ELLIS. I can't take a shower! (*Lynne slumps in her seat*)

NURSE EATON. You could have. With a peripheral catheter implanted in your arm.

ELLIS. You mean, I had a choice?

NURSE EATON. Certainly. (*Ellis drops tubex into bucket, sits with arms folded, staring*) Your catheter may be a little inconvenient, but I'm sure your veins will thank you. Hold the heparin needle between your fingers, open a prep pad, and clean off the heparin cap. (*Farmers Wife holds alcohol prep pad up for others. With needle between fingers, along with prep pad, class has trouble grabbing hold of heparin cap to wipe it. Nurse Eaton has five hands*) Insert the needle into the heparin cap and gently push the plunger. If you meet any resistance, don't push or you'll blow a hole right out of your catheter. (*All hands shoot up, minus Ellis's; Eaton perseveres*) I repeat, if you hear a pop; run to a doctor. Give heparin shots the same time daily, change op-sites once a week. (*Lynne fixes her hair with upraised hand*)

FARMER. Op-sites?

NURSE EATON. Figure twelve, page eight. (*In Rockettelike synchronization, all but Ellis reach below chair for pamphlet*)

ELLIS. (*Loudly to Farmer*) Did they tell you you couldn't take a shower? (*Class lowers eyes; Lynne cleans off her shoe*)

FARMER. (*Whispers*) Hell, they don't tell you nothin'.

NURSE EATON. When you change the op-site, feel around the incision. Is it red? Is it swollen? (*All hands shoot up; all but Ellis's*)

LYNNE. Could we get back to the "pop?" (*Chorus of whispered "Yah"s*)

NURSE EATON. Use a hemostat ...

ELLIS. What's a hemostat?

NURSE EATON. (*Holds up hemostat for Ellis to see*) ... to avoid getting germs on the hub.

ELLIS. What's a hub? (*Lynne cleans off her other shoe*)

NURSE EATON. Another name for a t-tube.

ELLIS. What's a t-tube? (*Singsongs with Eaton*) Figure six, page four. (*Beat*) Can I turn this in on a peripheral?

NURSE EATON. If you want to wait a week.

ELLIS. That's all we do is wait. (*All softly mutter; overlap*)

ELLIS. We wait in insurance, we wait in pharmacy, we wait in blood and urine.

FARMER'S WIFE. They keep you waitin' 'til ya don't care if you live or die. Then they tell ya, when ya don't care.

FARMER. I'd wait a week, if I know'd it was a week. But their weeks is two weeks.

NURSE EATON. (*Seeking an ally; chooses Lynne*) I'm sure the "waiting" causes frustration, but like I tell all my relatives, "If you're going to have cancer, have it in Houston." Patients have been known to make lifelong friends in this hospital.

ELLIS. (*Rises*) What's that? Three months? (*Storms off, Nurse Eaton catches Lynne's uncomfortable eye, smiles, as if she were a confederate*)

NURSE EATON. (*To Lynne*) She'll be back; she has no choice. (*Lynne squirms; nailed eye to eye. As Eaton drones on, Lynne slowly backs out of scene*) When changing the dressing, it is of the utmost importance to wear a sterile glove, keeping your ungloved hand away from the wound. In nurse's training, we learn by tieing the excess arm behind our back. (*Lights fade on bench area as Farmer, Farmer's Wife and Eaton exit with chairs and props*) It's filled with potentially harmful germs. Should the catheter become infected, get to a hospital. I repeat, get to a hospital immediately.

Lights up on bed area. Ellis is pacing, wrapped in a voluminous bath towel, eager to begin. Bed is dressed with L.A. quilt.

ELLIS. It's itchy.

LYNNE. (*Offstage*) I'm hurrying.

ELLIS. And it's cold.

LYNNE. (*Offstage*) Almost ready.

ELLIS. This isn't just a dressing change, you know.

LYNNE. (*Offstage*) I know.

ELLIS. One slip of the clamp and there's an air bubble. (*Lynne brings in a chair, covered with dressing kit, op-site bandage, chux, hemostat, and alcohol preps*) One slip and the emergency room. That tube leads right to my blood stream, right to my heart. (*Beat*) Think it's infected?

LYNNE. Don't worry.

ELLIS. "Don't worry." What a dumb thing to say, "Don't worry." Of course, I'm worried. Aren't you worried?

LYNNE. (*Leans instructions on back of chair*) Yes. (*Reads*) "Wash hands thoroughly." (*Exits narrowly into bathroom, blocking out the cat*) Move, Holbein.

ELLIS. (*Over sound of water*) My blood count's low! (*Pause for response*) One germ and it goes right to my blood stream. (*Pause for response*) She warned us. One germ and I've got infection. (*To herself*) All I need is infection. (*Beat*) Is that water hot?

LYNNE. (*Offstage*) Yes.

ELLIS. Very?

LYNNE. (*Enters narrowly, squeezing out cat. Closes door*) Very.

ELLIS. Wash your hands.

LYNNE. I just washed my hands.

ELLIS. Again.

LYNNE. Why?

ELLIS. You touched the doorknob. (*Lynne returns to bathroom, pushing cat out of way. Sound of water. Ellis lies down on bed. Vulnerable*) I'm not sure this bed's such a good idea!

LYNNE. (*Offstage*) Would you prefer a table?

ELLIS. No. (*Beat*) You sure that water's hot?

LYNNE. (*Offstage*) Trust me.

ELLIS. (*To herself*) Trust her. Terrific. (*Yells*) This is my life in your hands! (*To herself*) I hate this. I really do. (*Lynne enters, squeezing out cat, hands clinically high*) Be nice to have a mirror.

LYNNE. I just washed my hands.

ELLIS. Never mind.

LYNNE. (*Reads instructions*) "Place chux beneath shoulder." (*Ellis glares at Lynne, skeptically.*) While I get you a mirrow. (*Exits to bathroom, squeezing out cat*)

ELLIS. But you just washed your hands.

LYNNE. (*Offstage*) Something tells me to get you a mirror. (*Sound of water*)

ELLIS. Something tells me you're stalling.

LYNNE. (*Offstage*) I'm not stalling.

ELLIS. You're stalling and you're scared. (*Places chux beneath her shoulder*)

LYNNE. (*Enters with surgically poised hands. Mirror under arm. Narrowly squeezes out the cat*) Move, Holbein. (*Hips the door shut; passes mirror to Ellis; reads*) "Remove old dressing carefully." (*An op-site bandage covers the clavicle of Ellis's right shoulder, underneath that a piece of gauze, underneath that a small tube, the heparin tube, dangles auspiciously. Lynne removes the op-site as if she were defusing an H-bomb. Peeling it off slowly. Hours later*) That hurt?

ELLIS. It wouldn't if you'd go faster. (*Finally off, Lynne looks around for a basket, no basket. She tosses bandage on the floor. The small piece of gauze now separates Lynne from the surgical wound. Ellis watches her intently, as she inches off the gauze*) What do you see?

LYNNE. A tube going into your shoulder, held down with wings, held down with stitches. And dried blood from the operation.

ELLIS. (*Feigns casual, but her voice betrays her — in the vicinity of "Aida"*) Is it red?

LYNNE. No.

ELLIS. Any swelling?

LYNNE. Not that I can see.

ELLIS. What do you mean, not that I can see?

LYNNE. No. No swelling.

ELLIS. All I need is phlebitis.

LYNNE. (*Reads; while cleansing hemostat with alcohol prep*) "Check sutures to see if they're still tight." (*Pulls squeamishly on sutures*)

ELLIS. Are they tight?

LYNNE. Yes.

ELLIS. You sure?

LYNNE. (*Not sure at all, but fearful of yanking the sutures out*) Yes.

ELLIS. You don't sound sure.

LYNNE. "Open dressing kit." (*Pauses. Ellis waits impatiently. Lynne snaps open the kit and drops its plastic wrapping on the floor*)

ELLIS. Why don't you put it in a basket?

LYNNE. I don't have a basket.

ELLIS. You should have put a basket there.

LYNNE. Too late, now. (*The kit, a clear plastic bucket, is enclosed in butcher's paper, folded like Christmas wrapping. When opened carefully, the butcher's paper becomes the sterile field. She tentatively reaches for the first pointed corner*)

ELLIS. Don't touch the inside of it with your fingers, you're going to get germs all over it! That paper's the sterile field!

LYNNE. Okay, okay.

ELLIS. It's going to clot, I know it. All I need is a clot.

LYNNE. (*Pulls each corner of the overwrap to form the sterile field*) If your eyes get any narrower, you'll look like Charlie Chan. (*Reads*) "Don first sterile glove." (*Carefully lifts glove out of wrapper*)

ELLIS. By the inside cuff! If you touch the outside, it won't be sterile. The inside cuff.

LYNNE. Will you settle down! (*Struggles with glove — like an udder gone wild; eroding Ellis's confidence even more*) Shit.

ELLIS. It'd be alot easier without your ring.

LYNNE. (*Trying to maintain her dignity*) I know that.

ELLIS. Then why's it on?

LYNNE. Because.

ELLIS. Because why?

LYNNE. Because I forgot to take it off, Ollie. (*Ellis suffers in silence, while Lynne continues struggling with the glove*) I'll bet Marcus Welby didn't do this. I'll bet he had a stand-in.

Grab the cuff, pull, and snap—who're they kidding? Grab the cuff, pull, and snap—all five fingers in the same damn thumb hole. (*Finally on. With a large bulge*)

ELLIS. All this and thrombosis. (*Lynne puts her ungloved hand behind her back*) She suggested you tie your ungloved hand behind your back.

LYNNE. Too late, now.

ELLIS. Isn't it. (*Beat*) Constantly. (*Lynne turns toward audience, stares deadpan. Then reads*)

LYNNE. "Place items from container on sterile field, including 4×4's, 2×2's, saving receptacle for pharmaceutical debris." (*Huh? The bucket is filled with pharmaceuticals: gauze, scissors, swab sticks, ointments. Lynne dumps the contents onto the field and drops the bucket on floor. Ellis looks at her through slits*)

ELLIS. You're gonna need that for garbage. (*Lynne reaches to pick it up with sterile glove—oops. Instead, picks it up with regular hand and starts to put it on field—oops. Ellis watches, eyebrow arched, testing. Lynne drops it back on floor*) It's hard not to notice the ineptness of my "Significant Other."

LYNNE. (*Reads*) "Use alcohol swabs to clean." I feel like I'm assembling a toy.

ELLIS. Well, you're not. (*Lynne picks up packet of swab sticks, selects one, and gingerly cleans around wound*) Get it good and clean. (*Pause*) Scrub harder, I can stand it. First the wings. Then under the wings, under the sutures. Get it all out. (*Beat*) Clean away from the wound. Concentric circles away from the wound. Never go back inside the circle. Don't contaminate what's already been cleaned. (*Alarmed*) Did you go back inside?

LYNNE. (*Not sure*) No.

ELLIS. Why did you say "no?" You're not sure, I can hear it.

LYNNE. Because I fear your temper more than I fear negligent homicide. (*Throws swab stick out; gets another*)

ELLIS. Clean the whole area.

LYNNE. I am.

ELLIS. (*Uses hand mirror to look*) Harder.

LYNNE. I am.

ELLIS. I should be doing this myself. (*Lynne picks up envelope of solution, concentrating on what she can and cannot touch. Phone rings; both freeze*) At least the machine's on. (*Another ring*) Why isn't the machine on?

LYNNE. I unplugged it while I was painting.

ELLIS. Swell. (*Guiltily, Lynne grabs the package by her left, ungloved hand, scissors in right*) Could be a job offer. (*Guiltily, Lynne cuts the package of solution on a diagonal*) What if it's a job offer? (*Guiltily, Lynne dips gauze in solution, daubs wound. Phone stops ringing. There is a slight drip. Ellis is delighted*) It's running.

LYNNE. One drip.

ELLIS. (*Even tone*) It's getting on the bed.

LYNNE. Will you relax!

ELLIS. I told you this bed was a lousy idea.

LYNNE. Ellis, I swear I'll kill you.

ELLIS. That's obvious. (*Lynne leans over Ellis, daubing the pathetic drip with gauze. Her hair lightly touches the site. Tempo accelerates*) You got your hair in it!

LYNNE. No, I didn't!

ELLIS. You did! You got your hair in it!

LYNNE. Stop yelling! You're not helping!

ELLIS. It's making a mess! It's running over everything! (*Lynne continues to daub*) That's enough. That's enough! Don't clean it up with the gauze. You're going outside the sterile field. That's not sterile down there. Did you touch it?

LYNNE. (*Quietly, hoping not to get caught*) No.

ELLIS. You did, too. Jesus!

LYNNE. Will you stop yelling! You're making me a nervous wreck! The more you yell, the worse I get! You're like a goddam backstreet surgeon! (*Aware of her faux pas, Lynne retreats and opens the ointment, hoping Ellis was deaf. Pace slows, Ellis is silenced by Lynne's outburst, until*)

ELLIS. Backstreet surgeon?

LYNNE. You know what I mean.

ELLIS. You said, "backstreet."

LYNNE. I meant, "backseat."

ELLIS. You said, "backstreet."

LYNNE. Damn it! Stop it! (*Metamorphosis. Lynne becomes the Diabolical Doctor. Pulls off first glove, savagely. Pace speeds up as her next syllable sounds like a hiss*) Discard glove! (*Wiggles it;*

drops it tauntingly on floor) Don second glove! (*Dons the second with great prowess. Pulls down on the cuff and lets the glove fly back into place—à la Ben Casey. It is her grand gesture. Proceeds quickly, now—with confidence. Even if the glove has gone on like a cow's udder.*) "Scoop ointment onto site." (*Lynne does. Drops it onto floor. Reads*) "Blot dry with sterile gauze." (*Does; throws it defiantly onto floor. Reads*) "Cover site with 2×2's." (*Places two gauze squares on top*) "Discard glove." (*Tosses glove maniacally into air*) "Affix op-site." (*Takes cover off op-site, pulls off backing and slaps it on Ellis. Beat, then*) Shit.

ELLIS. What?

LYNNE. Shit.

ELLIS. What? What!

LYNNE. The bandage puckered.

ELLIS. Did you touch the sterile site?

LYNNE. Yes.

ELLIS. (*Delighted to be proved right. An idiot has been attending her medically. Oliver Hardy stare*) Then you'll have to start over, Stanley. (*Lynne exits as Ellis mutters*) I've had enough of this, I really have. Starting Monday, I'm gonna stop being a victim and learn to take care of myself. I'm going to go to gym, go to yoga, and run ten miles around the lake whether I'm tired or not. (*Clamps on headphones; defiantly snaps on Walkman full blast—intro to "Fame": "Baby, look at me." ... Lynne returns, sterile hands in air, as Ellis takes off headphones, sound out. Ellis yells defiantly*) Starting Monday, I'll be perfect.

Sound on as Ellis clamps on headphones. Lights fade out. House lights fade up slowly as music continues.

act 2

AT RISE: SOUND: *"Brandenburg Concerto."*

Fadeup. A cozy portrait. Helen is sitting on the bench, wrapping a Christmas present. Lynne is stretched out on floor reading an Isocal pamphlet while stirring a bucket of yellow paint.

LYNNE. (*Reads*) "Weight loss occurs because the disease and its treatments decrease appetite. Dry mouth decreases appetite; nausea decreases appetite; decreased appetite decreases appetite." Swell. (*Suddenly, there is a piercing cri de coeur from the kitchen*)

ELLIS. (*Offstage*) I can't stand it any longer! (*Lynne looks up, startled. Helen continues wrapping*) I don't know where anything is! There are pans in the plates, plates in the pans, forks in the knives, and every cupboard door is open! (*Bang*) Were we born in a barn!

LYNNE. (*Waits, "cri" over? Back to pamphlet. Then to Helen*) Oh, you're gonna love this. Things we can make: Isocal Eggnog, Isocal Banana Blush . . .

ELLIS. (*Offstage*) I can't stand it any longer! Everything in this refrigerator is moldy. The rice, the beans, the moo shu pork. And where's the jelly lid? Look at this! Look at this!

LYNNE. (*To Helen*) Look at what?

ELLIS. (*Offstage*) Look at this refrigerator! Little dabs of leftover everything. No wonder we can't find the eggplant. Mr. Keene *and all his lost persons* couldn't find the eggplant. I found the jelly lid! (*The news has little impact*) Even the jelly lid's moldy. And what's in the tin foil?

LYNNE. (*Under her breath to Helen*) Last week's pizza?

HELEN. Could be that, could be fish.

ELLIS. (*Offstage*) Tomorrow morning at 9:00 A.M., there will be an autopsy on this pizza. (*Helen stands up*)

LYNNE. I think she needs you.

HELEN. Uh, uh. Not in that mood. I learned a long time ago to leave her alone. (*Exits with wrappings. Silence, only the sound of the "Brandenburg Concerto." Lynne returns to pamphlet.*

Then: roar of an engine from offstage. Ellis careens around the corner pushing the front part or hose of a vacuum cleaner, sans canister. Lynne turns the pages of the pamphlet; Ellis yells above the roar)

ELLIS. The sea salt does not belong in the medicine cabinet. (*Lynne lifts feet on cue*) The toothpaste, however, does. (*Lynne stares deadpan at audience*) Every cup, saucer, and plate we own is in the dishwasher. Are we packing it to move? (*Ellis switches off vacuum*) Wonderful, now she's stirring paint in the living room. Are you stirring paint in the living room? (*Lynne nods her head yes*) Are you getting it on the floor? (*Lynne shakes her head no*) I'll bet you're getting it on the floor. Tell me that's not yellow. Is that yellow? (*Lynne nods her head yes*) The whole kitchen's yellow. The walls are yellow; the cupboards are yellow. Even the pepper mill's yellow. Why is the pepper mill yellow?

LYNNE. I had some paint left.

ELLIS. Well, I hope you ran out of stenciled roosters. (*Switches on vacuum, looks away from Lynne; Lynne looks at audience, shakes her head no; Ellis switches off vacuum*) I saw that!

LYNNE. You said you liked "country"!

ELLIS. That's not "country."

LYNNE. Then what is it?

ELLIS. Enchanted cottage.

LYNNE. You want it painted, or you want it perfect?

ELLIS. Aren't we late for my heparin shot?

LYNNE. Ooh, right. Just give me time to find a marker.

ELLIS. Time. Take your time. I've got all the time in the world.

LYNNE. (*Rips page out of pamphlet*) I found a marker.

ELLIS. I knew it was going to come to this.

LYNNE. Ellis, I'm here to help. Tell me how to help.

ELLIS. You can help by being less controlling.

LYNNE. (*Leaps up à la Rumplestiltskin*) I'm controlling! I'm controlling!

ELLIS. (*Winds vacuum cord with pseudo nonchalance, inwardly frightened by the intensity of Lynne's anger*) Yes.

LYNNE. Are you crazy! How, in God's name, am I the one that's controlling?

ELLIS. Demanding I be rational is controlling. (*Exits to bed area. Lynne is furious. A little Gleason*) Bang, pow, zoom! (*Pause. Then, to audience*) You know, she's right. (*Helen enters with tray containing mug, heparin needle inserted into tubex, alcohol prep, and assorted socks. Lynne gives bucket to Helen, drapes socks over her shoulder, takes tray while addressing audience. Helen exits*) I kept thinking about this kid I saw at a garden party — running round and round in a circle. Round the tables, round the buffet. Faster and faster. You could see she was exhausted but she'd just go faster. Then she began to scream: "Stop me! Stop me! Somebody, please, stop me!"

Cross-fade. Ellis is under L.A. quilt; nose deep in book. Lynne enters with tray.

LYNNE. (*Hesitant*) I brought you some soup. (*No response*) It's your favorite: cream of mushroom. (*No response*) Sixty calories. Eighty, if you use whole milk. We used whole milk. (*Sets tray on bedtable*)

ELLIS. Why do I do that? (*Beat*) Why do I do it?

LYNNE. (*A Viennese psychiatrist*) Tell me about your mother.

ELLIS. Speaking of whom?

LYNNE. (*Opens alcohol prep*) In the refrigerator. Looking for the eggplant.

ELLIS. She doesn't have to.

LYNNE. Try and tell her that.

ELLIS. (*Unbuttons top of shirt or blouse; holds heparin cap toward Lynne*) I told you you wouldn't like me when you saw all of me.

LYNNE. (*Cleans heparin cap with alcohol pad*) I saw all of you when we met. Slowly but surely, I'm seeing less and less.

ELLIS. Have you noticed these books say the same thing. "Let go of the oars." "Flow with the River." "Let it pass, let it be, let go." I keep thinking, that's so trite, that's so corny. They all say the same thing: Psychiatry, religion, A.A., Jesus Christ . . .

LYNNE. (*Expertly releases air bubble from needle*) Paul McCartney.

ELLIS. I don't need a relationship; I need a nanny. Why do you put up with it?

LYNNE. (*In her best Mousketeer*) "Why? Because we love you."

ELLIS. That's what I mean — why?

LYNNE. (*Gives Ellis heparin shot*) Your vulnerability.

ELLIS. I thought the world liked tough.

LYNNE. Vulnerability. And you've sure got a lot to love. Eat your soup. (*Ellis starts to eat*) Jesus God, it's cold in this house. (*Crawls under covers at foot of bed, folds socks. Ellis stops eating*) What's wrong?

ELLIS. (*Staring into soup*) I'm not very hungry.

LYNNE. But you love cream of mushroom.

ELLIS. (*Hesitation; not wanting to hurt*) It has lumps in it.

LYNNE. It always has lumps.

ELLIS. Not when Mom fixes it. I got a job offer today. (*Sets mug on tray*) Primetime television. Not an interview — a definite job offer.

LYNNE. When does it start?

ELLIS. Two months. (*Silence*) Well, we don't know if I'll be dead. Where should I have my ashes scattered? (*Beat*) How 'bout Island Beach? How 'bout the inlet at Barnegat Bay? (*Beat*) I can't hear out of my left ear.

LYNNE. (*Feels Ellis's shoulder*) Since when?

ELLIS. Since yesterday.

LYNNE. Why didn't you tell me yesterday?

ELLIS. I wasn't frightened yesterday. (*Laughs*) What are the signs of a brain tumor? (*Softly*) Help me.

LYNNE. How?

ELLIS. Push the fear away.

LYNNE. Let it in.

ELLIS. Oh, please. That's not what I need.

LYNNE. That is what you need. It is, Ellis. (*Entreats*) Don't turn away, listen to me. Will you listen? You're like a soldier defending a bunker, piling up layer after layer of sandbags to protect yourself from pain. And you know what the joke is? You're only sealing it in. What's down there that's so frightening? What's down there that's so bad?

ELLIS. A barn filled with slime.

LYNNE. Then clean it out. Why would you want to live in it? Clean it out.

ELLIS. I want to die unafraid. With dignity, unafraid.

LYNNE. First you have to live unafraid. I know, "look who's talking." (*Laughs*) We're quite a pair. I'm afraid to go outside; you're afraid to go inside.

HELEN. (*Hurries on stage*) I found the eggplant! (*Looks at watch*) My God, it's 2:00 A.M. (*Exits*)

ELLIS. There's a two-week intensive in Ojai [O-hi]. Lot of meditating. (*Silence*) Lot of people.

LYNNE. (*Shudders; long silence*) Look, I'll make a deal with you. I'll face the people; you face yourself.

ELLIS. You're asking me to dig out thirty-eight years of shit.

LYNNE. I'll grab a shovel, we'll work fast. (*Both laugh; Ellis coughs; takes Lynne's finger; studies it*) From making cole slaw. I grated my finger. (*Looks at Lynne's thumb*) Razor cut. From scraping beautiful Victorian windows. (*Looks at palms of hands*) Grass stains. Pulling vines. (*Lynne shows Ellis hairless arm*) Singed. Everytime I light the oven. (*Shows another spot on fingers*) Pinched. From setting up your mother's bed. (*Re-parts hair*) This is where Johnny Danielson hit me with a bat. (*Shows top of foot*) This is where Lois Eby [Ee-bee] stabbed me with a lead pencil.

ELLIS. You remember every scar?

LYNNE. Every scar.

ELLIS. Even the ones I give you?

LYNNE. Every scar.

ELLIS. Don't pay me back, okay?

Cross-fade. Ellis crosses to neutral area; Lynne puts tray and socks under bed, then crosses downstage to audience.

LYNNE. Picasso once said: a friend is someone you can sleep with. He wasn't talking about sex; he was talking about touch. There's a physical honesty as well as a mental honesty. I think it was Picasso. (*Lights on Ellis, eyes closed, meditating in lotus position*) I thought it was Picasso. (*Sits next to Ellis, shifts into lotus*) I'd like it to be Picasso. (*Sound: George Winston; to Ellis*) I want you to know we look ridiculous.

ELLIS. Concentrate on the mantra; exclude all thoughts.

LYNNE. Easy for you. (*To audience*) Would someone please explain this to my mother. I come from a sensible state.

Michigan. You don't do this in Michigan. And if you do, you lock the door. (*Beat*) I lost all sense of dignity. The first day we sat around in high lotus doing "Introductions." I hate "Introductions." I sit there rehearsing my name. Then we had to conjure up a power animal to be our guide. The first guy saw a tiger. My turn: I saw nothing. The next saw an eagle; the next a hawk. My turn: I saw nothing. They told me to let my mind drift, meander through the woods. And there, at the edge of a glen, I saw my power animal. I had to tell them it looked a lot like Thumper. (*Closes eyes, meditates*)

ELLIS. (*Opens eyes, to herself*) Ardis says temper tantrums are my specialty. I learned their power early. I think Mom found it easier to give in than live through one. When I was upset I'd go to my room and sulk, hoping she'd follow. She never did. I guess she just wanted to give me privacy. I thought she didn't care. Maybe that's why I care about Lynne. She doesn't stay outside the door. But sometimes I punish her for it. I don't know why. (*Closes eyes*)

LYNNE. (*Opens eyes; to audience*) I've always been terrified of hippies; I think they know something I don't. Truth be told, my other great terror was Ingmar Bergman movies. I was so relieved when I found out they weren't over my head. (*Beat*) Can a person with average intelligence flunk meditating? I mean, maybe I don't have a higher consciousness; maybe my brain stops at the mezzanine. Thank you for sharing. (*Closes eyes; meditates*)

ELLIS. (*Opens eyes; to herself*) For so long I wanted out. But I don't think that's true anymore. I have to admit, the house looks nice. When I'm not being perfect. When I'm not being a perfect shit. (*Beat*) I love my dog. I love my cat. (*Looks at Lynne; looks away*) I'd very much like to live. (*Closes eyes*)

LYNNE. (*To audience*) One night I dreamt that Ellis died alone. That was my biggest fear. It's such an intimate thing, death. Why in hospitals, why with strangers? (*Motions toward Ellis*) Look at her. I mean, that's serious meditating. I'll bet she's on the seventeenth floor.

ELLIS. (*To Lynne*) Bargain basement, smart ass. (*Looks at watch; stands up*) Three o'clock. Dance time.

LYNNE. I hate it.

ELLIS. I love it.

LYNNE. Sure. You look good in a leotard.

ELLIS. Then don't do it. Speak up.

LYNNE. (*Stands up*) Speak up, she says. Speaking up makes you visible. You want to walk around visible? I sure don't.

ELLIS. I thought we had a deal.

LYNNE. I'll speak up. (*Lighting change. Lynne exits. Benberg enters studying a chart; Trish carries a clipboard*)

TRISH. How you feeling?

ELLIS. Four months down; none to go. Shouldn't I be dead?

BENBERG. (*Feels her shoulder*) If you come here five years from now and call me an ass, I won't be surprised. Cancer's unpredictable.

ELLIS. I can't hear out of my left ear.

BENBERG. Pain?

ELLIS. Terror. (*Laughs; coughs*) What are the signs of a brain tumor?

BENBERG. I think we should try something else.

ELLIS. What's left?

BENBERG. A Chinese plant. (*Ellis looks at him*) Would I kid you? (*Trish hands Ellis paper to sign*) You'd be guinea pig Number 3. And you'd have to stay in Houston, as an inpatient.

ELLIS. (*Looks at paper*) Homoharringtonine?

TRISH. Great stuff. (*Escorts Ellis across stage to bed area as Benberg exits. Swirl of activity as Ellis goes offstage and changes into hospital gown. Trish changes the bed to hospital white. Nurse brings in IV pole and places it upstage of bed. Male Nurse brings in a blanketed cot stage right, Ellis's robe on top, and sets it between Ellis's bed and window, paralleling the bed. Nurse and Male Nurse exit*). Where's Lynne?

ELLIS. (*Offstage*) Getting me toothpaste. (*Enters*) See these are the biggies, do you get travel size or economy size when you're told you have three months to live? (*Coughs. Trish tucks Ellis in bed; inserts IV line into Ellis's arm; takes remote off bedtable and turns on flying TV. Sound: Academy awards bump loudly on: applause, music, the reading of the nominees. Trish uses remote to lower the sound. Ellis gets out journal*)

LYNNE. (*Enters stage left with grocery bag; to audience*) It was April, 1983. I remember because it was Academy Award night. Better known as "The Night They Ignored E.T." Best Film Editing: "Ghandi." Best Screenplay: "Ghandi." Best Location Caterer: "Ghandi."

ELLIS. (*From hospital bed*) At least they didn't get "Best Cancer Patient." I got best cancer patient. (*Trish sits at foot of bed, glances up at TV. Ellis writes in journal, thinks, erases. Lynne crosses to bed area. She is a whirlwind of movement: sets grocery bag on bedtable; refolds Ellis's robe, sets it on side of bed*)

LYNNE. They put patients' first names outside each door. Your "S" fell off. You're now "Elli Crowley." (*Looks at TV*) Who's that?

TRISH. He just won for best short animated ... and won't get off the stage. (*Ellis writes; erases*) What're you doing?

ELLIS. Ardis says to list all the ways to punish people without punishing myself.

LYNNE. She's been at that for two days.

ELLIS. Even my moderation is excessive.

BLOOD NURSE. (*Enters with blood caddy. Talks to Ellis loudly, as if she's deaf. Talks softly to others*) I have to get some blood, Mrs. Crowley.

ELLIS. Miss. It's Miss Crowley.

LYNNE. They just did that this morning.

BLOOD NURSE. It won't hurt.

ELLIS. Yes, it will. (*To Blood Nurse*) I hope you're the best. I don't have any veins left.

BLOOD NURSE. Only take a minute.

LYNNE. (*Watches, helplessly, while Blood Nurse swabs Ellis's arm, stabs, and Ellis winces; mumbles into bag*) They just did that this morning. (*Takes out groceries; holds each on high before setting on bedtable*) Papaya Sunrise, 250 calories ... Toothpaste ... (*Takes an enormous tube of toothpaste out of bag*)

ELLIS. (*Coughs*) That's a little optimistic, don't you think?

LYNNE. Häagen-Dazs vanilla fudge ... (*Takes off lid*) twenty glorious calories every glorious spoonful. (*Inserts spoon*) Eat. (*Sets ice cream on bedtable*)

ELLIS. (*Continues to write; erase*) I ate.

LYNNE. You tossed. Eat. You've only had 650 calories so far today. (*Takes toothpaste into bathroom*)

ELLIS. It burns.

LYNNE. (*Offstage*) Ice cream burns?

TRISH. It's the medicine.

LYNNE. (*Comes out of bathroom; to Trish*) Her mouth's so dry it burns?

ELLIS. (*Writes in journal, erases*) Will you slow down? Sit. Watch the show. (*Points to TV*)

LYNNE. (*Sits, watches Blood Nurse withdraw needle and stab again. Mutters*) They just did that this morning. (*Lynne looks away*)

TRISH. (*Tries to divert Ellis's attention from needle*) How much television did you direct?

ELLIS. None of them count.

LYNNE. Plenty count. What about the soap? Doesn't a year on a soap count?

ELLIS. How can it? I got fired.

LYNNE. (*For the last time*) You *weren't* fired. (*To Trish*) Why the hell she'd choose directing, I'll never know. Out of 60,000 hours of prime-time television only 135 were directed by women.

ELLIS. Thirty-five of those by Ida Lupino. (*Ellis winces; wince turns to cough*)

BLOOD NURSE. You got a cough, too? I had a cough all day yesterday. Took Nyquil and slept like a baby. Just took Nyquil. (*Withdraws needle; stabs again*) Your vein keeps rolling.

LYNNE. (*Looking at TV*) Oh oh.

ELLIS. What?

LYNNE. They've been raiding the motion picture home again.

TRISH. (*Looking at TV*) My God, is he still alive?

LYNNE. He'll never make it to the podium.

TRISH. Is he still alive?

LYNNE. Why do they wait to honor them in their nineties?

ELLIS. They prefer near death. Or just after. You're no longer a threat.

LYNNE. He'll never make it to the podium.

BENBERG. (*Enters*) Evening ladies.

TRISH. You still here?

BENBERG. I'm still here; you still here? (*Glances at TV*) My God, is he still here? (*All watch. Male Nurse wanders on, watches. Long pause*)

LYNNE. He made it! (*Cheers*)

ELLIS. I hate to throw a damper on all this enthusiasm, but he still has to open the envelope. (*Overlapping mutters*)

MALE NURSE. Well, guess I'll go finish my coffee.

BENBERG. Are there any donuts left?

TRISH. Donuts? Did someone say donuts?

BLOOD NURSE. (*Withdraws needle; to Trish*) Her veins keep rolling.

TRISH. (*Stops at door; softly*) Who's the best? Are you the best?

BLOOD NURSE. Christine's the best. (*Trish continues to look at her*) I'll get Christine. (*Exits*)

TRISH. (*To Lynne*) It's cold by that window. I'll find you more blankets. (*Exits*)

ELLIS. (*Writes, erases*) Damn.

LYNNE. What?

ELLIS. There aren't any ways to punish people without punishing myself.

LYNNE. I wondered how long it'd take you to figure that out.

ELLIS. Did you pay her?

LYNNE. (*Turns off TV with remote control on bedtable; to audience*) We finally settled down for sleep. (*Sits on cot; covers herself*) But the night was far from over. (*Reaches up to switch; turns off light*)

Blackout. Fadeup faint light: the moon the only source. Lynne is between the bed and the window, sleeping on the cot. She pulls sheetblanket around her ears, freezing. Ellis sits up in bed, looks around, climbs out, and walks to the window. The IV pole, however, remains by her bed. As the tubes are still attached to her body, the lines become taut with each step. They wake Lynne with a start as they snake across her bed. She sees the pole tipping precariously and bolts up.

LYNNE. What are you doing!

ELLIS. (*Looks at Lynne; puzzled by the alarm, then calmly*) Looking out the window.

LYNNE. But the pole!

ELLIS. (*Calmly*) What?

LYNNE. The pole! Don't move!

ELLIS. (*Calmly*) Why are you yelling?

LYNNE. Don't move! (*Leaps out of bed; switches on light; grabs pole*) You're going to pull the catheter right out of your arm. Trust me, don't move. (*Walks Ellis toward the bed*) God, you scared me. Geezus, it's 5:00 A.M.

ELLIS. (*Like a child, an amnesiac*) I'm sorry.

LYNNE. It wasn't your fault. Your're still asleep. (*Helps her into bed*) I've never seen you like that.

ELLIS. Like what?

LYNNE. Like that. So out of it.

ELLIS. Why are you sleeping?

LYNNE. Pardon me?

ELLIS. (*Points at pole*) Why are you sleeping? (*Her voice even, low — emotionless. Almost robotic*)

LYNNE. Are you trying to say pole?

ELLIS. Yes.

LYNNE. Honey, you're not making any sense.

ELLIS. You're not either.

LYNNE. But you're pointing at the pole.

ELLIS. Yes. (*Begins picking at her hospital gown*)

LYNNE. (*Long pause*) Ellis, what's wrong?

ELLIS. Nothing.

LYNNE. Do you know where you are?

ELLIS. In a hospital?

LYNNE. You're not sure?

ELLIS. It looks like a hospital.

LYNNE. It is a hospital.

ELLIS. (*Her questions are soft, sweet*) Am I sick?

LYNNE. You don't know?

ELLIS. I guess I am.

LYNNE. Ellis . . . you have cancer.

ELLIS. (*Emotionless*) Oh.

LYNNE. You don't remember?

ELLIS. No.

LYNNE. Not anything?

ELLIS. (*Picks at her gown*) No.

LYNNE. What year is this?

ELLIS. 1978.

LYNNE. Where do you live?

ELLIS. West 87th.

LYNNE. New York?

ELLIS. Yes.

LYNNE. (*A little too harshly; alarmed*) You live in L.A. (*Ellis, puzzled silence; chastised. Lynne is terrified, but gentler*) Don't be scared.

ELLIS. (*Her voice remains emotionless*) I'm not scared.

LYNNE. Ellis, think. Please. What year is this?

ELLIS. 1967.

LYNNE. Where do you live?

ELLIS. East 14th.

LYNNE. I'll be right back. Stay in bed; I'll be right back. (*Runs off. Hurries back trailed by Nurse Eaton and Male Nurse. He scans his clipboard*)

NURSE EATON. (*As if addressing a four-year-old*) Hello, Elli.

ELLIS. (*Like said four-year-old*) Hello.

LYNNE. (*Overlap; softly*) Ellis. It's Ellis.

NURSE EATON. How are you feeling?

ELLIS. Okay.

NURSE EATON. Do you know where you are?

ELLIS. A hospital.

NURSE EATON. Do you know why?

ELLIS. (*Sweetly*) Yes.

NURSE EATON. Why?

ELLIS. I have cancer.

NURSE EATON. (*Looks at Lynne with "she's fine"*) What year is this?

ELLIS. 1953.

NURSE EATON. Where do you live?

ELLIS. Westbury Avenue. (*Nurse Eaton looks to Lynne for varification; as does Ellis*)

LYNNE. Long Island?

ELLIS. Yes. (*Wanting to please*) Is that wrong?

LYNNE. When she was nine. (*Offhand*) Is it in the brain?

NURSE EATON. (*To Male Nurse*) Call Chawla. (*Both exit. Lynne sits on side of bed. Ellis watches her closely, like a child who has done something wrong. They have nothing to say to each other.*

Nurse Eaton returns with pill and papercup)
LYNNE. What's that?
NURSE EATON. Benadryl. (*Hands pill to Ellis*)
LYNNE. Isn't it possible — with all these drugs she's getting —
isn't it possible they backed up on her. That she overdosed?
NURSE EATON. Possible.
LYNNE. If the liver can't detox poisons, it can't detox drugs
either. Isn't it possible?
NURSE EATON. Possible.
LYNNE. Can't you wait; can't we find out?
NURSE EATON. (*Hands papercup to Ellis*) The doctor prescribed
it.
LYNNE. When? Just now? Before? Is it in the brain? (*Watches
helplessly. Ellis takes pill as Male Nurse and Nurse enter*)
NURSE EATON. (*Begins a rote exchange preoccupied with IV bottle*)
How are you, Elli? Do you know where you are?
MALE NURSE. What year is it? What month? Do you know
where you are? (*Litany continues softly, overlapping Lynne and
eventually Trish*)
NURSE EATON. What year is it? What month?
MALE NURSE. Do you know where you are?
NURSE. What year is it? What month? Do you know where you
are?

*Lynne paces apron as muted litany continues. Lighting changes to
early morning. Trish enters wearing a coat; crosses directly to
Lynne.*

TRISH. Do you have power of attorney? Anything signed?
(*Lynne shakes head no*) You're not related, that's trouble. If
they put her on life supports, you can't get her off. She
needs your protection and right now you can't protect her.
Where's her mother?
LYNNE. On a plane, Newark to L.A. Or picking up the animals. I
tried to leave her a message at the house, but the machine's
not picking up. Is it in the brain?
TRISH (*Puts hand on Lynne's shoulder*) They don't know.
LYNNE. Oh God, don't be kind. I'll never make it if you're
kind.
TRISH. (*Hurries to join questioners*) Ellis, it's Trish.

MALE NURSE. What year is it? What month?

NURSE EATON. Do you know where you are?

ELLIS. In the hospital.

NURSE EATON. Why?

ELLIS. I'm sick.

NURSE EATON. With what?

ELLIS. Cancer.

MALE NURSE. What year is it?

ELLIS. 1983. (*Lynne stands; attentive*)

TRISH. What month?

ELLIS. April.

TRISH. Where do you live?

ELLIS. Los Angeles.

TRISH. (*Points to Lynne*) Who is this?

ELLIS. Lynne.

NURSE EATON. Is she your sister?

ELLIS. No. (*Beat*) She's my friend. (*Trish helps Ellis off. Nurse changes bed to L.A. quilt; Male Nurse adds clothes to bed, puts pillow on floor, presetting robbery scene, then exits carrying empty IV bottle. Lynne walks out of scene*)

LYNNE. (*To audience*) I was never so glad to see anyone in my life. It *was* an overdose. And I was so glad, I cried. I was so glad, I more than cried. I was so glad, I had a teensy nervous breakdown in the corner. Ellis saw it. Ellis shouldn't have seen it. Ellis shouldn't have seen this, either.

Sound: airport traffic — ground and air. Lights cross-fade from bed area to apron. Lynne hurries across stage.

SKYCAP. (*Offstage*) You can't park there, lady!

LYNNE. (*Yells to Skycap, stage left*) I'm not parking, I'm just loading ...

SKYCAP. (*Offstage*) You can't park there!

LYNNE. But my friend's sick, I have to ...

SKYCAP. (*Offstage*) Okay, two minutes.

LYNNE. Right. Two minutes. (*Hurries off. Los Angeles Cop enters, wearing motorcycle helmet; saunters to car; looks at plates; takes out book, starts to write parking ticket. Lynne enters pushing Ellis in wheelchair; yells to him, confident of explanation*) He said, "Two minutes." He said I could park there for two minutes.

L.A. COP. You lose, Ma'am. (*Shrugs; keeps writing*)

LYNNE. (*Leaves Ellis stage right; runs over to L.A. Cop to confide*) Look, she's sick, we've got a mound of luggage, I've gotta race to the carousel, race back ... give me a break.

L.A. COP. (*Keeps writing*) I already wrote out the ticket.

LYNNE. Then unwrite it.

L.A. COP. I can't unwrite it.

LYNNE. Then I'll unwrite it!

L.A. COP. (*Calmly*) Go right ahead, Ma'am, and you'll cool off in jail. (*Hands her ticket*)

LYNNE. But he said, "Two minutes." (*He moves to next car; turning his back on her. Long pause. Ellis watches as Lynne explodes*) Don't you dare turn away from me. Don't you dare! I'm talking to you, Charlie! (*He looks at plates of next car; writing up another ticket*) That's right shrug your shoulders! Turn away and shrug your shoulders! You lose, Ma'am? Just like that, you lose? Big guy with a badge, writing parking tickets. Big guy with a badge! You must be some brave hero to your kids, you sadistic son of a ... !

L.A. COP. (*Turns; nose to nose*) Don't push me, Lady! I swear I'll haul you in. Don't push me! Now get in that car and get out of here! (*They glare at each other; he turns, walks off. As he disappears off stage, Lynne watches his back, Ellis watches Lynne. Then Lynne screams*)

LYNNE. "Two minutes!" HE SAID, "TWO MINUTES!"

Lynne pushes Ellis in wheelchair as Lights cross-fade to bed area. The bed is mussed, pillow is on floor.

HELEN. (*Enters*) They got the lamps. The police said make a list. They got the lamps; they got the TV. They got your jewelry; they got the answering machine. They got the washer; they got the dryer ...

LYNNE. (*Looks at the devastation*) They get the checkbooks?

HELEN. They got the checkbooks; they got the stereo.

LYNNE. Should we go to a hotel? (*Ellis shakes head no*) But you can't sleep here, this room's a mess. (*Cleans off bed; three or four pieces of clothing fall to the floor*)

HELEN. Want some soup? Cereal? (*Ellis shakes head no*)

Cinnamon toast, lots of butter? (*Ellis coughs*) I'll make some toast. (*Exiting*) They got the scale; they got the typewriter. They got the clock; they got the other clock. (*Ellis gets out of wheelchair*)

LYNNE. (*Rushes to help*) Careful, there's glass. (*Helps her slowly into bed*) How many you think there were? Two, three? (*Taking off Ellis's shoes*) I'll clean this up right away. At least the clothes. I'll wash the clothes. No I won't. (*Mimics Helen*) They got the washer, they got the dryer. (*Exits with wheelchair*)

HELEN. (*Offstage*) They got the juicer; they got the can opener. (*Head around corner*) They got the toaster. No toast. (*Beat*) Want a malt? Never mind, they got the blender. How 'bout ... (*Ellis shakes head no; Helen feels chastized*) Look at Holbein. She loves to sleep on that chair. Ever since Lynne got that cover, she stopped sleeping on the couch.

LYNNE. (*Enters*) She's no fool; it's got cat hair.

HELEN. (*Exiting*) They got the Polaroid; they got the photos ...

ELLIS. (*Coughs, a deep wrenching cough*) May I have some water?

LYNNE. Sure. (*Exits to bathroom; sound of water. Offstage*) The good news is: they cleaned out the medicine cabinet. The bad news is: they left the water-pic. (*Enters; hands cup to Ellis; sits on bed. Ellis coughs. Silence, then, with difficulty*) Trish thinks we should talk about contingencies.

ELLIS. What contingencies?

LYNNE. I should know your wishes, get power of attorney.

ELLIS. Why now?

LYNNE. It can wait till tomorrow.

ELLIS. But why now?

LYNNE. I guess she's just thinking ahead.

ELLIS. Way ahead, don't you think?

LYNNE. I didn't ...

ELLIS. You sure didn't. (*Beat*) Does it mean you'd have power over me?

LYNNE. I could run off with the funds.

ELLIS. You could, you know.

LYNNE. Jesus. (*Long pause*) Better get some sleep. I'll tiptoe when I come in.

ELLIS. Do you have to?

LYNNE. Come in? (*Yes*) Course not. (*Stands up; takes cup from Ellis*) Don't be alone, if you don't have to, okay? (*Beat*) Well. Need a pillow. (*Picks pillow up*) Wonderful, they took the pillow case. (*Kneels on floor; looks under bed*) I just saw one. Hang on, I'm out of here. (*Rummages further; faster*) Hell with it, I'll use a sweatshirt. (*Rummaging*) Now where's a sweatshirt? (*Beat*) Forget the sweatshirt, I'm out of here. (*Waits; wants more; gets nothing. Exits. A beat, then Helen enters*)

HELEN. They got the card table; they got the chairs. (*Sits on bed; looks at Holbein*) Look at Holbein. Animals are so peaceful.

ELLIS. Of course, they are. They don't know they're gonna die.

HELEN. (*Chides with humor*) What a thing to say. (*Ellis grabs on to Helen*) It'll be okay. (*Holds her*) It'll be okay. (*Continues to hold her*) Don't worry. It'll be okay. (*Jumps up; reverts to cheerleader*) I've got it! Root-beer float! You used to love root-beer floats! I'll fix you a root-beer float! (*Helen exits. Cross-fade to Lynne, neutral area*)

LYNNE. (*Holding bowl of soup; to audience*) Ellis went so far inward, we couldn't find her. It was like "Invasion of the Body Snatchers." Remember that movie? All the towns-people are zombies, except for Kevin McCarthy and Dana Wynter, who are in love and trying to escape. He keeps begging her, "Stay awake, don't fall asleep! Stay awake!" Then he leaves her in a cave and she nods off; when he returns, she looks at him with lifeless eyes. Same face, same mannerisms, but lifeless eyes. No love in them. (*Beat*) That was the most horrifying moment in any horror movie I ever saw. (*Delivers bowl to Ellis*) There aren't any lumps. We strained it with cheese cloth. (*Waits for response; no response; to audience*) We were the butt end of a cosmic joke: When she pulled away, I grabbed on. And the more I clutched, the more she pulled away. It was a wonderful cycle. And did I get good. (*Helen enters, sets blankets for next scene at foot of bed, takes bowl from Ellis, exits*) Boy, did we get good. For five days, we cooked, we sewed, we cooked, we painted. The more she withdrew, the gooder we got. (*Kneels on bedroom floor; to audience*) I bought her a VCR. (*Adjusts *machine*) Took me ten years to hook it up. (*To Ellis*) "Ragtime" or "Midnight Express?"

ELLIS. Either.

LYNNE. "Midnight Express." (*Turns it on. Sound of movie*) Hey, it works! (*Looks to Ellis for applause. Ellis stares at set in silence. To audience*) The illness became our universe. I was three months behind on the Falkland Islands. I had no idea who won. But I had learned one thing: Cancer eats up 2000 calories a day. All by itself. (*Helen enters, sweeps floor with a broom. Lynne turns to Ellis who is writing in journal*) There's a two-week intensive next week in the desert. They said they'd make room for two more.

ELLIS. Can we afford it?

LYNNE. I've got credit cards.

ELLIS. Aren't they at their limit?

LYNNE. I'll get new ones; I'll borrow from friends.

ELLIS. What if I get worse?

LYNNE. I'll bring you home.

ELLIS. Who's going to monitor my blood?

LYNNE. They said there's a doctor, he can take your blood. Then I'll take it to a hospital in Barstow.

ELLIS. Next time you make plans, want to include me?

LYNNE. Sorry. (*Dares*) But why don't you sleep on it. (*Silence; jokes*) Stay out of your personal sphere? (*Silence*) Ellis, talk to me.

ELLIS. (*Furious*) Stop telling me what to do! (*Helen starts to tiptoe off with broom*)

LYNNE. (*Backs off, quickly*) Sorry. I'm really sorry.

ELLIS. (*To Lynne*) And stop tiptoeing! (*Helen stops tiptoeing abruptly; exits*)

LYNNE. I said I was sorry.

ELLIS. You make me feel like a monster! Always tiptoeing! (*Lynne is silent*) Swell, now she's gonna pout. You gonna pout? You're acting just like my mother. (*Beat*) I can't do this. I really can't. We met speaking a different language. We're still speaking a different language. I really can't take this turmoil. I need time alone.

LYNNE. I've left you alone.

ELLIS. I need time alone.

LYNNE. Are you saying tonight? (*Silence*) Are you saying tomorrow? (*Silence*) What are you saying? (*Silence*) Small word. Three letters. Sounds like . . .

ELLIS. Sometimes I don't think I love you as much as you love me.

LYNNE. Jesus, where'd that come from? (*It landed*) I'll make a deal with you. I won't ask you to love me more; if you don't ask me to love you less. (*Silence*) Okay? (*Silence*) Okay? (*Silence*) Obviously, not okay. (*Silence*) I don't believe this. (*Silence*) You want me to leave? Is that what you're saying? (*Silence*) You want me to pack up and leave? (*Silence*) Ellis, don't do this. (*Touches her*)

ELLIS. Don't touch me!

LYNNE. What!

ELLIS. Don't touch me! You always wanna talk things out! Talk things to death! I don't know how the hell we've lasted!

LYNNE. Because you chose me! I'm your friendly neighborhood dentist. That's why you chose me! You want me to reach down and wrench out your feelings because you don't have the guts to do it yourself. That's why you chose me! So don't give me "you overanalyze, you always want to confront, you always want to talk." Because you chose me! You want me out, I'm out!

ELLIS. When does the fucking pain stop!

LYNNE. When we're dead! (*Lynne crosses out of scene to apron; furious. Paces angrily — one, two, three; one, two, three; one, two, three. Stops. Thinks. Marches back into room just as defiant*) I don't care what you say, I'm not leaving!

ELLIS. Thank God.

LYNNE. (*Plops on floor, rests against bed. Neither looking at the other, exhausted*) Wanna go to the desert?

ELLIS. They'll split us up, you know. For two weeks, they'll split us up.

LYNNE. Wanna sleep on it?

ELLIS. Why are you letting a four-year-old run your life? (*Without rancor, explaining*) I hate your energy, you know. I don't want to, but I do. (*Lynne realizes the irony. Pause*) If I lose your strength; I lose everything.

LYNNE. Is that what this is about? Because I cried in the hospital? Because I got nutsy with a cop?

ELLIS. Yes. (*Thinks*) No. (*Thinks*) I think it's about Mom and last Friday.

LYNNE. What about Mom and last Friday? (*Beat*) You got this far. (*Ellis hands her the journal. Lynne addresses audience*) This is what she wrote.

ELLIS. Today she held me while I cried. I'm thirty-eight years old and she held me while I cried and because she loves me she said, "It'll be okay." But it's not okay, I'm dying. (*Quietly*) She's my mother. She should have magical powers, she should be able to make it better. But she can't make it better and I feel betrayed by her, not it—and I want to protect myself from her, not it. (*Angrier*) I want to punish her. I want to punish her because she's not magical. I want to punish her because she's not all-giving. I want to punish her because she's not God. She is merely, my mother. (*Beat*) I want to deny her. I want to deny her the most serious thing I can deny her. I want to deny her me. (*Hears the enormity of what she's said*) I want to deny her me.

LYNNE. See how easy that was.

ELLIS. You're out of the will.

Sound: Crickets and George Winston. Lights: Blackout, except for stars stretched across the horizon. A flashlight bumps on. Light picks up Ellis stage left writing in her journal with the help of Duracell. Knapsack by her side.

ELLIS. I slept out last night—the first time I've ever slept out under the stars. Actually, I didn't sleep; I didn't want to miss anything. (*Stops writing*) I watched the stars traverse the sky from east to west—I don't think I ever really knew that—that the stars rise in the east and set in the west. And this morning, the best of all. This morning, I wanted to get up. I wasn't even afraid of snakes. (*Cross-fade on Lynne, stage right, in advanced state of hypothermia. Random swatting. Pulls blanket around shoulders; to audience*)

LYNNE. I can't believe I'm doing this. Out here. On some lousy hill. In the middle of the desert. In the middle of the night. Fasting to death and freezing my chaconees off.

Frankly, I don't know how Christ did it. (*Slaps arm; sound of very loud coyote*) Oh, swell. Explain this to my mother. "Your daughter was eaten alive by a pack of coyotes in the Mojave desert while becoming one with the universe." (*Slaps elbow*) God, I'm hungry. Two more hours to breakfast. Probably tofu on toast. (*Slaps neck; cross-fade*)

ELLIS. (*Writes*) There's this poem by some guy named Wang Zoo. (*Looks up*) If a man's in a skiff heading for shore and an empty boat bumps into his, what does he do? He keeps on heading for shore. But if there's a person in the other boat, what does he do? He rants, he raves, he bellows, he kicks, and stops heading for shore. His ranting and raving won't change anything. But he's seduced into thinking it can. (*Beat*) I sat in that boat and ranted away a lifetime and never got any closer to shore. It's becoming very clear I can't change what's about to happen. I can't hold back death. And the wierdest thing? There's a peacefulness in that. There's not a damn thing I can do. The joke is that was true with everything else in my life. The seduction was to think I could.

LYNNE. (*Flashlight crosses the stage. Lynne sings à la Mister Rogers*) "It's a *be*-oo-tiful day in the neighborhood, a beautiful day in the neighborhood. Could you be mine? (*Enters Ellis's light*) Would you be mine?" (*Sun begins to rise slowly*)

ELLIS. What are you doing here!

LYNNE. That's what I've been asking myself for twelve days. Want to make sandcastles, Chickee?

ELLIS. What if we get caught?

LYNNE. What are they gonna do? Lash us with a soba noodle? Take away our "I Ching" [Ee-ching]?

ELLIS. How you doin'? (*Shivers; Lynne sits down next to her and shares the blanket*) I'm having a lot of trouble with "unconditional love." For starters, I hate the cook.

ELLIS. God, it's good to see you.

LYNNE. It's good to see you saying, "It's good to see you." (*Flicks flashlight on Ellis's face*) Geez, Ellis, if I didn't believe in this stuff before I do now. You look radiant. (*Flashlight off*)

ELLIS. Last night, I dreamt I was sitting on a fence, teetering between choosing life and choosing death. I wanted to choose life ... but was afraid of making a commitment. (*Beat*) We shouldn't be doing this. We're supposed to keep silence.

LYNNE. We're here to make changes, right? I'm working on defying authority. What are you working on?

ELLIS. Trying to stop my terror of negative thoughts. I'm up to ten a day. (*Beat*) Why do you think we keep death out of life?

LYNNE. There's pain in death.

ELLIS. There's pain in birth. What'll I do if the fear comes back.

LYNNE. Let it.

ELLIS. Let it?

LYNNE. Let it.

ELLIS. Gotcha. I need to itch.

LYNNE. Where?

ELLIS. My right shoulder.

LYNNE. (*Scratches Ellis's right shoulder*) Boy, for someone who feared dependency.

ELLIS. Funny, isn't it. We'd never be together, you know. If I weren't dying. (*Beat*) And this whole year. This whole year. I've never been more alive. (*Beat*) Why did you stay?

LYNNE. It never occurred to me to leave. (*Thinks*) Because I love you. (*Beat*) Because I fear dying alone.

ELLIS. You won't die alone.

LYNNE. Will you be there?

ELLIS. I'll be there. You won't die alone. My world; I make the rules.

LYNNE. (*Dives into Ellis's knapsack*) Got any peanut butter in here?

ELLIS. You can cry.

LYNNE. It's selfish.

ELLIS. You can cry. (*Lights fade on both as Ellis exits with blanket. Lynne addresses audience*)

LYNNE. Now, I'm not dumb enough to suggest two weeks on a low mount in the high desert turned her life around. But when we got back everything had changed. Ellis made more phone calls, wrote more proposals, AD'd a live stage production for PBS, but when we walked in the woods, she dawdled. She seemed to have lost all fear. Fear of death, fear of life, fear of me. She even bought a pair of Mary Janes. A kind of symbolic break. Seemed delightfully ironic that Mary Janes became synonymous with "fuck you." (*Music starts softly, "Eye of the Tiger" from "Rocky III"*) Benberg had said three months. It was now eighteen and rising. The cough was still there, her mouth was still dry, but the lump in the shoulder? It was going down. And waiting? Oh, had she learned to wait.

Sound of music level rises to blasting. Ellis enters and sits as lights come up on bench area, now the waiting area in Houston. Ellis has headphones on. Totally relaxed in chair, she colors and taps her foot to the music. Lynne talks to her, no sound is heard. Ellis is oblivious. Lynne shrugs, sits; her movements unaffected by the music. Nurse Eaton enters, walking counterpoint to the music; calls out a name, no sound is heard. Ellis lifts headphones. Sound out.

ELLIS. (*Yells to Lynne*) What color looks good on Shirley Partridge?! (*Nurse Eaton casts a glance. As she exits, Lynne hastily scans waiting room; then reverts to her "mortified" slump. Surreptitiously whispers into Ellis's ear*)

LYNNE. Housedress or when she's playing the tambourine?

ELLIS. (*Yells*) Housedress!

LYNNE. (*In her ear*) Try periwinkle blue. Want some soup? (*Ellis nods yes, replaces headphones. Sound on: "Tiger" again blares forth as she searches for periwinkle blue. Lynne reaches for thermos behind bench, pours soup into top, nudges Ellis, Ellis sets one speaker off ear, takes soup. Sound out*)

ELLIS. (*Yells*) How long have we been waiting?!

LYNNE. Four hours.

ELLIS. (*Yells*) What's the record?!

LYNNE. Mrs. Headley at nine.

ELLIS. (*Yells*) Is this too loud?!

LYNNE. (*Yells*) No, but you are! (*Ellis anchors headphones around her neck; stares into her soup*) Oh God, you find a lump? Is there a lump? (*Looks into soup; sucks in breath in high outrage*) One. One lump.

ELLIS. (*Laughs*) Well, would I change in two years? (*Gets serious*)

You know, I was just thinking. . . . You were there when I had the hysterectomy, you were there when they diagnosed cancer, you were there when I overdosed. I was just thinking. . . .

LYNNE. What?

ELLIS. You're a fucking jinx.

LYNNE. Where'd you hear that one?

ELLIS. (*Coughing*) Some guy in the chemo ward. (*Coughing gets worse*) I can't get air. (*Beat*) I can't get air.

NURSE EATON. (*Hurries in*) What's wrong?

ELLIS. (*Gulps for air*) Isn't that silly? (*Gulps air*) I can't get air.

Lights fade slightly. Sound of muffled voices. Male Nurse and Nurse rush in, clustering around Ellis, escort her into bed area. Another swirl of activity setting the next scene: Male Nurse brings in blanketed cot; Nurse brings in IV pole; Nurse Eaton attaches tubing to Ellis. Lynne crosses downstage and addresses audience as frantic movements in the dark continue.

LYNNE. Ellis began to vomit that night. And vomit and vomit. I was emptying basins as fast as I could run. Then the male nurse climbed on the bed and stuck a tube down her throat. She now had oxygen tubing in her nose, IV's in her arms, and tubing in her stomach. For someone who wanted freedom, she was attached like a Bil Baird marionette.

TRISH. (*Enters; hands Lynne gloves, mask, and papercup; helps her into isolation gown*) Change whenever you enter her room. New mask, new gown, new gloves. Her white blood count's low.

LYNNE. They said a thousand.

TRISH. It's a hundred. Someone added an extra 0. (*Exits*)

LYNNE. (*Dons gloves*) I phoned her mother in Barnegat Bay but she was sick herself—her legs, arms rubbed raw from infection, a product of the sun. She died two months later of skin cancer, screaming for *her* mother. (*Beat*) Three days later, I had a job interview, eighty miles out of town. I wanted to cancel but Ellis insisted; I didn't get back until late. On my return, I learned one thing very quickly.

When someone becomes helpless, latent vultures begin to circle. And the healthy line up with the healthy.

Lights full up. Sound of gastric sump tube; sound of oxygen. Ellis is lying in hospital bed on a forty-five-degree angle to audience next to an upstage IV pole, bedtable with chart, and chair. Downstage guardrail is up. There is a blanketed cot just below the window stage center, paralleling the bed. Ellis is connected to a bank of tubing: oxygen attached around the ears to her nose; IV's in her arm; sump tube in her nose. Her mouth is so dry from medicine, it's now affecting her speech. There are sheets on the floor, emesis basin and Kleenex on bedtable. Lynne enters wearing mask, carrying a paper cup.

LYNNE. Hi, Kiddo!

ELLIS. (*Relief*) Oh, good.

LYNNE. Good what? Good to see me? (*Sits on bed; Ellis smiles yes*) Oh, good. (*Offers her the paper cup. Side-of-mouth, like a gangster*) No one was looking, so I stole ya some ice chips.

ELLIS. Shh.

LYNNE. Shh, what? They're for your mouth.

ELLIS. Will it make them angry?

LYNNE. Make who angry?

ELLIS. Let'sh not make them angry, okay?

LYNNE. (*Puzzled; relents*) Okay. (*Sets cup on table; leans over*) Grab my neck. (*Ellis does. Lynne pulls her up*) Scootch. (*Ellis does*) Better?

ELLIS. Yesh.

LYNNE. Here. (*Hands Ellis cup. Ellis is hesitant. Nurse Eaton enters from bathroom wearing isolation gown, no mask, gloves. Tucks in bedding*)

NURSE EATON. She messed her bed again. Third time tonight. (*Loudly, as if chiding a small child*) You've been a naughty girl, haven't you, Mrs. Crowley?

ELLIS. Yesh.

NURSE EATON. (*Loudly to Ellis; pointing to ice cup*) Careful, or you'll spill your water. Did you spill your water? (*Aside to Lynne*) They don't make it easy, do they? (*Picks up emesis basin from bedtable; exits to bathroom. Lynne stands dumbfounded.*

Eaton returns) Just when we'd finish cleaning her up, we'd clean her up again. (*Loudly to Ellis*) You've really been a naughty girl. (*Walks to door. Intimately to Lynne*) She just keeps shitting. (*Exits. Lynne continues to stare in disbelief at Nurse Eaton's receding back*)

LYNNE. (*Takes Kleenex from bedtable, moistens it in ice cup, sits on bed, and dabs Ellis's mouth*) You're bleeding again. Open wide. Can you open wide? (*Ellis does. Lynne dabs her mouth*) She's treating you like you're two.

ELLIS. Poetic jushtish.

LYNNE. She's never done that before. She's never dared. (*Moistens Kleenex; dabs mouth*) Your mouth's a mess. Am I hurting you? (*Beat*) Should I steal some more peroxide? Can you gargle with peroxide? (*Beat*) What are you thinking? (*Laughs*) Well, would I change in two years?

ELLIS. We'll do thish again.

LYNNE. What again? Us again? (*Beat*) In another life? (*Ellis nods yes*) Think we'll know each other?

ELLIS. In a minute, Chickee. (*Silence; then, like a tiny child*) Let'sh go home.

LYNNE. Now?

ELLIS. Yesh, can we?

LYNNE. (*Sets ice cup on table*) It's awfully late. Can we wait 'til tomorrow? (*Ellis thinks about it*) I promise. Tomorrow. If you still want to go. I'll spring you from this joint, okay? (*Beat*) Your world. You make the rules. (*Ellis blinks with both eyes*) Is that a wink? You telling me it's okay? (*Ellis nods*) Does it hurt to talk? (*Ellis nods*) In that case ... (*Looks at watch*) It's 7:30. Time for "Family Feud." (*With remote on bedtable, Lynne turns on television: "Family Feud" droans in the distance. Ellis stares drowsily at TV. Lynne sits on cot, focusing on Ellis. Both are very tired. Lighting change to suggest time change. Sound fades out; fades in with theme for "Hillstreet Blues"*)

ELLIS. Oh, oh.

LYNNE. What?

ELLIS. I meshed the bed again.

LYNNE. (*Laughs*) Oh, oh.

ELLIS. (*In little girl voice*) Will she be mad?

LYNNE. She wouldn't dare.

ELLIS. Will she be mad?

LYNNE. It's not your fault.

ELLIS. I'll bet she'sh mad.

LYNNE. (*Beat*) Tell you what. I'll clean you up, okay?

ELLIS. Better not.

LYNNE. She'll never know, I promise. She'll never know, okay? (*Beat*) Would it embarrass you?

ELLIS. Not if you do it.

LYNNE. She'll never know, hang on. (*Rushes out. Sound of X-ray machine lumbering down the hall. Sound of someone whistling [or semi-singing] "Bye Bye, Blackbird." A Technician, wearing mask and gloves, rolls in [or mimes rolling in] a skeletal representation of a large X-ray machine, pushes it into position over the bed*)

TECHNICIAN. (*Loudly*) I have to take X rays, Mrs. Crowley. (*Plugs it into wall*) Can you sit up? (*Ellis maneuvers an inch*) A little more? (*Ellis tries*) Here. (*Sets her in uncomfortable position; holding guardrail, staring out the side of the bed, like a Raggedy Ann doll*) Okay, now hold that pose until I count ten. (*Leaves the room, whistling. Ellis falls out of position. Technician returns*) Please, Mrs. Crowley, the sooner you hold, the sooner it's over. (*Ellis holds shakily onto rail. He leaves the room. Lynne hurries into doorway, carrying a ream of sheets*) You can't go in there! (*To Ellis*) Now hold to ten. One, two, three, four ... (*Ellis holds, staring out the side of the bed. He looks at watch; continues to whistle. Ellis falls back*) Did you hold to ten?

LYNNE. She held, you weren't counting.

TECHNICIAN. Maybe I'd better get another one.

LYNNE. She held, please, she held. (*Enters room, crosses into bathroom. Technician shrugs, unplugs machine, packs up, and exits, whistling, Lynne returns with washcloth and emesis basin filled with water*)

LYNNE. Quick, roll on your side. Can you roll on your side? (*Ellis doesn't move. Urgently*) Roll on your side, chum. (*Ellis does with effort*) Here. (*Races around to downstage side*) Grab my arm. (*Nothing. Grabs Ellis's arm and pulls her on her side*) Hold on to the guardrail. Okay? (*Kneels down, puts Ellis's hands on guardrail. Ellis holds on like a child*) Okay, now roll over. Roll over a little more. (*Hurries around upstage side*) A little more. Please, honey, a little more. (*Pulls out bottom sheet, balls it, tosses it on floor. Quickly cleans Ellis with washcloth*) She won't be mad. She'll never know. Trust me. She'll never know.

ELLIS. Let'sh go home.

LYNNE. Tomorrow, okay? I promise, tomorrow. (*Picks up clean sheet; hears someone approaching*) Roll back, someone's coming. Roll back, honey. (*Stashes clean sheet under cot blanket. While juggling the emesis basin, she grabs dirty sheets and races to bathroom. Ellis remains in the same position*) Roll back! (*Ellis falls back. Lynne sets basin down as Male Nurse enters carrying a jug and a long needle; sets it on floor*)

MALE NURSE. You'll have to leave now.

LYNNE. (*Almost laughs*) What!

MALE NURSE. Doctor's going to do a lung tap. (*Studies chart*) Sorry but you'll have to leave.

LYNNE. They let me stay before.

MALE NURSE. (*Disturbed by something on chart*) Who let you stay?

LYNNE. Benberg.

MALE NURSE. For a lung tap?

LYNNE. For three lung taps.

MALE NURSE. (*Doesn't hear; preoccupied*) When the doctor comes, you'll have to leave. (*Exits*)

LYNNE. (*Moves quickly to bed*) Hold on to the side. Hold on, okay. I need to put this sheet down. (*Ellis doesn't move*) If it's missing, they'll know. Hold on, okay? (*Lynne hurries around to downstage side of bed; pulls her toward guardrail*) When the doctor comes, should I leave? Would it be easier for you if I left? (*Ellis shakes her head no over and over*) Okay, then hold on, okay. Just for a second. (*Runs around to upstage side; Ellis falls back*) Can't you hold on? (*Runs to downstage side; pulls her toward guardrail*) Please, Ellis, hold on. You have to help me. Hold on. (*Runs around to upstage side*) Your eyes are so red. Are you overdosing again? Does it feel like an overdose? (*Ellis falls back*) Please, hold on! (*Lynne shoulders Ellis up; forces sheet under*) There! Good! (*Ellis falls back on bed in a slightly neck-breaking position: slumped down, below the pillow*) Grab my neck. (*Beat*) Grab my neck. If she sees you, she'll know. Grab my neck.

(*Leans down; puts Ellis's arms around her neck; tries to inch her toward the pillow*) Now, scooch up. (*Beat*) Just scooch like you always do. (*Tries to move her*) You're dead weight. Can't you help me? Please, honey, hike up. (*Ellis tries hard, inches gained. Lynne lets her head down slowly. It is now barely on the pillow. Nurse Eaton enters with box of medicine. Male Nurse follows with heparin needle; goes directly to Ellis, prepares catheter, administers heparin shot*)

NURSE EATON. You'll have to leave now. (*Picks up jar and needle; sets it on bedtable*)

LYNNE. (*Rote*) I won't get in his way.

NURSE EATON. I said, you'll have to leave. (*Holds up box of medicine*) For diarrhea. No side effects. It'll just make her mouth exceedingly dry.

LYNNE. You can't do that! Her mouth's so dry it's bleeding!

NURSE EATON. The fact remains, the doctor prescribed it.

LYNNE. Which doctor prescribed it?

NURSE EATON. (*Opens box of medicine*) The doctor on duty.

LYNNE. He's never been in here!

NURSE EATON. The doctor prescribed it. She's getting dehydrated. Besides, we can't spend the night cleaning her up.

LYNNE. I'll clean her up. If it happens again, I'll clean her up.

NURSE EATON. (*Walks to tubing; unscrews bottle of medicine*) That's not the point.

LYNNE. That is the point.

NURSE EATON. No, here's the point. The doctor prescribed it.

LYNNE. Then unprescribe it! Look at her mouth! (*Male Nurse takes needle out of catheter, inserts it again. Lynne attempts to calm down; addresses Male Nurse*) They did that this morning. They did that at ten. (*Catches nervous look from Male Nurse to Nurse Eaton*) Didn't they do that at ten?

NURSE EATON. (*Fills eyedropper*) You'll have to leave now.

LYNNE. (*Rote*) They let me stay before.

NURSE EATON. (*Finality*) I said, you'll have to leave.

LYNNE. (*Male Nurse takes needle, inserts it into catheter once again*) What's wrong? Is it clotted? (*Beat*) Did they wait too long? Is it clotted?

MALE NURSE. (*Hurries to door; Lynne follows*) If it's clotted, we'll unclot it. No cause for alarm. (*Exits*)

LYNNE. I know, but is it clotted? (*Nurse Eaton opens sump tube to*

Ellis's stomach and is about to put medicine down it. Lynne rushes over, whips her hand over the tube, blocking it. She lowers her voice) I'm telling you, you're not giving her something that'll make her mouth dryer.

NURSE EATON. (*Same tone; medicine dropper poised*) And I'm telling you, it's been prescribed.

LYNNE. What about her heparin, wasn't that prescribed? Wasn't that prescribed at ten?

NURSE EATON. You're getting emotional.

LYNNE. You bet I am. Wasn't that prescribed at ten!

NURSE EATON. (*Guides Lynne to apron*) Okay, now calm down. Can we calm down? (*Lynne takes a deep breath*) Just calm down and listen, okay? (*Lynne does*) In my job I follow orders, I follow doctor's orders. I have no choice, I just obey. Understand? (*Waits; Lynne absently nods*) Good. Now. If a doctor prescribes medicine — whether or not I agree with that medicine — I have no choice, I just obey. Understand? (*Waits; Lynne nods*) Good. Now a doctor has ordered a lung tap. Not just any doctor, but a particular doctor, a particular doctor with a particular preference. So. (*Doesn't wait for Lynne to react*) Before the doctor enters a room, he prefers I empty the room. Not your choice; not my choice; but his choice. Understand?

LYNNE. (*Quietly*) Putting it that way, I can't help but understand. Of course, it's the doctor's choice. (*Beat*) So. (*Beat*) When the doctor enters the room, and finds my body still in the room, he can choose to leave the room; do a lung tap with me in the room; or, find a less particular doctor with a less particular preference who will let me stay in the room.

BLOOD NURSE. (*Barely enters room with caddy*) I have to get a blood test, Mrs. Crowley.

LYNNE. (*Does not take her eyes off Eaton*) Are you Christine!

BLOOD NURSE. No.

LYNNE. Get Christine! (*Blood Nurse hurries out*)

NURSE EATON. (*Explodes*) You can't countermand a doctor's orders! You're not a relative! You have no say!

LYNNE. (*Hesitant; puzzled*) I have power of attorney.

NURSE EATON. (*Pause*) In that case (*Shrugs: "just doing my job"*) fine. (*Puts eyedropper back in medicine bottle, screws on cap, without a trace of animosity. Lynne watches — surprised by the power of her remark. Nurse Eaton walks out, a study in composure*)

LYNNE. You look so uncomfortable. Don't you care? (*Ellis stares into the distance, squinting, as if by focusing intensely with her outward eyes she can see her inner life*) Don't you care? (*Ellis makes an incomplete circle with her thumb and index finger, as if the index finger was stretching to touch the thumb*) What? (*Beat*) A circle? (*Ellis shakes her head no. Makes another incomplete circle with the index finger, stretching the index finger over and over, trying to touch the thumb*) A "C?" (*Ellis shakes her head no. Lynne finally begins to understand, brakes the urgency*) Your life? (*Beat*) Is it closing? (*She nods yes*) Was it all sad? (*Ellis looks intently at Lynne; smiles; shakes her head no. Her breathing becomes irregular. Breathing in becomes weaker; breathing out becomes stronger and longer*) Ellis. (*Beat*) Are you dying? (*Long delays between each breath — as if there'll never be another*) I'm here, Kiddo. I'm here. (*Then there's another*) Go with it, Chum. Let go. (*Then nothing. Lynne takes off mask and gloves*) I'm getting you out of here, Chickee. We're going home. (*Peels the tape off Ellis's arm and removes the IV*) We're blowing this joint, Kiddo. (*Takes the oxygen tubing out of her nose, the straps from around her ears*) We're going home. (*Walks out of scene; to audience*) On a warm Monday morning in summer, driving south on the Jersey Turnpike, along the Jersey Shore, I took Ellis home. To scatter her ashes at Island Beach, where we'd walked near the inlet at Barnegat Bay. (*Beat*) I remembered our first drive to the shore — Ellis quoting from John's First Epistle: "There is no fear in love; but perfect love casteth out fear." I thought she was celebrating our friendship. (*Smiles*) Little did I know she was trying to ward off sheer terror. (*Sound of ocean and gulls*) I arrived at the entrance at 6:00 A.M., but the barrier gate was down: "No cars allowed 'til eight." I'd have to hurry; I'd have to walk, to avoid the summer crowd. I figured it was six miles to the inlet, six miles back; a four-hour hike. I learned it was eleven miles to the inlet, eleven miles back; an eight-hour hike. (*Beat*) I noticed everything on that walk: the blackbirds, the spikemoss. I was aware of a fly buzz, a friendly fly that followed me along the tarmac, darting in and out of the bramble. Seven-thirty jogged by, eight. I shifted my knapsack to my other shoulder — surprised by the weight. Why the inlet; why not any beach? No, Ellis wanted the inlet. I lost track of the fly. (*Beat*) Eight-thirty, nine. A car went by; another car. Turn off, take any bay. Or you'll have ashes catching the wind in a maze of Frisbees. No, Ellis wanted the inlet. Another car, walk faster. Another car, let go. Nine-thirty, ten. The ashes slammed against my back. Another car, walk faster. Another car, let go. (*Beat*) I turned off on a narrow pathway, climbed one sandy rise after another, until I gazed out at the morning ocean. The beach was deserted, the sea calm, the sky a Maxfield Parrish blue. And I knew Ellis wasn't minding this spot at all. (*Sits*) I sat down on a ridge of sand ... (*Takes off shoes and socks*) Took the box of ashes out of the tote bag, and shuddered. A friend said I'd see bone. (*Slowly pushes it open, like a cigar box*) Inside was a clear plastic bag with a wire tie; inside that, the solidness of gray and white, salt and pepper. The fear left. (*Beat*) I waded into the ocean, the water cold against my legs, undid the tie. I poured the ashes slowly between the waves. They swirled in the foam. Then I heard a voice from the deepest part of me, a voice that sounded very much like Ellis and it said, "Now, live." (*Beat*) "Don't wait for Monday." (*The lights fade out*)

philip kan gotanda
yankee
dawg you
DIE

American theatre should represent America. When one walks down the streets of any large city, what does one see? A vast array of peoples from diverse cultural and ethnic backgrounds, all of whom are Americans. And if theatre in America is to be an alive, vital medium, it must begin to include the stories of all her people.

For the past ten years I have been writing plays about Asian Americans. Whether it be my satirical *Yankee Dawg You Die*, dealing with Asian stereotypes in the Hollywood film and TV industries, or *The Wash*, exploring the tensions of acculturalization in a contemporary Japanese American family, I have tried to bring a better understanding of one particular American group to the stage.

I have often been asked whether my perspective is a "narrow" one, the assumption being that the term "Asian American writer" is limiting. I feel rather it is just the opposite case. To explore one's own cultural specificity affords all of us a more expansive look into who and what America really is. It is my belief that America is a cultural pluralism rather than a melting pot of indistinguishable humanity. And the better the understanding of her peoples' unique and special differences, the more evident becomes the universality of those groups.

Certainly given the volatility of the times in regard to racial and cultural tension, we all need to begin to see the world from the other person's vantage point, be brave enough to examine socialized biases we all carry within us and challenge them, or America is truly in for a tumultuous time ahead.

Sometime in 1985 I was sitting in a coffee shop with a good friend, Eric Hayashi, the Artistic Director of the Asian American Theater Company in San Francisco. We got into a discussion about old World War II movies and soon found ourselves trying to remember our favorite "classic lines" the evil Japanese soldier would invariably hiss out in "Hollywood Orientalese." The one phrase that seemed continually to pop into mind was "Yankee dog you die." Whether that was ever really said or it was a kind of distillation of all those silly Sargeant Moto diatribes, I'm not sure. But we soon found ourselves locked in a raucous game of dueling sterotypes. Eric would say "Yankee dog you die" in thick Hollywood Orientalese, then I would say "Yankee dog you die" with an even thicker and more ridiculous accent, each continuing to challenge the other till our performances had reached grotesque cartoon proportions. In other words, our performances were now perfect for the portrayal of Asians in American movies.

Now at the same time I had been working with many of the Asian American actors through my work as a playwright writing plays specifically Asian American in theme. And as I got to know them, they began to share with me stories of their experiences in the movie, television, and theatre fields. Some were humorous, some hilarious, and some infinitely sad. Some of the experiences had happened to them, others had happened to friends — but all were entertaining and certainly informative as to the particular nuances a person of color in the industry had to live with day after day.

And at some point five years ago, between the "Yankee Dog" game at the coffee shop and me getting to know these special people, I decided to write *Yankee Dawg You Die*. Too many good stories to keep to myself, a silly coffee shop game to set it in motion, and I was at work. It was to be my tribute to Asian American actors, the ones who had breathed so much life into my works and to whom I owed so much.

Now here's where the practical side to writing for theatre comes into play — I had recently encountered some difficulty getting my most recent work produced because of its large cast. Thus, I decided that this new play would be a two-character piece. A play about actors, letting the real-life actors have the entire stage to themselves. Let these Asian American players have their "moments." And let me have a play that would get produced.

My original intention was to make the two characters such that they could be played by either males or females. However, once into the material I realized that each gender had its own set of very specific issues. Most of the plot I had already developed more readily fit a two-male cast so I proceeded with that story line with hopes of one day getting back to writing a play with two female characters.

I first workshopped the play at the Los Angeles—based East West Players in 1986. I directed it and the two actors were Sab Shimono as Vincent and Michael Paul Chan as Bradley. I workshopped it again at the Bay Area Playwrights Festival in 1987 with Richard E. T. White directing and Dennis Dun as Vincent and Marc Hayashi as Bradley. The world premiere took place at the Berkeley Repertory Theatre in 1988 with Sharon Ott directing and Sab Shimono playing Vincent and Kelvin Han Yee playing Bradley. Subsequent productions have been staged at the Los Angeles Theatre Center, The Group Theatre in Seattle, Wisdom Bridge in Chicago, Playwrights Horizons in New York, and the Asian American Theater Company in San Francisco.

characters

VINCENT CHANG: Actor. Mid to late 60s. Former hoofer.

BRADLEY YAMASHITA: Actor. Mid to late 20s.

set

Minimal with a hint of fragmentation and distortion of perspective to allow for a subtle dreamlike quality. Upstage, high-tech shoji screens for title and visual projections. Set should allow for a certain fluidity of movement. Allow for lights to be integral in scene transitions. Suggested colors— black with red accents.

lighting

Fluid. Interludes should use cross-fades. Dream sequences might experiment with color and shafts of light cutting at askew angles, film-noirish.

music

Minimal instrumentation. Classical in feel.

introduction

Darkness. Filmic music score enters. Then, on the projection screens upstage we see emblazoned the following titles:

"[Name of Producing Theatre] PRESENTS ..."

"VINCENT CHANG ..."

Vincent lit in pool of light, staring pensively into the darkness. The music dips and we hear the faint beating of a heart. A hint of blood red washes over Vincent as he lightly touches his breast near his heart area. Fade to black.

"AND INTRODUCING ..."
"BRADLEY YAMASHITA"

Bradley lit in pool of light. Restless, shifting his weight back and forth on his feet. The music dips and we hear the light rustling of large wings. As he looks skyward, a large shadow passes over head. Fade to black.

"IN ..."
"YANKEE DAWG YOU DIE ..."

The entire theatre — stage as well as audience area — is gradually inundated in an ocean of stars. Hold for a moment, then a slow fade to black.

act 1

INTERLUDE ONE

Lights come up. Vincent portraying a "Jap soldier." Lighting creates the mood of an old '40s black and white movie. Thick Coke-bottle glasses, holding a gun. Acts in an exaggerated, stereotypic — almost cartoonish manner.

Sergeant Moto pretends to be falling asleep while guarding American prisoners. The snakelike lids of his slanty eyes drooping into a feigned slumber. Suddenly Moto's eyes, spitting hate and bile, flash open, catching the American prisoners in the midst of their escape plans.

VINCENT. (*As Moto*) You stupid American G.I. I know you try and escape. You think you can pull my leg. I speakee your language. I graduate UCLA, Class of '34. I drive big American car with big-chested American blond sitting next to ... Heh? No, no, no, not "dirty floor." Floor clean. Class of '34. No, no, not "dirty floor." Floor clean. Just clean this morning. 34. No, no, not "dirty floor." Listen carefully. Watch my lips. (*He moves his lips but the words are not synched with them à la poorly dubbed Japanese monster movie*) 34. 34! 34!!! (*Pause. Return to synched speaking*) What is wrong with you? You sickee in the head? What the hell is wrong with you? Why can't you hear what I'm saying? Why can't you see me as I really am? (*Vincent as Sergeant Moto dims to darkness*)

SCENE ONE

"YOU LOOKED LIKE A FUCKING CHIMPANZEE"

Night. Party. House in Hollywood Hills. Vincent Chang, a youthful, silver-maned man, in his late 60s, stands on the back terrace balcony sipping on a glass of red wine. Stares into the night air. Bradley Yamashita, 27, pokes his head out from the party and notices Vincent. Stops, losing his nerve. Changes his mind again and moves out on the terrace next to Vincent. Bradley holds a cup of club soda.

Silence. Vincent notices Bradley, Bradley smiles, Vincent nods. Silence. They both sip on their drinks.

BRADLEY. Hello. (*Vincent nods*) Nice Evening. (*Silence*) God. *What a night.* Love it. (*Silence. Looking out*) Stars. Wow, would you believe. Stars, stars, stars. (*Pause*)
VINCENT. Orion's belt. (*Bradley doesn't follow his comment. Vincent*)

points upwards) The constellation. Orion the Hunter. That line of stars there forms his belt. See?

BRADLEY. Uh-huh. (*Pause. Sips his drink. Vincent points to another part of the night sky*)

VINCENT. And of course, the Big Dipper.

BRADLEY. Of course.

VINCENT. And, using the two stars that form the front of the lip of the dipper as your guide, it leads to the ...

BRADLEY. The North Star.

VINCENT. Yes. Good. Very good. You will never be lost. (*Both quietly laugh*)

BRADLEY. Jeez, it's a bit stuffy in there. With all of them. It's nice to be with someone I can feel comfortable around. (*Vincent doesn't understand*) Well, I mean, like you and me. We're—I mean, we don't exactly look like ... (*Nods towards the people inside*)

VINCENT. Ahhh. (*Bradley laughs nervously, relieved that Vincent has understood*) Actually, I had not noticed. I do not really notice, or quite frankly care, if someone is Caucasian or Oriental or ...

BRADLEY. (*Interrupts, correcting Asian. Vincent doesn't understand*) It's Asian, not Oriental. (*Vincent still doesn't follow. Bradley, embarrassed, tries to explain*) Asian, Oriental. African American, Negro. Woman, girl. Gay, homosexual ... Asian, Oriental.

VINCENT. Ahhh. (*Pause*) Orientals are rugs? (*Bradley nods sheepishly*) I see. (*Vincent studies him for a moment, then goes back to sipping his red wine*) You don't look familiar.

BRADLEY. First time.

VINCENT. You haven't been to one of these parties before? (*Bradley shakes his head*) Hah! You're in for a wonderful surprise. Everyone here is as obnoxious as hell.

BRADLEY. I noticed.

VINCENT. (*Laughs, extends his hand*) Vincent Chang ...

BRADLEY. (*Overlapping*) Chang! (*Bradley grabs Vincent's hand and manipulates it through the classic "right-on" handshake. Vincent watches it unfold*) You don't have to tell me. Everybody knows who you are. Especially in the community. Not that you're not famous—I mean, walking down the street they'd notice you—but in the community, whew! Forget it.

VINCENT. Ahhh. And you?

BRADLEY. What?

VINCENT. Your name.

BRADLEY. Oh. Bradley Yamashita. (*Pronounced "Yamasheeta" by him. Bradley shakes his hand again. Vincent repeats name to himself, trying to remember where he's heard it. He pronounces the name correctly*) This is an amazing business. It really is. It's an amazing business. One moment I'm this snotty nose kid watching you on TV and the next thing you know I'm standing next to you and we're talking and stuff and you know ... (*Silence. Sips drink. Looks at stars*) Mr. Chang? Mr. Chang? I think it's important that all of us know each other. Asian American actors. I think the two of us meeting is very important. The young and the old. We can learn from each other. We can. I mean, the way things are, the way they're going, Jesus. If we don't stick together who the hell is going ...

VINCENT. (*Interrupts, waving at someone*) Ah, Theodora. Hello!

BRADLEY. Wow ...

VINCENT. Theodora Ando. The *Asian American* actress.

BRADLEY. God, she's gorgeous.

VINCENT. (*Coldly*) Don't turn your back on her. (*Bradley doesn't follow. Vincent mimes sticking a knife in and twisting it*)

BRADLEY. (*Staring after a disappearing Theodora*) Oh ... (*Silence. They sip and stare out into the darkness. Bradley begins to turn and smile at Vincent in hopes that Vincent will recognize his face. Vincent does not*) New York. Jesus, what a town. Do you spend much time out there? (*Vincent shrugs*) Yeah. I've been out in New York. That's where they know me most. Out in New York. I come from San Francisco. That's where I was born and raised. Trained—ACT. But I've been out in New York. I just came back from there. A film of mine opened. New York Film Festival. Guillaume Bouchet, the French critic, loved it.

VINCENT. (*Impressed*) Guillaume Bouchet.

BRADLEY. Uh-huh. Called it one of the ten best films of the year.

VINCENT. It's your film? You ... directed it? (*Bradley shakes his head*) Wrote it?

BRADLEY. No, no, I'm in it. I'm the main actor in it.

VINCENT. (*Mutters under his breath*) An actor . . .

BRADLEY. It's a Matthew Iwasaki film.

VINCENT. I have heard of him, yes. He does those low-budget . . .

BRADLEY. (*Interrupts, correcting*) Independent.

VINCENT. Ahhh. *Independent movies* about . . .

BRADLEY. (*Interrupts, correcting again*) Films. Independent films, they play in art houses.

VINCENT. Ahhhh. *Independent films* that play in *art houses* about people like . . . (*Nods to Bradley and to himself*)

BRADLEY. Uh-huh

VINCENT. I see. Hmmm.

BRADLEY. I'm in it. I star in it. Eugene Bickle . . .

VINCENT. (*Interrupts*) Who?

BRADLEY. Eugene Bickle, the film critic on TV. You know, everybody knows about him. He used to be on PBS and now he's on the networks with that other fat guy. He said I was one of the most "watchable" stars he's seen this year.

VINCENT. Really?

BRADLEY. He said he wouldn't mind watching me no matter what I was doing.

VINCENT. *Really?*

BRADLEY. Well, that's not exactly—I'm sort of paraphrasing, but that's what he meant. Not that he'd wanna watch me doing anything—you know, walking down the street. But on the screen. In another movie.

VINCENT. Film.

BRADLEY. What?

VINCENT. You said "another movie."

BRADLEY. Film.

VINCENT. Ahh.

BRADLEY. My agent at William Morris wanted me to come to L.A. I have an audition on Monday. One of the big theatres.

VINCENT. (*Impressed, but hiding it*) William Morris?

BRADLEY. (*Notices that Vincent is impressed*) Uh-huh. (*Pause*) Who handles you?

VINCENT. Snow Kwong-Johnson.

BRADLEY. Oh. (*Pause*) I hear they handle mainly ...

VINCENT. (*Interrupts*) She.

BRADLEY. Oh, yes. *She* handles mainly ... (*Motions to Vincent and himself*)

VINCENT. Yes. Mainly ... (*Motions to Bradley and to himself*)

BRADLEY. Ahhh, I see. Well. (*Silence*)

VINCENT. It's a bit warm tonight.

BRADLEY. I feel fine, just fine. (*Vincent takes a cigarette out and is about to smoke. Bradley begins to steal glances at Vincent's face. Vincent remembers to offer one to Bradley*) I don't smoke. (*The mood is ruined for Vincent. He puts the cigarette away. About to take a sip of his red wine. Bradley notices Vincent's drink*) Tanins. Bad for the complexion. (*Holds up his drink*) Club soda.

VINCENT. I imagine you exercise, too?

BRADLEY. I swim three times a week. Do you work out?

VINCENT. Yes. Watch. (*Lifts drink to his lips and gulps it down. Pause. Vincent notices Bradley looking at his face. Bradley realizes he's been caught, feigns ignorance, and looks away. Vincent touches his face to see if he has a piece of food on his cheek, or something worse on his nose. Vincent's not sure of Bradley's intent. Perhaps he was admiring his good looks Vincent's not sure*) Bradley? Was there something? You were ... looking at me? (*Vincent motions gracefully towards his face. Pause. Bradley decides to explain*)

BRADLEY. This is kind of personal, I know. I don't know if I should ask you. (*Pause*) OK, is that your real nose?

VINCENT. What?

BRADLEY. I mean, your original one—you know, the one you were born with?

VINCENT. (*Smile fading*) What?

BRADLEY. Someone once told me—and if it's not true just say so—someone once told me you hold the record for "noses." (*Barely able to contain his giggling*) You've had all these different noses. Sinatra, Montgomery Clift, Troy Donahue—whatever was *in* at the time. Sort of like the "Seven Noses of Dr. Lao ..." (*Notices Vincent is not laughing*) That's what they said. I just thought maybe I would ask you about ...

VINCENT. (*Interrupts*) Who told you this?

BRADLEY. No one.

VINCENT. You said someone told you.

BRADLEY. Yes, but . . .

VINCENT. (*Interrupts*) Someone is usually a person. And if this person *told you* it means he probably has lips. Who is this person with *big fat moving* lips.

BRADLEY. I don't know, just someone. I forget — I'm not good at remembering lips.

VINCENT. No. (*Bradley doesn't follow*) No, it is *not* true. This is my natural nose. As God is my witness. (*Silence. Vincent sipping drink. Turns to look at Bradley. Repeating the name to himself*) Yamashita . . . Ya-ma-shita . . . You worked with Chloe Fong in New York? (*Bradley nods*) Ahhh.

BRADLEY. What? (*Vincent ignores Bradley's query and goes back to staring out at the night sky. Occasionally, glances at Bradley knowingly*) What? (*Pause*)

VINCENT. Now this is kind of personal. And tell me if I am wrong. I heard you almost got fired in New York.

BRADLEY. Who said that — what?

VINCENT. You are the fellow who was out in that play in New York, correct? With Chloe?

BRADLEY. Yeah, so?

VINCENT. I heard — and tell me if I am wrong, rumors are such vicious things — I heard they were not too happy with you, your work.

BRADLEY. What do you mean, "not happy with me?"

VINCENT. Now, this is probably just a rumor — I do not know — But, that is what I . . .

BRADLEY. (*Interrupts*) That's not true. That's not true at all. I was a little nervous, so was everybody. And I never, "almost got fired." Did Chloe say that?

VINCENT. No, no, no.

BRADLEY. Cause I was OK. Once I got comfortable I was good. You ask Chloe. The director came up afterwards and congratulated me he liked my work so much. White director.

VINCENT. Ah, rumors.

BRADLEY. (*Mutters under his breath*) Bull shit . . . (*Silence. Vincent takes a cigarette out, lights it and takes a deep, satisfying drag*)

VINCENT. Ahhh. I needed that. (*Pause*)

BRADLEY. Who said I almost got fired? Was it Chloe? She wouldn't say something like that. I know her. (*Beat*) Was it her?

VINCENT. It is just a rumor. Take it easy. Just a rumor. Remember this? (*Taps his nose*) Dr. Lao? It comes with the terrain. You must learn to live with it. It happens to everyone. Sooner or later. *Everyone.* You are walking along, minding your own business, your head filled with poems and paintings — when what do you see coming your way? Some ugly "rumor," dressed in your clothes, staggering down the street impersonating you. And it is not you but no one seems to care. They want this impersonator — who is drinking from a brown paper bag, whose pant zipper is down to here and flapping in the wind — to be you. Why? They like it. It gives them glee. They like the lie. And the more incensed you become, the more real it seems to grow. Like some monster in a nightmare. If you ignore it, you rob it of its strength. It will soon disappear. (*Beat*) You will live. We all go to bed thinking, "The pain is so great, I will not last through the night." (*Beat*) We wake up. Alive. C'est dommage. (*Pause*) Have you seen my latest film? It has been out for several months.

BRADLEY. Was this the Ninja assassin one?

VINCENT. No, that was three years ago. This one deals with life after the atomic holocaust and dramatizes how postnuclear man must deal with what has become, basically, a very very hostile environ ...

BRADLEY. (*Interrupts*) Oh, the one with the mutant monsters — they moved all jerky, Ray Harryhausen stuff — and the hairy guys eating raw meat? You were in that film? I saw that film.

VINCENT. I got billing. I got ...

BRADLEY. You were in it?

VINCENT. ... the box.

BRADLEY. I'm sure I saw that film. (*Looking at Vincent's face*)

VINCENT. I came in after everyone signed so my name is in the square box. My name ...

BRADLEY. Nah, you weren't in it. I saw that film.

VINCENT. . . . is in all the ads. There is a big marquee as you drive down Sunset Boulevard with my name in that box.

BRADLEY. (*Staring at Vincent's face, it's coming to him*) Oh, oh . . . you were the husband of the woman who was eaten by the giant salamander? (*Bradley is having a hard time suppressing his laughter*)

VINCENT. (*Shrugging*) It was a little hard to tell, I know. The makeup was a little heavy. But it was important to create characters that in some way reflected the effects . . .

BRADLEY. (*Overlapping, can no longer contain himself and bursts out laughing*) Makeup a little heavy? Jesus Christ, you had so much hair on your face you looked like a fucking chimpanzee! (*Bradley stops laughing as he notices Vincent's pained expression. Awkward silence. Vincent smokes his cigarette. Bradley sips on his soda. Bradley occasionally steals a glance at Vincent. Vincent watches the North Star. Dim to darkness*)

SCENE TWO

"WIN ONE FOR THE NIPPER"

Audition waiting room at a theatre. Vincent seated, reading a magazine. Bradley enters, carrying script.

BRADLEY. (*Calls back*) Yeah, thanks, ten minutes. (*Bradley sees Vincent, cautiously seats himself. Vincent pretends not to notice Bradley and turns away from him, still buried in his magazine. They sit in silence. Breaking the ice*) Mr. Chang, I'm sorry. I really didn't mean to laugh . . .

VINCENT. (*Interrupts*) Excuse me young man, but do I know you?

BRADLEY. Well, yes . . . we met at that party over the weekend in the Hollywood Hills . . .

VINCENT. (*Interrupts*) What did you say your name was?

BRADLEY. Bradley. Bradley Yamashita.

VINCENT. And we met at that party.

BRADLEY. Yeah, On the balcony. (*Vincent stares intently at Bradley who is becoming uncomfortable*)

VINCENT. You look familiar. You must forgive me. I go to so many parties. Did I make a fool of myself? I do that sometimes. I drink too much and do not remember a thing. That makes me an angel. You see, angels have no memories. (*Vincent smiles and goes back to reading*)

BRADLEY. Look, whether you want to remember or not, that's your business. But I'm sorry, Mr. Chang. I sincerely apologize. I can't do more than that. I shouldn't have laughed at you. (*Silence*)

VINCENT. You say your name is Bradley? Bradley Yamashita? (*Bradley nods*) Which part in the play are you reading for?

BRADLEY. The son.

VINCENT. They want me for the part of the father. I am meeting the director. We could end up father and son. It might prove to be interesting.

BRADLEY. Yeah.

VINCENT. Then again, it might not. (*Silence. Awkward moment. Vincent studies Bradley*) Maybe they will cast Theodora Ando. As your sister. Make it a *murder* mystery. (*Vincent mimes stabbing with a knife and twisting the blade. Bradley recalls Vincent's earlier reference to Theodora at the party and laughs. Vincent laughs, also. Pause*)

BRADLEY. You know, Mr. Chang, when I was growing up you were sort of my hero. No, really, you were. I mean, I'd be watching TV and suddenly you'd appear in some old film or an old Bonanza or something. And at first something would always jerk inside. Whoo, what's this? This is weird, like watching my own family on TV. It's like the first time I made it with an Asian girl—up to then only white girls. They seemed more outgoing—I don't know—more normal. With this Asian girl it was like doing it with my sister. It was weird. Everything about her was familiar. Her face, her skin, the sound of her voice, the way she smelled. It was like having sex with someone in my own family. That's how it was when you'd come on the TV. You were kind of an idol. (*Pause*)

VINCENT. You know who I wanted to be like? You know who my hero was? Fred Astaire. (*Noticing Bradley's look*) Yes, Fred Astaire.

BRADLEY. You danced?

VINCENT. (*Nods*) Un-huh.

BRADLEY. I didn't know that.

VINCENT. Yes, well ... (*Awkward pause. Both want to pursue conversation but unsure how to. Vincent starts to go back to his magazine*)

BRADLEY. What kind of dancing did you do? I mean, Fred Astaire kind of dancing or Gene Kelly—like, or, or, like the Nicholas Brothers—flying off those risers, landing doing the splits—ouch!

VINCENT. (*Laughs*) You know who the Nicholas Brothers are?

BRADLEY. Yeah, sure, of course. And Fred Astaire—Jesus, so smooth. I loved him in *Silk Stockings*. And Cyd Charisse was great.

VINCENT. No, no, Ginger Rogers, *Top Hat*. The two of them together, Ahhh. (*Silence*)

BRADLEY. Would you show me something? (*Vincent doesn't follow*) Some dance moves.

VINCENT. Now? Right here?

BRADLEY. Yeah, come on, just a little.

VINCENT. No, no, I haven't danced in years.

BRADLEY. Come on, Vincent. I'd love to see you ...

VINCENT. (*Overlapping*) No, no, I can't.

BRADLEY. ... dance. No one's around. Come on. Vincent, I'd love to see it.

VINCENT. Well. Alright. (*He gets up*) A little soft-shoe routine ... (*Vincent does a small sampling of some dance moves ending with a small flourish*)

BRADLEY. (*Applauds*) Great! That was great!

VINCENT. Back then you did everything. Tell jokes, juggle, sing—The Kanazawa Trio, great jugglers. Oh, and Jade Wing, a wonderful, wonderful, dancer. The Wongettes— like the Andrews Sisters. On and on, all great performers. We all worked the Chop Suey Circuit.

BRADLEY. Chop Suey Circuit?

VINCENT. In San Francisco you had of course, Forbidden City, Kubla Kan, New York's China Doll—some of the greatest Oriental acts ever to go down. That's my theatre background. (*Vincent tries to catch his breath*) See, there was this one routine that Jade—Jade Wing, she was my partner— and I did that was special. We had developed it ourselves and at the end we did this spectacular move where I pull her up on my shoulders, she falls back, and as she's falling I reach under, grab her hands and pull her through my legs thrusting her into the air ... and I catch her! Tadah! We were rather famous for it. This one night we performed it — we were in town here, I forget the name of the club — and as the audience began to clap, these two people at one of the front tables stood up, applauding enthusiastically. Everyone followed. It was an amazing feeling to have the whole house on their feet. And then we saw the two people leading the standing ovation. We couldn't believe our eyes — Anna Mae Wong, the "Chinese Flapper" herself, and Sessue Hayakawa. The two most famous Oriental stars of the day. They invited us to their table, Hayakawa with his fancy French cigarettes and his thick accent. It was a good thing that I spoke Japanese.

BRADLEY. You speak Japanese?

VINCENT. A little, I speak a little. But Anna Mae Wong spoke impeccable English. In fact, she had an English accent, can you believe that? "Vincent, you danced like you were floating on air." We nearly died then and there. Jade and I sitting at the same table with Anna Mae and Sessue.

BRADLEY. God, wasn't Anna Mae gorgeous.

VINCENT. Yes. But not as pretty as Jade Wing. I think Anna Mae Wong was a little jealous of all the attention Sessue was paying to Jade. God, Jade was beautiful. She was 23 when I met her. I was just 19. She was a burlesque dancer at the Forbidden City.

BRADLEY. What? Did you two have a thing going on or something?

VINCENT. For a while. But things happen. You are on the road continuously. She wanted one thing, I wanted another. I was pretty wild in those days. There were things about me she just could not accept. That was a long, long time ago.

BRADLEY. What happened to her?

VINCENT. I do not know. I heard she ended up marrying someone up in San Francisco who owned a bar in Chinatown. I forget the name of the bar — "Gumbo's" or some such name. I always meant to go and see her.

BRADLEY. I've been there a couple of times. There's ...

VINCENT. (*Overlapping*) I think she may have passed away. She was ...

BRADLEY. ... this old woman who runs it, a grouchy old bitch ...

VINCENT. ... so beautiful ... (*Awkward pause. Vincent had heard Bradley speak of the old woman*) Remember this? (*Reenacting a scene from his most famous role*) "A sleep that will take an eternity to wash away the weariness that I now feel."

BRADLEY. I know that, I know that ... *Tears of Winter*, opposite Peter O'Toole. You were nominated for best supporting actor! It's out on video, I have it. I know it by heart. (*Vincent feels good. Decides to launch into the whole scene. Saki is mortally wounded*)

VINCENT. (*As Saki*) Death is a funny thing Master Abrams. You spend your entire life running from its toothless grin. Yet, when you are face to face with it, death is friendly. It smiles and beckons to you like some long-lost lover. And you find yourself wanting, more than anything in the world, to rest, to sleep in her open inviting arms. A sleep that will take an eternity to wash away the weariness that I now feel. (*Vincent stumbles towards Bradley*)

BRADLEY. Vincent? (*Vincent collapses into Bradley's unexpecting arms. They tumble to the ground. Vincent, cradled in Bradley's arms, looks up at him*) You surprised me.

VINCENT. Don't speak,

BRADLEY. What?

VINCENT. Don't speak. That's your line, Peter O'Toole's line. *Don't speak.*

BRADLEY. Oh-oh. Don't speak, Saki. You must save your strength. We did the best we could. All is lost my little "nipper." The dream is dead. (*Saki is fading fast. Starts to close eyes. Then suddenly*)

VINCENT. *No!* A dream does not die with one man's death, Master. Think of all the women, children, and babies who will suffer if we are defeated. You must smash the enemy! You must win! (*Pause. Coughs up blood. Continues with heroic efforts*) Then I can sleep the final sleep with only one dream, the most important dream to keep me company on my journey through hell. (*Vincent nudges Bradley to feed him his line*)

BRADLEY. What dream is that Saki?

VINCENT. The dream of *victory*! (*Saki gasps for life*) Master ...

BRADLEY. Yes?

VINCENT. Win one for the ... Nipper. (*Saki dies in his master's arms*)

BRADLEY. Saki? Saki? (*He bows his grief-stricken head in Saki's breast. Then, recovering*) Oh, you were great in that film. Great.

VINCENT. You weren't so bad yourself. (*Bradley helps Vincent to his feet*) I'm ready for the director now.

BRADLEY. Can I run my audition piece for you? This is the first Asian American play I ever saw. Characters up there talking to me, something inside of me, not some white guy. I'd never experienced anything ...

VINCENT. (*Interrupts*) Just do it, do it. Don't explain it away. (*Bradley stands in silence. Closes eyes. Shrugs, fidgets, clears throat. Opens eyes, finally, and begins*)

BRADLEY. It was night. It was one of those typical summer nights in the Valley. The hot dry heat of the day was gone. Just the night air filled with swarming mosquitoes, the sound of those irrigation pumps sloshing away. And that peculiar smell that comes from those empty fruit crates stacked in the sheds with their bits and pieces of mashed apricots still clinging to the sides and bottom. They've been sitting in the moist heat of the packing sheds all day long. And by evening they fill the night air with that unmistakable pungent odor of sour and sweet that only a summer night, a summer night in the San Joaquin Valley can give you. And that night, as with every night, I was lost. And that night, as with every night of my life, I was looking for somewhere, someplace that belonged to me. I took my Dad's car 'cause I just had to go for a drive. "Where you going son? We got more work to do in the sheds separating out the fruit." "Sorry, Dad ..." I'd drive out to the Yonemoto's and pick up my girl, Bess. Her mother'd say, "Drive carefully and take good care of my daughter—She's Pa and me's only girl." "Sure,

Mrs. Yonemoto . . ." And I'd drive. Long into the night. Windows down, my girl Bess beside me, the radio blasting away. . . . But it continued to escape me — this thing, place, that belonged to me. . . . And then the DJ came on the radio, "Here's a new record by a hot new artist, 'Carol' by Neil Sedaka!" Neil who? Sedaka? Did you say, "Sedaka." (*Pronunciation gradually becomes Japanese*) Sedaka. Sedaka. Sedaka. *Sedaakaa.* As in my father's cousin's brother-in-law's name. Hiroshi Sedaka? What's that you say — the first Japanese American rock 'n' roll star! Neil Sedaka. That name. I couldn't believe it. Suddenly everything was alright. I was there. Driving in my car, windows down, girl beside me — with a goddamned Buddhahead singing on the radio . . . Neil Sedaakaa! I knew. I just knew for once, wherever I drove to that night, the road belonged to me. (*Silence*)

VINCENT. Bradley? Neil Sedaka is not Japanese.

BRADLEY. Yes, I know.

VINCENT. I have met him before. He's Jewish, or was it Lebanese. Very nice fellow. But definitely not Japanese.

BRADLEY. Yes, yes, I know. It's by Robinson Kan, the sansei playwright. It shows the need we have for legitimate heroes. And how when you don't have any, just how far you'll go to make them up.

VINCENT. Yes, yes. Well . . . (*Awkward pause*) Say, do you sing?

BRADLEY. "Scoshi," a little.

VINCENT. Do you know the musical I was in, *Tea Cakes and Moon Songs*? Sure you do. Let's do Charlie Chop Suey's love song to Mei Ling. I'll play Charlie the Waiter and you play Mei Ling.

BRADLEY. Mei Ling?

VINCENT. (*Dragging Bradley about*) Your part is easy. All you have to do is stand there and sing, "So Sorry, Charlie." You hit the gong. (*Standing side by side. Vincent provides classic sing-songey intro*) Da Da Da Da — Dah Dah Dah Dah Dah Da Da Da Dah Dah DAH! (*Vincent looks expectantly at Bradley who doesn't have a clue and is feeling ridiculous*) You hit the gong. You hit the gong. (*Vincent demonstrates, then quickly hums intro and starts the song. Bradley feels awkward but is swept*

along by the enthusiasm of Vincent. Vincent singing)
Tea cakes and moon songs
June bugs and love songs
I feel like dancing with you.
Roast duck and dao fu
Lop chong and char siu
Strolling down Grant Avenue
Chorus: Da Da Da Da — Dah Dah Dah Dah Dah
So Solly Cholly.
(*As they dance around, Bradley coquettishly hiding behind a fan, Vincent urges him to make his voice more female sounding*)
Higher, make your voice higher! Da Da Da Da — Dah Dah Dah Dah Dah.

BRADLEY. (*Struggling to go higher*) So Solly Cholly!

VINCENT. Higher! Higher!

BRADLEY. (*Falsetto*) So Solly Cholly! (*They are whirling around the stage. Vincent singing and tap dancing with Bradley in tow singing in a high pitched falsetto. Both are getting more and more involved, acting out more and more outrageous stereotypes. Bradley slowly starts to realize what he's doing*) Wait, wait, wait, what is this — WAIT! What am I doing? What is this shit? (*Then accusingly to Vincent who has gradually stopped*) You're acting like a Chinese Steppin Fetchit. That's what you're acting like. Jesus, fucking Christ, Vincent. A *Chinese Steppin Fetchit.* (*Bradley exits. Vincent glares in the direction of his exit*)

INTERLUDE TWO

Vincent lit in pool of light accepting an award.

VINCENT. This is a great honor. A great honor, indeed. To be recognized by my fellow Asian American actors in the industry. I have been criticized. Yes, I am aware of that. But I am an actor. Not a writer. I can only speak the words that are written for me. I am an actor. Not a politician. I cannot change the world. I can only bring life, through truth and craft, to my characterizations. I have never turned down a role. Good or bad, the responsibility of an actor is to do that role well. That is all an actor should or has to be concerned about. Acting. Whatever is asked of you, do it. Yes. But do it with dignity. I am an actor. (*Vincent dims to darkness. Flash! Bradley lit in pool of light. Holding a camera that has just flashed. Wearing stereotypic glasses. He is at an audition for a commercial*)

BRADLEY. What? Take the picture, then put my hand like this—in front of my mouth and *giggle*? Yeah, but Japanese men don't giggle. How about if I shoot the picture and like this ... just laugh. (*Listens*) I'm sorry but I can't do that. Look, it's not truthful to the character. Japanese men don't giggle. What? (*Listens. Turns to leave*) Yeah, well the same to you Mr. Asshole Director. (*Dim to darkness on Bradley. We hear a glitzy, Las Vegas version of "Tea Cakes and Moon Songs." Vincent lit in a pool of light. Wearing a big cowboy hat. He is the master of ceremonies at a huge Tupperware convention in Houston. Holding mike*)

VINCENT. Howdy! Howdy! It is good to be here in Houston, Texas. In case you don't know me, I'm Vincent Chang. (*Applause*) Thank you, thank you. And if you do not know who I am, shame on you! And, go out and buy a copy of *Tears of Winter*. It is out on video now I understand. Hey, you know what they call Chinese blindfolds? *Dental Floss!* (*Laughter*) And I would especially like to thank Tupperware for inviting me to be your master of ceremonies at your annual national—no, I take that back—your *international* convention. (*Applause, and more applause*) Yeah! Yeah! What's the word? (*Holds mike out to audience*) TUPPERWARE! Yeah! What's the word? (*Vincent holds mike out to the audience. Black-out on Vincent. Bradley lit talking to his Asian actor friends*)

BRADLEY. I can't believe this business with the Asian American awards. I mean it's a joke—there aren't enough decent roles for us in a year. What? An award for the best Asian American actor in the role of Vietnamese killer. (*Mimicking sarcastically*) And now in the category of "Best Actress with Five Lines or Less ... " That's all we get. Who're we kidding. This business. This goddamned fucking business. And I can't believe they gave that award to Vincent Chang. *Vincent Chang*. His speech—"I never turned down a role." Shi-it! (*Dim to darkness*)

SCENE THREE

"THEY EDITED IT OUT"

After an acting class. Vincent is upset. Bradley packing his duffle bag.

VINCENT. You do not know a thing about the industry. Not a damn thing. Who the hell ...

BRADLEY. (*Interrupts, calling to someone across the room*) Yeah, Alice — I'll get my lines down for our scene, sorry.

VINCENT. (*Attempts to lower his voice so as not to be heard*) Who the hell are you to talk to me that way. Been in the business a few ...

BRADLEY. (*Interrupts*) Look, if I offended you last time by something I said I'm sorry. I like your work, Mr. Chang. You know that. I like your ...

VINCENT. (*Interrupts*) A "Chinese Steppin Fetchit" — that is what you called me. A "Chinese Steppin Fetchit." Remember?

BRADLEY. I'm an angel, OK, I'm an angel. *No memory.*

VINCENT. And you do not belong in this class.

BRADLEY. My agent at William Morris arranged for me to join this class.

VINCENT. This is for *advanced* actors.

BRADLEY. I've been acting in the theatre for seven years, Mr. Chang.

VINCENT. Seven years? Seven years? Seven years is a wink of an eye. An itch on the ass. A fart in my sleep, my fine feathered friend.

BRADLEY. I've been acting at the Theatre Project of Asian America in San Francisco for seven years — acting, directing, writing ...

VINCENT. Poppycock, cockypoop, bullshit. Theatre Project of Asian America — "Amateur Hour."

BRADLEY. "Amateur Hour?" Asian American theatres are where we do the real work, Mr. Chang.

VINCENT. The business, Bradley, I am talking about the business, the industry. That Matthew Iwasaki movie was a fluke, an accident ...

BRADLEY. (*Interrupts*) Film, Mr. Chang.

VINCENT. *Movie!* And stop calling me Mr. Chang. It's Shigeo Nakada. "Asian American consciousness." Hah. You can't even tell the difference between a Chinaman and a Jap. I'm Japanese, didn't you know that? I changed my name after the war. Hell, I wanted to work . . .

BRADLEY. (*Mutters*) You are so jive, Mr. Chang . . .

VINCENT. You think you're better than I, don't you? Somehow special, above it all. The new generation. With all your fancy politics about this Asian American new-way-of-thinking and seven long years of paying your dues at Asian Project Theatre or whatever it is. You don't know shit my friend. You don't know the meaning of paying your dues in this business.

BRADLEY. The business. You keep talking about the business. The industry. Hollywood. What's Hollywood? Cutting up your face to look more white? So my nose is a little flat. Fine! Flat is beautiful. So I don't have a double-fold in my eyelid. Great! No one in my entire racial family has had it in the last 10,000 years. My old girlfriend used to put scotch tape on her eyelids to get the double fold so she could look more "Cau-ca-sian." My new girlfriend—she doesn't mess around, she got surgery. Where does it begin? Vincent? All that self hate, *where does it begin*? You and your Charley Chop Suey roles . . .

VINCENT. You want to know the truth? I'm glad I did it. Yes, you heard me right. I'm glad I did it and I'm not ashamed, I wanted to do it. And no one is ever going to get an apology out of me. And in some small way it is a victory. Yes, a victory. At least an Oriental was on screen acting, being seen. We existed.

BRADLEY. But that's not existing—wearing some goddamn monkey suit and kissing up to some white man, that's not existing.

VINCENT. That's all there was, Bradley. That's all there was! But you don't think I wouldn't have wanted to play a better role than that bucktoothed, groveling waiter? I would have killed for a better role where I could have played an honest-to-god human being with real emotions. I would have killed for it. You seem to assume "Asian Americans" always existed. That there were always roles for you. You didn't exist back then buster. Back then there was no Asian American consciousness, no Asian American actor, and no Asian American theatres. Just a handful of "Orientals" who for some god-forsaken reason wanted to perform. *Act.* And we did. At church bazaars, community talent night, and on the Chop Suey Circuit playing China-towns and Little Tokyos around the country as hoofers, jugglers, acrobats, strippers — anything we could for anyone who would watch. You, you with that holier-than-thou look, trying to make me feel ashamed. You wouldn't be here if it weren't for all the crap we had put up with. We built something. We built the mountain, as small as it may be, that you stand on so proudly looking down at me. Sure, it's a mountain of Charley Chop Suey's and slipper-toting geishas. But it is also filled with forgotten moments of extraordinary wonder, artistic achievement. A singer, Larry Ching, he could croon like Frank Sinatra and better looking, too. Ever heard of him? Toy Yet Mar — boy, she could belt it out with the best of them. "The Chinese Sophie Tucker." No one's ever heard of her. And Dorothy Takahashi, she could dance the high heels off of anyone, Ginger Rodgers included. And, who in the hell has ever heard of Fred Astaire and Dorothy Takahashi? Dead dreams, my friend. Dead dreams, broken backs and long forgotten beauty. I swear sometimes when I'm taking my curtain call I can see this shadowy figure out of the corner of my eye taking the most glorious, dignified bow. Who remembers? *Who* appreciates?

BRADLEY. See, you think every time you do one of those de-meaning roles, the only thing lost is *your* dignity. That the only person who has to pay is you. Don't you see that every time you do that millions of people in movie theaters will see it. Believe it. Every time you do any old stereotypic role just to pay the bills, someone has to pay for it — and it ain't you. *No.* It's some Asian kid innocently walking home. "Hey, it's a Chinaman gook!" "Rambo, Rambo, Rambo!" You older actors. You ask to be understood, forgiven, but you refuse to change. You have no sense of social responsibility. Only me ...

VINCENT. (*Overlapping*) No ...

BRADLEY. ... me, me. Shame on you. I'd never play a role like that stupid waiter in that musical. And ...

VINCENT. You don't know ...

BRADLEY. ... I'd never let them put so much makeup on my face that I look like some goddamn chimpanzee on the screen.

VINCENT. (*Overlapping*) You don't know ...

BRADLEY. I don't care if they paid me a million dollars, what good is it to lose your dignity. I'm not going to prostitute my soul just to ...

VINCENT. (*Overlapping*) There's *that* word. I was wondering when we'd get around to that word. I hate that word! I HATE THAT WORD!

BRADLEY. ... see myself on screen if I have to go grunting around like some slant-eyed animal. You probably wouldn't know a good role if it grabbed you by the balls!

VINCENT. I have played many good roles.

BRADLEY. Sure, waiters, Viet Cong killers, chimpanzees, drug dealers, hookers ...

VINCENT. (*Interrupts*) I was the first to be nominated for an Academy Award.

BRADLEY. Oh, it's pull-out-the-old-credits time. But what about some of the TV stuff you've been doing lately. Jesus, TV! At least in the movies we're still dangerous. But TV? They fucking cut off our balls and made us all house boys on the evening soaps. (*Calls out*) "Get your very own neutered, Oriental houseboy!"

VINCENT. I got the woman once. (*Bradley doesn't understand*) In the movie. I got the woman.

BRADLEY. Sure.

VINCENT. And she was *white*.

BRADLEY. You're so full of it.

VINCENT. And I kissed her!

BRADLEY. What, a peck on the cheek?

VINCENT. ON THE LIPS! ON THE LIPS! *I GOT THE WOMAN.*

BRADLEY. Nah.

VINCENT. Yes.

BRADLEY. Nah?

VINCENT. YES.

BRADLEY. (*Pondering*) When was this? In the '30s. Before the war?

VINCENT. (*Overlapping*) No.

BRADLEY. Because that happened back then. After the war forget it. Mr. Moto even disappeared and he was played by Peter Lorre.

VINCENT. No, no. This was the '50s.

BRADLEY. Come on, you're kidding.

VINCENT. 1959. A cop movie. (*Correcting himself*) Film. *The Scarlet Kimono*. Directed by Sam Fuller. Set in L.A. Two police detectives, one Japanese American and one Caucasian. And a beautiful blond, they both love.

BRADLEY. Yeah ... I remember. And there's this violent kendo fight between you two guys because you both want the woman. (*Realizing*) And you get the woman.

VINCENT. See, I told you so. (*Pause. Bradley seated himself*)

BRADLEY. Except when I saw it you didn't kiss her. I mean I would have remembered something like that. An Asian man and a white woman. You didn't kiss her.

VINCENT. TV?

BRADLEY. Late Night. (*Bradley nods. Vincent making the realization*)

VINCENT. They edited it out. (*Silence. Vincent is upset. Bradley watches him. Dim to darkness*)

INTERLUDE THREE

Darkness. Bradley lit in pool of light. Silently practicing "tai-chi," with dark glasses on. His movements are graceful, fluid. Stops. Poised in silence like a statue. Suddenly breaks into savage kung-fu kicks with the accompanying Bruce Lee screams. Stops. Silence. Bradley shakes himself as if trying to release pent-up tension. Quietly begins the graceful "tai-chi" movement. Bradley dims to darkness and Vincent lit in pool of light.

VINCENT. (*On the phone to Kenneth*) I can not. You know why. Someone might see us together. (*Listens*) You do not know. People talk. Especially in this Oriental community and then what happens to my career. I am a leading man. (*Kenneth hangs up on him*) I am a leading man. (*Dim to darkness*)

SCENE FOUR

"THE LOOK IN THEIR EYES"

After acting class, Vincent and Bradley in a crowded, noisy bar having a drink. They play a raucous verbal game.

BRADLEY. Mr. Chang, it's a . . .

VINCENT. (*Interrupts, calls to a waitress*) Excuse me! Tanquery martini, straight up with a twist. Dry.

BRADLEY. (*Pretending to be a casting agent making an offer*) Mr. Chang, it's a two-day contract.

VINCENT. (*No accent, straight, not much effort*) Yankee dog, you die.

BRADLEY. (*Trying to suppress his laughter*) Mr. Chang, it's a one-week contract. And don't forget the residuals when this goes into syndication.

VINCENT. (*Big "oriental" accent. Barely able to contain his laughter*) Yankee dawg, you die!

BRADLEY. Mr. Chang, it's a three-month shoot on location in the Caribbean Islands. Vincent, we're talking a cool six figures here. You can get your condo in Malibu, your silver Mercedes, you'll . . .

VINCENT. (*Overlapping. An outrageous caricature, all the while barely containing his laughter*) YANKEE DAWG YOU DIE! YANKEE DAWG YOU DIE! YANKEE DAWG YOU DIE!

BRADLEY. . . . BE LYING ON SOME BEACH IN ST. TROPEZ, GETTING A TAN, HAVING A GOOD OLE TIME! . . .

VINCENT. My drink . . . (*Both calm down*)

BRADLEY. I talked my agent into getting me an audition. It's that new lawyer series. He was very reluctant, the role wasn't written for an Asian. I said, "Jason, just get me in there." I showed up for the audition. I said, "I can do it, I can do it." They said, "No, the character's name is Jones." I said, "I can play a character named Jones." They said, "No." "I was adopted." "No." "I married a women and gave up my name." "No." Hell, if some white guy can play Chan, some yellow guy can play Jones. (*Pause. Sipping drinks*)

VINCENT. Do you remember that film, *Bad Day At Black Rock*?

BRADLEY. (*Remembering*) Yeah, yeah . . .

VINCENT. That role, that role that Spencer Tracy plays?

BRADLEY. Yeah, but it's about some Nisei 442 vet, right?

VINCENT. That's who the story revolves around but he does not appear. He's dead. Got killed saving Tracy's life in Italy. After the war Tracy goes to the dead soldier's home town to return a war medal to his Issei parents. Only they don't appear either. Their farm is burned down, they are missing, and therein lies the tale. I should have played that role.

BRADLEY. Whose role? Spencer Tracy's?

VINCENT. It's about a Nisei.

BRADLEY. Yeah, but none appear.

VINCENT. But he could have been a Nisei, Tracy's character. And I have always felt I should have played it.

BRADLEY. Me. Robert De Niro, *Taxi Driver*. "You talking to me? You talking to me?"

VINCENT. *Harvey*.

BRADLEY. Keitel?

VINCENT. No, no. The film with Jimmy Stewart.

BRADLEY. With the rabbit? The big fucking rabbit nobody can see?

VINCENT. God, Stewart's role is wonderful. Everyone thinks he is mad, but he is not. He is not. Original innocence.

BRADLEY. Mickey Rourke in *The Pope of Greenwich Village*. "Hit me again — see if I change."

VINCENT. James Dean, *East of Eden*, Salinas, a farm boy just like me. (*As Vincent enacts a scene from the movie, Bradley appears quiet and momentarily lost in thought*)

BRADLEY. (*Interrupts*) Forget what I said about Mickey Rourke. He's an asshole — he did that *Year of the Dragon*. I hated that film.

VINCENT. Not that film again. It is . . . just a "movie." (*Calls after waitress who seems to be ignoring him*) My drink! (*They sip in silence. Bradley reaches into his bag and pulls out a script)*

BRADLEY. Vincent? Want to work on something together?

VINCENT. We already are taking the same class ...

BRADLEY. (*Interrupts*) No, no, over at the Asian American Theatre. The one here in town.

VINCENT. No, no, all those Orientals huddling together, scared of the outside world—it is stifling to an actor's need for freedom.

BRADLEY. It's a workshop production, a new play by Robinson Kan—a sci-fi, political drama about ...

VINCENT. (*Interrupts*) You should be out there doing the classics, Bradley. It is limiting, seeing yourself just as an Asian. And you must never limit yourself. Never. (*Bradley reaches into his bag and pulls out a small Godzilla toy*)

BRADLEY. It's got Godzilla in it.

VINCENT. Godzilla? (*Moving it playfully*) Godzilla. Aahk. (*Calling to waitress*) My drink, *please.*

BRADLEY. You can do and say whatever you want there.

VINCENT. An actor must be free. You must understand that. *Free.*

BRADLEY. And they will never edit it out. (*Awkward silence. Sipping*) I was in a theatre in Westwood. I was there with a bunch of Asian friends. And then that "movie" starts. Rourke struts into this room of Chinatown elders like he's John Wayne and starts going on and on, "Fuck you, fuck you. I'm tired of all this Chinese this, Chinese that. This is America." And then these young teenagers sitting across from us start going, "Right on, kick their butts." I started to feel scared. Can you believe that? "Right on Mickey, kick their asses!" I looked over at my friends. They all knew what was happening in that theatre. As we walked out I could feel people staring at us. And the look in their eyes. I'm an American. Three fucking generations, *I'm an American.* And this goddamn movie comes along and makes me feel like I don't belong here. Like I'm the enemy. *I belong here.* I wanted to rip the whole goddamn fucking place up. Tear it all down. (*Silence. Vincent picks up Godzilla*)

VINCENT. Godzilla? Robinson Kan, a workshop production?

(*Bradley nods*) Well. "I never turn down a role." (*They both laugh. Vincent picks up script*) Let's see what we have here. (*Dim to darkness*)

SCENE FIVE

"GODZILLA ... AAHK!"

Darkness. Godzilla-like theme music. High-tension wires crackle across the projection screens.

VINCENT. (*Voice over*) I can't believe I let you talk me into this!

BRADLEY. (*Voice over*) Take it easy, take it easy.

VINCENT. (*Voice over*) I should have never let you talk me into this Asian American thing! And this costume ...

BRADLEY. (*Voice over. Interrupts*) We're on! (*Bradley lit in pool of light downright. He plays a reporter out of the '50s. He wears a hat and holds one of those old-style announcer microphones*) Good evening Mr. and Mrs. America and all the ships at sea. Flash! Godzilla!

VINCENT. (*On tape*) AAHK!

REPORTER. A 1957 TOHO production. Filmed in Tokyo, to be distributed in Japan *and* America. Starring Kehara Ken, the scientist who develops the anti-oxygen bomb that wipes out Godzilla ...

GODZILLA. (*On tape*) AAHK!

REPORTER. ... and Raymond Burr, an American actor who was so popular as Perry Mason that he just might be the drawing card needed to bring in those American audiences. Godzilla! ...

GODZILLA. (*On tape*) AAHK!

REPORTER. Rising, rising from the depths. In Japan it's released as *Gojira*. In America, it's Anglicized and marketed as *Godzilla!* ... (*Vincent, dressed up in a Godzilla outfit, bursts through the projected high-tension wires as the projection screens turn to allow him to enter. Smoke and flashing lights*)

GODZILLA. AAHK! (*During the following, Godzilla acts out what the Reporter is describing*)

REPORTER. It breaks through the surface just off the shores of San Francisco. SPPLAASSHH!!! It's swum the entire Pacific

Ocean underwater and is about to hyperventilate. It staggers onto the beach and collapses. It looks like a giant zucchini gone to seed. A huge capsized pickle with legs.

VICTOR. (*Struggling to get up*) Bradley! Bradley, I'm stuck! (*Bradley helps Victor up*)

REPORTER. Five days later — refreshed and revived, it continues its trek inland. It takes the Great Highway up to Geary Boulevard, hangs a right on Gough and follows that sucker right onto the Bay Bridge. It pays no toll. Cars screech, children cry, mothers with babies scream. The men don't. They're "manly." Godzilla! ...

GODZILLA. AAHK! (*Godzilla strolls over to the Reporter/Bradley, takes the hat and mike and now he becomes the Reporter. Bradley, in turn, now becomes the Little Boy acting out what is said by Vincent*)

REPORTER/GODZILLA/VINCENT. A little boy. A little boy watching TV. A little boy watching TV on Saturday night and it's "Creature Features" on Channel 2. Tonight the feature is "Godzilla ... " (*Reporter momentarily becomes Godzilla*) AAHK! (*Back to reporting*) ... And a little boy watching, watching, has a hunger, a craving for a hero, for a symbol, for a secret agent to carry out his secret deeds ... Godzilla!

GODZILLA/LITTLE BOY. AAHK! (*Bradley grabs the hat and mike back and becomes the Reporter once again. Vincent as Godzilla acts out the blow by blow account*)

REPORTER. ... In its anger it lashes out. It gouges out eyes of people who stare, rips out the tongues of people who taunt! Causes blackouts of old World War II movies! Godzilla! ...

GODZILLA. AAHK!

REPORTER. It takes the 580 turnoff and continues to head inland into the San Joaquin Valley. And there in the distance ... STOCKTON! Stockton, a small aggie town just south of Sacramento, population 120,000 and the home of a little boy. A little boy who knows, understands, and needs Godzilla ...

GODZILLA. AAHK!

REPORTER. And who Godzilla ...

GODZILLA. AAHK!

REPORTER. ... with his pea-sized brain, regards with supreme affection and would do anything the little boy asked it to do. And this is what the little boy asked ... (*Bradley puts hat and mike aside and becomes the Little Boy*)

BRADLEY/LITTLE BOY. Godzilla, ya know Sammy Jones. She's this little fancy pants girl. She said she was watching this old war movie last night and that there was this female nurse—the *only* female in the whole entire army—and that a Japanese sniper shot her dead in the first ten minutes of the movie. Then she said I was the enemy. And *then* she called me a "dirty Jap." (*Godzilla looks appalled, then angry*) You know what to do. (*Godzilla turns, picks up a "Sammy Jones" doll, looks down, and then dramatically stomps his foot down as if he were crushing a bug*) OH BOY! OH BOY! (*End of scene. Bradley and Vincent laughing. They had a good time together. They do a "right on" handshake. Godzilla-like music swells. Dim to darkness*)

act 2

INTERLUDE ONE

Vincent lit in a pool of light. Body microphone. Visual projections.

VINCENT. I have this dream. In this dream there is a man. And though this man is rich, successful, famous—he is unhappy, so very unhappy. He is unhappy because the love around him, the love in the hearts of those he cared for most, was beginning to shrivel and wither away. And this, in turn, made his own heart begin to grow in order to make up for the love that was disappearing around him. And the more the love in the hearts of those around him shriveled up, the bigger his own heart grew in order to make up for the growing emptiness that he now began to feel. So the love kept withering away and his heart kept growing bigger. Until one day there was so little love around him and his own heart so big—it burst into a thousand red petals that filled the sky and fell slowly, so very slowly, to the earth. And the people, his friends, the ones who had withheld their love, began to swallow the petals, these remains of the man's glorious heart as they fell from the sky. Hungrily, they fed. Greedily they swallowed. They pushed and shoved each other, gorging themselves on these petals because they felt then, they too, would become like the man. Rich, famous, beautiful, lonely ... (*Vincent dims to darkness*)

SCENE ONE

"WE WENT TO SEE THE MOVIE"

Bradley reading from a Shakespeare book. Rehearsing. Vincent coaching.

BRADLEY. Or art thou but/a dagger of the mind, a false creation,/Proceeding from the heat-oppressed — (*Vincent entering, correcting*)

VINCENT. Oppres-sed. Oppres-sed. (*Bradley, frustrated continues*)

BRADLEY. ... heat oppres-sed brain?/I see thee yet, in form as palpable/As this which I now draw. (*Bradley draws a knife. Uncomfortable holding it*)

VINCENT. (*Overlapping towards end of Bradley's speech*) ... which now I draw.

BRADLEY. ... now I draw, now I draw.

VINCENT. You should be elated you are doing Shàkespeare. This is a great opportunity for you.

BRADLEY. (*Holding up a script*) But this is *Macbeth*. I'm doing *Romeo and Juliet*, Vincent — I'm doing Romeo.

VINCENT. (*Holding his book up*) You must learn them all while you are still young. "Is this a dagger which I see before me, the handle towards my hand? Come, let me clutch thee." There is music to its language and you must know its rhythm so you can think clearly within its verse. I studied Shakespeare when I was younger. And I was — all modesty aside — the best Shakespearean actor in my class. But the only role I got was carrying a spear. And here you are with a gem of a role and you don't want to work.

Come on, come on, let's hear it (*Bradley puts his script aside and reads from his book*)

BRADLEY. Is this a dagger which I see before me,/The handle toward my hand? Come, let me clutch thee./I have thee not and yet I see thee still/Art thou not, fatal vision, sensible/To feeling as to sight, or art thou but/A dagger of the mind, a false creation,/Proceeding from the heat-oppressed brain?/I see thee yet, in form as palpable/As this which now I draw.

VINCENT. Thou marshal'st me the way that I was going— (*Bradley lowers his knife. Vincent notices*) Grip it. Hold it. You must be able to imagine it, feel it. Know the experience from the inside. Of course, you may not have wanted to kill someone. You must know the feeling.

BRADLEY. (*Overlapping after "kill someone"*) I'm having trouble with this one, Vincent. I just can't. I can't. OK.

VINCENT. This is ridiculous. You're too tense, way too tense. Lie on the floor. (*Bradley resists*) Lie on the floor. (*While speaking Vincent lights up a cigarette. He needs a break and can do this rote. Not paying attention to Bradley sprawled out on the ground, trying out different shapes*) Become a ... rock. You are a rock. Find your shape. Are you big, small, flat, oblong? Keep looking until you find your own particular shape. (*Bradley slowly gets up into an upright position. Vincent puffing, doesn't notice*) Got it?

BRADLEY. Yeah.

VINCENT. What do you feel? (*Vincent turns to see the standing Bradley*)

BRADLEY. Alive. Conscious. But there is no hunger, no wanting. And no sense of time. It is now. Yes, that's it. Everything is *now*.

VINCENT. A rock that stands. With no appetite.

BRADLEY. No, no really I know. This is what a rock feels.

VINCENT. I have no reason not to believe.

BRADLEY. I have been a rock before.

VINCENT. Now I have a reason.

BRADLEY. I have. On acid. LSD. The first time I dropped acid I walked into a forest in the Santa Cruz mountains and became a rock.

VINCENT. Why did you do this?

BRADLEY. I was in college.

VINCENT. Alright. Let's work with it. Since we finally have something. (*Putting out cigarette*) Go with it Bradley. Relive the experience. Relive it moment by moment. Pebble by pebble. (*Suppressing giggle*) I'm sorry.

BRADLEY. I am walking. There is a tightness I feel in the back of my neck — I guess it's the acid coming on. With each step I go deeper into the forest. And with each step I can feel the civilized part of me peeling away like an old skin. Whoo, my mind is beginning to cast aside whole concepts. God, the earth is breathing. I can feel it. It's like standing on someone's tummy. And this rock. This big, beautiful rock. Our consciousnesses are very similar. I do a Vulcan Mind-meld. (*Touching the rock*) "I am waiting for nothing. I am expecting no one." (*Releases Vulcan Mind-meld*) It is beautiful in its own rockness.

VINCENT. Good. OK, let us work with ...

BRADLEY. I began walking again.

VINCENT. OK.

BRADLEY. Thoughts of great insight float in and out of my mind like pretty butterflies. Skin holds the body together. And the head holds the brain together. But what holds the mind together? *What holds the mind together?* I panic! I feel my mind beginning to drift away. There is nothing to hold my mind together. Soon bits and pieces of my consciousness will be scattered across the universe. I'll NEVER GRADUATE! What? What's this? Cows. Ten, twenty, sixty, hundreds. Hundreds and hundreds of cows. Where did they come from? They spot me. They see that I am different. One cow steps forward. He is the leader. He wears a bell as a sign of his authority. He approaches me cautiously, studying me. This head cow nods in approval. He knows I am no longer a civilized human, but somehow different, like them. He turns and signals the others. They all begin to move towards me. Soon I am surrounded in a sea of friendly cows. Hello, hi — It's like old home week. Suddenly I hear a noise coming from far away. It tugs at something inside me. I turn to see where the noise is coming from. I see ...

I recognize . . . Jeffrey. My best friend. Calling my "name." I look at the cows. They are waiting to see what I will do. I look at Jeffrey, his voice ringing clearer and clearer, my name sounding more and more familiar. I look at the cows — they are beginning to turn away. Should I stay and run wild and free with the cows? Or, should I return to the dorms on campus? "HOWDY JEFFREY!" As I run back to see, the cows are once again pretending to be cows. They slowly lumber away, stupid and dumb. Moo, moo. (*Bradley notices Vincent staring at him*) It's a true story.

VINCENT. Cows?

BRADLEY. Yes.

VINCENT. Cows that have a double life? (*Bradley nods*) The dumb facade they show to the outside world and their true cow selves that they show to one another when they are alone? Moo, moo? Well, back to the real world. Perhaps. Anyway, to the task at hand. The role you are playing. Let me rethink this. (*Holding book*) "Is this a dagger which I see before me, the handle towards my hand? Come, let me clutch thee . . ."

BRADLEY. (*Quietly*) I killed someone.

VINCENT. What?

BRADLEY. I think I killed someone.

VINCENT. Like in a person? A human being? (*Bradley nods*) My God.

BRADLEY. I'm not sure. I may have. But I'm not sure. It was stupid. So stupid. I was about 16. I used to hang around a lot with some Chinatown boys, gangs and that sort of thing. I was walking down Jackson Street with my girlfriend, we were going to see the movies, when these two guys — they must have been college students come to gawk at all the Chinese people — turned the corner. Well, as they walked passed, one of them looked at my girlfriend and said, "Hey, look at the yellow pussy." So I walked over to the one guy, "What did you say? What did you say?" He just laughed at me. So I pulled a knife and stabbed him. (*Shocked silence*)

VINCENT. What happened then?

BRADLEY. We went to see the movie. (*Pause*) I don't know. Sometimes it just builds up. The anger. (*Pause*) That was over ten years ago. I hope he's OK. I hope with my heart he's OK. (*Dim to darkness*)

INTERLUDE TWO

Darkness. Over house speakers we hear: "Un Bel Di Vedremo" from Madame Butterfly. *Vincent lit in pool of light. He relaxes at home, wearing a velvet bathrobe. He is seated, looking at himself in a mirror.*

VINCENT. (*Repeated two times with different interpretations*) "You will cooperate or I will kill you." (*Pause*) "You will cooperate or I will kill you." I will take my moment. They expect me to just read my lines and get the hell out of there, another dumb North Vietnamese general. "You will cooperate or I will kill you." Yes, I will take my moment. And I am not going to let the director know. I won't tell Robert. I am just going to do it. (*Pause. Smiling to himself*) Yes, I will take my moment. Vincent Chang is an actor. (*Vincent dims to darkness. Music lowers in volume. Bradley lit in a pool of light*)

BRADLEY. (*On the phone*) But why? I don't understand, Jason. I thought we had an agreement, an understanding. I know the series fell through, but I'm going to get other roles. I'm a leading man. You told me so yourself. How many young Asian American leading men are there? (*Beat*) I'm not *like* the rest of them. What? (*Listening*) Yeah ... I've heard of Snow Kwong Johnson. (*Bradley dims to darkness. Music up. Vincent lit in a pool of light*)

VINCENT. Why do you keep threatening to do it? I hate that. You know you won't do it. Besides I am not going to change my mind. (*Pause*) We can still see each other. (*Beat*) As friends. (*His eyes follow someone out of the room. Music fades. Vincent dims. Music out. Bradley lit in a pool of light. He is talking to a friend*)

BRADLEY. That's not true. Who said that about me? That's not true at all. What? I was an "ex-con"? I was a "hit man" for the *what*? (*Pause. Butterfly's suicide aria in*) Who told you this? Huh? Who told you this? (*Music swells and peaks as lights go down on Bradley*)

SCENE TWO

"... HIT MAN FOR THE CHINESE MAFIA ..."

Vincent's apartment. Bradley has stormed in. Vincent is trying to put on his coat and pack a small duffle bag at the same time.

VINCENT. (*Putting things back into bag*) I cannot talk now. I cannot. Now, *please.*

BRADLEY. (*Angry*) Who else could have told them, Vincent? You're the only one who knows.

VINCENT. (*In a great hurry*) Can't we talk about this later. I have to go somewhere. (*Pushing Bradley out of the way, continuing to pack*)

BRADLEY. I told you in confidence. Haven't you heard of "confidentiality?" What do they call it, what do they call it — "privilege." Doctor-patient privilege. Lawyer-client privilege. *Actor — acting teacher privilege.* (*Vincent is all packed. Trying to get his coat on which has been dangling off his left shoulder*)

VINCENT. I have to go Bradley. I have a very important appointment.

BRADLEY. (*Interrupts*) Fuck your audition! What about *my* career? You told him, didn't you. Goddamn it. You told everybody I was an ex-con, a hit man for the *Chinese Mafia!* (*Pause*) What if the casting agencies hear about it? Huh? Think they'll want to hire me?

VINCENT. (*Quietly*) My friend is dying ...

BRADLEY. (*Not hearing*) What happens to my ...

VINCENT. (*Interrupts*) My friend is dying! (*Silence*) He overdosed. Took a whole bottle of pills. I have to go to the hospital. Now, get out of may way, Bradley. (*Pushing a stunned Bradley aside*) There are some things in this world more important than *your* career. ... What has happened to you Bradley? What the hell has happened to you?

BRADLEY. (*Quietly*)I just wanted to know. That's all. If you

told him. I haven't gotten a call lately and I thought you
know ... (*Pause. Vincent feels badly about his remarks*)

VINCENT. Look. I am sorry ...

BRADLEY. You better go Vincent, your friend ...

VINCENT. (*Starts to leave, stops*) He always does this. My friend
is just ... lonely. He wants me to come running.

BRADLEY. You said he took a whole bottle of sleeping pills?

VINCENT. Last time it was a whole bottle of laxatives. One
week in the hospital. He was so happy. He lost fifteen
pounds. (*Pause*) Maybe I did. (*Bradley doesn't follow his
comment*) Mention it. About what happened in Chinatown.
Just to a few people. I just never had someone tell me they
killed ...

BRADLEY. (*Overlapping*) He's probably OK, now. I'm sure the
guy's fine.

VINCENT. ... someone before. I had to tell somebody. And I
never said you were a hit man for the Chinese Mafia, or
whatever ... (*Pause*) I am sorry, Bradley. Remember?
(*Taps his nose*) Dr. Lao? I have to go. The nurses may need
some help with the bed pans. (*Notices Bradley*) We all go
through these periods when the phone does not ring. I,
too, have had them. Of course, far and few between, but I,
too. Try some "ochazuke" with some "umeboshi" — it's on
the stove. My mother used to make me eat it when I was
upset. Soothes the nerves. (*Vincent turns to exit*) `

BRADLEY. Vincent? I was going to kick your ass. I was. (*Vincent
stops. Stares at Bradley*) I just sit in my room, waiting for the
phone to ring. Why won't the phone ring, Vincent? Huh?
Why won't the goddamn phone ring? (*Dim to darkness*)

INTERLUDE THREE

*Darkness. We hear Bradley's voice. Gradually lights are brought up
as he speaks. Upstage area, lit in a pool of light. Body
microphone. Visual projections.*

BRADLEY. I have this dream. In this dream, I'm lying on a
park bench. I wear only a very ragged black overcoat.

Then, I fall asleep. My mouth wide open. It is a kind of perfect sleep. No hunger, no desire ... no dreams. My heart stops beating. The blood comes to rest in my veins. (*Noticing*) It's quite pleasureful. The whispering of warm breezes through my hair. Big, colorful maple leaves of red and orange that flutter down and cover my eyes like coins. Ahh. ... What's this? Two dark clouds circling high above. Now they swoop down, down, towards my sleeping corpse. I see what they are. Two magnificent vultures. I think of something to offer. "Here, here, take my fingers. Yes, yes ... don't be afraid. Here, take the rest of my hand." That should be enough. No. They want more ... they've jumped on my chest. They're beginning to rip me open. It feels ... so ... so ... (*Dim to darkness*)

SCENE THREE

"I SEE MYSELF THIRTY-FIVE YEARS AGO"

Thunder. Bradley seated on a bench in a small outdoor shelter. Raining. Umbrella on ground. Vincent runs to the shelter holding two cups of hot coffee.

VINCENT. (*Hands coffee to Bradley*) Black, right? (*Bradley nods, takes coffee. Sips, watches rain*)

BRADLEY. I finally got a call. I just came from an audition. It was for one of those evening soaps, everybody was there. Butler gig, glorified extra. I didn't get the role. I walked outside and I started crying. And I was crying, not because of the humiliation. But because, *I wanted the role.* I keep thinking, if I got it, the part, could I go through with it? I mean, actually show up and do that stuff?

VINCENT. When you walk on that set and there is all that expectation from everyone — the director, the writer, the other actors to be that way, it is so ... I was watching TV last week. They had on this story about Martin Luther King. He was picked up by some night riders. Drove him to the outskirts of town, dragged him out of the car and surrounded him. And that night he felt something inside he never felt before — impotent, like the slave, willing to go along, almost wanting to comply. After that, he realized he had to fight not only the white man on the outside, but that feeling, the slave inside of him. It is so easy to slip into being the "ching-chong-Chinaman." (*Vincent looks at Bradley, knowingly*) Moo, moo.

BRADLEY. It's still raining pretty hard. I felt kind a bad about last time. That's why I called you up. Your friend OK? (*Vincent nods. Pause*)

VINCENT. I love the rain. It is like meditating. It seems to quiet all the distractions around you so you can better hear the voice of your own heart. The heart. A mysterious thing. Kind. Cruel. At times you would like to rip it out. It feels too much, gives you too much pain. And other times— aah, the ecstasy. You wish it were a huge golden peach so that everyone might taste of its sweetness. (*Pause. Thinks*) It is also like a mirror. Yes, a mirror. And if one is brave enough to gaze into it, in it is reflected the truth of what we really are. Not as we would like to be, or as we would like the world to see us. But as we truly are. (*Vincent looks at Bradley intently*) Would you like to know what I see? (*Bradley motions to himself, questioningly. Vincent nods*)

BRADLEY. That's OK, I'd rather you didn't tell me. An ego-maniac, right? A selfish, arrogant, insecure actor.

VINCENT. No, no, quite the contrary. I see a sensitive, shy and compassionate soul. (*Pause*) And I see a driven, ambitious, self-centered asshole. In other words, I see myself thirty-five years ago. (*They laugh quietly*)

BRADLEY. I know this sounds kind of silly. I've never told anyone. You know how everyone has these secret goals. You know what mine were? Obie, Oscar, Tony. OOT. (*They quietly laugh*)

VINCENT. I was so cocky after my Oscar nomination. No more of those lousy Chinaman's parts for me anymore. This was my ticket out of there. Hell, I might even call my own shots. *My agent kept warning me though. "Vincent, you're an Oriental actor. It's different for you." I said, "No way. Not anymore. From now on only good roles are coming my way."

BRADLEY. Did the offers for good roles come in?

VINCENT. No* (*Pause*). I have this dream. I am standing in the middle of a room with all these people staring at me. At first I think they are friendly towards me. Then I think, no, they are evil people out to get me. Then suddenly again, I think this is exactly where I want to be, it feels wonderful. Then I am seized with a strange fear and I feel I must get the hell out of there. A spotlight flashes on me. I am disoriented. Someone hands me a script. (*Vincent glances at the lines*) "Why do I have to do this?" Then this warm, soothing voice says, "Is there a problem Vincent? All we want you to do is fuck yourself. Take all the time you want. We'll get the most expensive lubricant if you need. Vincent, is there a problem? We hear Sly Stallone's doing it, so it must be OK. OK?" "Read the lines this way." (*Pause*) I know what is going on, Bradley. I am not stupid. I know what I am doing. That is the problem. (*They sip their drinks in silence. Watch the rain*)

BRADLEY. Maybe you should call Gumbo's, that bar in San Francisco. Right now. Come on, let's be crazy!

VINCENT. What? And find out that my beautiful memory of Jade Wing has turned into — what did you say? A grouchy old bitch? No. I could not bear to kill any more of my dreams.

BRADLEY. That was probably just the bartender. Jade is probably rich, still beautiful, living in some expensive home in Pacific Heights, wondering this very instant, "What ever happened to Shig Nakada?" (*Vincent sadly shakes his head*)

VINCENT. We were married. Jade and I. No one ever knew that. Just us. We were so young. (*Pause*) She left me one night. Never saw her again. I don't blame her. She caught me in bed with someone.

BRADLEY. Vincent.

VINCENT. Actually, she did not mind the idea of me playing around. Or rather she minded but she could live with it. What she could not stomach was who I was playing around with. (*Pause*) Well. It is getting late. And the rain seems to

---

* Dialogue between asterisks based on a scene from the film *Yuki Shimoda* by John Esaki and Amy Kato.

have finally abated. (*Both get up*) Bradley? Would you like to come over to my place? For a drink? (*Awkward pause*)

BRADLEY. No, Vincent. No, I can't.

VINCENT. Right. Well. Good night. (*Pause*)

BRADLEY. It's OK. (*Vincent doesn't follow*) It's OK, Vincent. It doesn't matter to me.

VINCENT. I do not know what you are talking about.

BRADLEY. It doesn't matter, Vincent. People don't care nowadays.

VINCENT. I do not know what you are talking about Bradley. I do not. It is late. Good-bye.

BRADLEY. Good night, Vincent. (*Bradley sadly watches Vincent exit. Dim to darkness*)

INTERLUDE FOUR

Bradley lit in pool of light, sitting.

BRADLEY. (*Bragging*) They want me to play this Chinese waiter. I'll go, OK, take a look. I get there and look at the script. Jesus. I read the lines straight. No accent, no nothing. They say, "No, no, we need an accent." You know, THE accent. I told my agent — What? No, I quit them — if they pay me twice the amount of the offer, OK. I'll do it anyway they want. Otherwise forget it. They paid it. The dumb shits. They paid it. (*Laughing smugly*) On top of it, they liked me. Yeah, they liked me. (*Cross-fade to an empty pool of light. The aria from* Madame Butterfly *softly underscoring this scene. Vincent enters dancing. He is wearing headphones with a Walkman and is practicing one of his old routines. Gradually the TV light and sound are brought up. We hear the Sergeant Moto monologue. Vincent stops dancing, takes off headphones and watches the TV light. Upset. Reaches for the phone and dials for his agent*)

VINCENT'S VOICE ON TV. You stupid American G.I. I know you try and escape. You think you can pull my leg. I speakee your language. I graduate UCLA, Class of '34. I drive big, American car with big-chested American blond sitting next to — Heh? No, no, not "dirty floor." Floor clean. Class of

'34. No, no, not "dirty floor." Floor clean, just clean this morning. 34. No, no, not "dirty floor." Listen carefully. Watch my lips. 34. 34! 34!!! What is wrong with you? You sickee in the head? What the hell is wrong with you? Why can't you hear what I'm saying? Why can't you see me as I really am? (*Dim to darkness on Vincent dialing the phone*)

SCENE FOUR

"AHHH ... THE NORTH STAR"

Six months later. Party at the same home in the Hollywood Hills. Balcony. Night. Vincent sips on a drink and stares into the night sky. Bradley appears. Walks over and stands beside him. They watch stars in silence.

VINCENT. (*Notices Bradley's drink*) Tanins are bad for your complexion. (*They both laugh, clink glasses and sip*) It's been a while. What, six months or so? I tried calling your service.

BRADLEY. It's been a little hectic. My girlfriend moved down from San Francisco.

VINCENT. Oh, I didn't know. I've been seeing more of my friend ... Kenneth.

BRADLEY. Ahh, Kenneth. (*Pause*)

VINCENT. You look good. Different. (*Looking closer at Bradley*) What is it? Your hair? Your nose?

BRADLEY. Oh, yeah. I was having a sinus problem, so I thought, you know, while they were doing that they might as well ...

VINCENT. Ahhh. It looks good.

BRADLEY. You look good.

VINCENT. Always.

BRADLEY. God. The night air. Ahhh. It was getting a bit stuffy in there.

VINCENT. I thought you liked being around Asians.

BRADLEY. Yeah, but not a whole room full of them. (*They both laugh*) No way I can protect my back side. (*Mimes jabbing a knife*)

VINCENT. Ahhh. (*Awkward pause. Bradley embarrassed that Vincent didn't laugh at the knife joke. Vincent looks up at the night sky.*

Pointing) The Big Dipper. Follow the two stars that form its lip and ...

BRADLEY. The North Star.

VINCENT. Voila! You will never be lost, my dear friend. Never. (*Silence. They sip their drinks*) Something interesting happened to me last week. I was offered a very well paying job in that new film everyone is talking about, *Angry Yellow Planet.*

BRADLEY. I read for that movie, too.

VINCENT. Playing "Yang, the Evil One."

BRADLEY. Yang! Hah! I read for the part of Yang's number one son. We could be father and son. Might be interesting.

VINCENT. Yes.

BRADLEY. Then again it might not. (*Both laugh at the old joke*) You know what, Vincent? You won't believe this ...

VINCENT. I turned it down. (*No response*) I just could not do it. Not this time. (*Pause*) It feels ... it feels good. Almost. I turned it down to be in Emily Sakoda's new film. It is about a Japanese American family living in Sacramento before the war. Just like my childhood. Sixteen milimeter, everyone deferring pay. And my role, it's wonderful. I get to play my father. (*Mimics father*) "Urusai, yo!" That. It's my father. And this ... "So-ka?" I mean, it's so damn exciting, Bradley. I had forgotten what it feels like. What it is supposed to feel like. Do you know what I mean?

BRADLEY. I took it. (*Vincent doesn't follow*) I took *it*. The role.

VINCENT. Oh ...

BRADLEY. I took the role of Yang's number one son. He's half Chinese and half rock.

VINCENT. I see.

BRADLEY. It's a science fiction movie.

VINCENT. Ahhh.

BRADLEY. I figure once I get there I can change it. I can sit down with the producers and writers and explain the situation. Look, if I don't take it then what happens? Some other jerk takes it and plays it like some goddamned geek.

VINCENT. Yes. Well.

BRADLEY. I'll sit down and convince them to change it. I will. Even if it's a bit. Just a small change, it's still something. And, even if they don't change it, they'll at least know how we feel and next time, maybe next time ...

VINCENT. Yes.

BRADLEY. And in that sense. In a small way. It's a victory. Yes, a victory. (*Pause*) Remember this? (*Sings*) Tea cakes and moon songs ... (*They both laugh. Pause. Bradley looks at Vincent*) Moo, moo. (*Muttering to himself*) Fucking cows.

VINCENT. Remember this? (*Starts Sergeant Moto monologue with the same stereotypic reading as in the opening interlude, but quickly loses accent. And, ultimately, performs with great passion*) You stupid American G.I. I know you try to escape. You think you can pull my leg. I speakee your language. (*Accent fading*) I graduated from UCLA, the Class of 1934. I had this big car ... (*Accent gone*) What? No, no, not "dirty floor." The floor is clean. Class of '34. No, no, not "dirty floor." I had it cleaned this morning. How many times do I have to tell you. 34. Class of '34. No, no, not "dirty floor." Listen carefully and watch my lips. 34. 34! 34!! What is wrong with you? What the hell is wrong with you? I graduated from the University of California right here in Los Angeles. I was born and raised in the San Joaquin Valley and spent my entire life growing up in California. Why can't you hear what I'm saying? Why can't you see me as I really am? (*Vincent stops. Bradley is truly moved. Bradley quietly applauds his performance. They smile at each other. They turn to look out at the night sky. They are now lit in a pool of light. Bradley points to the lip of the Big Dipper and moving his hand traces a path to the North Star*) Ahhh. The North Star. (*Vincent and Bradley begin a slow fade to black. At the same time, the theatre is again filled with a vast array of stars. The music swells in volume. As Vincent and Bradley fade to black, the stars hold for a beat. Then, surge in brightness for a moment. Then, blackout. Screen: "THE END." Screen darkens*)

richard strand
the
BUG

I got fired.

That was quite a few years ago now. And it was a lousy job that I got fired from. In fact, I had already quit the job before they fired me. I gave two weeks notice, my boss persuaded me to stay for four weeks and then, after two, he canned me. I have always believed that he manipulated that situation so that he could tell people he fired me instead of having to tell people I quit. It was a close call, but I did get fired, and getting fired, even from a lousy job, is a humiliating experience.

The experience warped my thinking. I had always had good relationships with employers in the past, but getting fired has made me suspicious of every boss I've had since. The next job I held—taking phone sales at an L-shaped desk—was no better than the one I had been fired from but I became desperately worried that I would be fired again. If my boss asked how I was doing, I viewed it as a criticism. If he was silent—and he usually was—I assumed he was plotting. I asked him periodically if he was happy with my work and he would say yes and I would assume he was lying. It was a tense time in my life.

My fears seemed confirmed when it slipped out that the company intended to hire two new salesmen. Counting me, there were already three salesmen and the company only owned four L-shaped desks. Hiring two more salesmen would make a total of five and I could see that the salesman/ desk ratio was getting top heavy. I became convinced that before the week was out, someone would be fired to make room for the new salesmen. And I never considered the idea that that someone might be someone else.

I went to work each day with a knotted stomach and a gloomy expression. I took calls and waited for my boss to stick a knife in my back. But it seemed I was working for a master of brinkmanship—he was going to wait until the last possible moment on the last possible day to tell me I was, once again, fired.

The not-too-surprising ending to this story is that I was not fired; the company bought a fifth desk. In gratitude, I worked for six dollars an hour for the next three years taking orders over the telephone at an L-shaped desk. My boss (whose last name is spelled Radziejeski—not Rajeski) is no longer my boss, but he is my friend. He quit almost a year before I did. It took me three years to persuade myself that, if I was ever going to leave that job, I was going to have to quit.

During that three years, I wrote *The Bug*. In 1988, several different theatres gave the script staged readings that greatly aided its development. Those theatres were The Victory Gardens Theater in Chicago, Vermont Repertory Theatre, The Open Eye in New York, and Ukiah Players in Ukiah, California.

The Bug was premiered by Actors Theatre of Louisville at the Thirteenth Annual Humana Festival in 1989. It has had several subsequent productions in this country as well as a German radio production under the translated title *Fehler im System.*

Writing and producing *The Bug* was made possible, in part, by a grant from the Illinois Arts Council, a state agency, and by The National Endowment for the Arts.

characters

DENNIS: An assembler at Jericho Corporation.

LINDA: An administrator.

KIMBERLY: A higher-level administrator.

DAVID: The highest-level administrator.

act 1

The administrative office of Jericho Inc., a large corporation that designs and manufactures factory automation systems. Mark Kropp is the president of this corporation. The door to his office is on the upstage wall. His name is printed on his door. Downstage, and to the side, is the door leading to the remainder of the building. Through the translucent glass pane on this door we can read the words, "JERICHO, INC. — ADMINISTRATION." However, these words are intended for people on the other side of the door; to us the letters are backwards. Between these two doors are three desks, protecting Mark Kropp's office from the outside world.

The desk furthest upstage belongs to DAVID RAJESKI. We can only see his torso, however. His lower body is blocked by his desk; his face is blocked by a computer monitor which is on a swiveling arm contraption.

Moving further downstage, and off to one side, is the desk belonging to KIMBERLY MILES. She is seated at her desk, her monitor, like David's, obstructing our view of her face. There is a bag of trail mix on her desk from which she occasionally snacks.

The desk closest to us — and on the opposite side of the stage from Kimberly's — belongs to LINDA TAYLOR. She is typing on her computer, inputting data from a stack of papers on her right. Periodically she will take the sheet on the top of the stack to her right and place it, face down, on a stack of papers to her left. Her face, like the others, is obscured by her monitor.

The office is noncommittally tasteful. It is well designed the same way a refrigerator might be well designed. The same could be said of the office's occupants. They are dressed in the latest in don't-make-waves. Their nails are clean. Their movements are vaguely mechanical. They are serene.

The bulk of this office is covered with an expensive carpet. The forestage, however, is tiled. This creates a sort of tile barrier — a D.M.Z. — between the office occupants and the audience. The door to the outside enters onto this D.M.Z.. We hear a knock at that door. Somebody in the office — it is difficult to tell who but in fact it is Linda — calls out in response to the knocking.

LINDA. Who's there? (*Dennis enters. This is Dennis's first trip to the upstairs office. He is in all ways out of place here. He is tweedy and tasteless. His clothes are loud and uncoordinated. He wears sneakers and a sportscoat. His hair does not lie down well, although Dennis often tries to push it into place. He moves about nervously and erratically, bouncing off the furniture and walls as he passes them. He looks like he has been set loose in a giant pinball machine. No one in the office so much as moves his head when Dennis enters)*

DENNIS. Excuse me. *(He waits for a response without getting any. He looks uncomfortably around at the people without heads)* Hello! *(He tries in vain to position himself so that he can catch a glimpse of someone's face)* Uh, hi! Listen, uh, I need to talk with someone. Not sure who, really. Someone. Just someone. *(No one responds)* See, I work here. I mean, not up here. Not with the big boys. No. I'm just a little guy. Hookin' wires together. No big deal. Only, I gotta talk with someone. Someone in authority. *(Pause)* Not sure who, really. *(Pause)* Just someone. *(Dennis looks around at the faceless people)*

LINDA. *(Without interrupting her typing)* What is this in regard to?

DENNIS. HO! A VOICE! Which one of you guys said that?

LINDA. *(Waving a hand)* Over here.

DENNIS. Whoa. Great. For a minute I thought you guys were all robots. *(He starts to cross to Linda's desk by walking on the carpeted area)*

LINDA. STAY ON THE TILE!

DENNIS. *(Freezing in midstride)* What?

LINDA. Please, stay on the tile. You're supposed to stay on the tile.

DENNIS. Why?

LINDA. Only employees are allowed on the carpeted area.

DENNIS. Oh, well, I'm an employee.

LINDA. Employees of THIS office. Are you an employee of THIS office?

DENNIS. I work in Assembly. Downstairs.

LINDA. Only employees of THIS office are allowed on the carpeted area.

DENNIS. I work in Assembly.

LINDA. Then please stay on the tile.

DENNIS. *(Muttering)* On the tile. I feel like the dog.

LINDA. What?

DENNIS. Nothing! On the tile. You want me on the tile so I'll be on the tile. That's fine. Only, the thing is, I can't see your face.

LINDA. Uh huh.

DENNIS. Why is it that I can't see your face?

LINDA. My computer monitor is in the way.

DENNIS. Right. Right. Listen, I don't want to make trouble. I can be as good a company man as anybody.

LINDA. Do you have any business up here?

DENNIS. Business up here? Right. Well, yes, I got business up here. Sort of. See, my name is Dennis Post and I work in Assembly and there's a sort of situation that has come up that causes a problem for me. Not a big problem! But personal, you know? I mean, no reason the company needs to get all bent out of shape about my personal problems, right? Only, I wonder if I could talk with someone about a little bit of a personal problem that I have with the company.

LINDA. With whom did you wish to speak?

DENNIS. NOT THAT I'M COMPLAINING! No! Not a bit. I love my job. It's a great job. Doesn't pay much, but hell, how much does a guy like me really need?

LINDA. With whom did you wish to speak?

DENNIS. You know, this is real hard talking to you when I can't see your face.

LINDA. WHO DO YOU WANT TO TALK TO?!

DENNIS. Right. Good idea. I should just come right out and say what I want, right? I was thinking about maybe talking to the prez?

LINDA. (*Pause*) You wish to speak to Mr. Kropp?

DENNIS. Right. Bad idea. I know. Bad idea. "Nobody sees the Wizard." See, I understand that he's got plenty to do without listening to some guy in Assembly bellyaching just because he doesn't want to go to St. Louis. Only, who DO I talk to about this?

LINDA. (*Pause*) About . . . St. Louis?

DENNIS. Yeah. See, the thing is—

LINDA. You wish to speak to Mr. Kropp about St. Louis?

DENNIS. Right. See, the thing is—

LINDA. Mr. Post, you can't just go around talking to anyone you feel like talking to about anything that might be on your mind. There are channels to go through. That's how things run here. Even I don't see Mr. Kropp, and I work for him. He comes in on his private elevator. When he wishes to speak to me he calls me on the intercom. Now, I know it may seem like a bother sometimes—sometimes it even seems silly to me—but without proper channels the system falls apart. Really.

DENNIS. Yeah. I know.

LINDA. It would be like letting you men in Assembly hook the wires up any old place. You know what I mean?

DENNIS. Uh huh.

LINDA. Do you really? I don't want you to think I'm being rude. Do you really understand what I'm saying?

DENNIS. Sure! You're saying that before I can talk to the prez I'm going to have to get past all three of you guys.

LINDA. That's not exactly—

DENNIS. See, the thing is . . . . You know, this is just about impossible for me. I just gotta see your face if we're going to continue this conversation. (*Dennis picks up Linda's monitor*) Let's just set this thing on the floor so that . . . (*Linda screams. Everyone in the office rises to stare at Dennis. All have perfectly acceptable-looking faces. Dennis begins to act like a looter who has just been caught with a hot television*) DON'T ANYBODY SHOOT! Ha ha! I just wanted to see her face. That's all. Just the face. I wasn't going to walk off with this or anything. (*He forces some laughter*) Just wanted to see the face here. (*He looks at the face*) Oooo! Pretty. Nice face.

LINDA. Give me the monitor.

DENNIS. It was an impulse. I didn't mean to upset everybody.

LINDA. Give me the monitor.

DENNIS. I mean, I wasn't going to steal it.

LINDA. GIVE ME THE MONITOR!

DENNIS. HERE! (*He places it back on the swivel contraption. Linda swivels it off to the side, out of the way of her face*)

LINDA. Is that better, Mr. Post?

DENNIS. A thousand percent! Really. This is so much better. Thank you! Really. This is going to help my attitude a lot.

(*David and Kimberly disappear again behind their monitors*) Listen, do you think I could get a chair?

LINDA. A chair?

DENNIS. I won't walk on the carpet. I can lean over and grab hold of this chair ... (*He does so as he speaks*) I ain't stealing it. (*Kimberly and David are watching him suspiciously*) Just going to set it down over here on the tile so that we can have a chat.

LINDA. Mr. Post ...

DENNIS. (*Seating himself*) There! No problem. What say we start back on square one, okay? Hi. My name is Dennis Post and your name is ... (*Linda does not respond. Dennis picks up the name plate on her desk and continues talking*) ... your name is Linda unless you stole somebody else's name plate. See, Linda, the problem is that I think they're going to transfer me to St. Louis, but this is my home, you know what I'm saying? And if I let people start shipping me around the country, I start to feel like a cog in a machine. NOT THAT I'M NOT ALL FOR AUTOMATION! But companies are still made up of people, right? And people can't be machines, can they?

LINDA. No. No, they can't.

DENNIS. Good. I'm glad we agree about that. See, I need to feel more autonomous. I think. Autonomous? Is that the right word? What does autonomous mean?

LINDA. I think it means you drop your leaves once a year.

DENNIS. Really? No. That can't be right. Is it?

LINDA. Maybe not.

DENNIS. (*Trying it again*) Autonomous. Hmmm. What word am I looking for?

LINDA. Automaton?

DENNIS. Automa—?! Oh. I see. You're making fun of me. (*He really does think it's funny*) Very good. Funny. Automaton.

LINDA. (*Her shell is cracking now; she is human after all. She laughs a little self-consciously, then checks to make sure she has not disturbed Kimberly or David. She speaks in a more friendly and confidential tone to Dennis*) Mr. Post, why don't we drop the formality?

DENNIS. Oh. I'm sorry. Was I being too formal?

LINDA. Can I call you Dennis?

DENNIS. Sure. That might be fun.

LINDA. Dennis, what makes you think anyone wants to send you to St. Louis?

DENNIS. Well, St. Louis is our only other office in this country, right?

LINDA. Well, yes.

DENNIS. Well, SOMEBODY'S getting shipped to St. Louis. I figure it's going to be the youngest guy with no wife. That's usually the way they do it, isn't it?

LINDA. Well . . .

DENNIS. Well that's me: Young, with no wife. Only I really don't want to go. Is there somebody I can talk to about this? It's been playing with my sleep. My stomach is all knotted up. Have I been doing something wrong? We don't get much feedback. Have you been getting negative reports about me?

LINDA. (*Confidentially, not wanting to be overheard*) Listen, Dennis, this isn't really my job to tell you this, but I don't think you have anything to worry about. See, all transfers have to go through me. I have to put 'em into this computer. And I've got no record of a Dennis Post being transferred. To anywhere. I'd remember.

DENNIS. Well, maybe they forgot to tell you.

LINDA. No, no. See, that'd be impossible. If they don't tell me to transfer you then you don't get transferred. It's that simple. It's actually scary how much power I have with this thing. (*She is patting her computer*)

DENNIS. That's easy for you to say. What do I do on Monday when they put me on the bus to St. Louis?

LINDA. Hmmm. I don't know how to put this to you any simpler. If you were gonna be transferred to St. Louis, that information would be in my computer. It's not in my computer so you are not going to St. Louis. See, that's the one good thing about red tape: you can't cut through it. Believe me, if I didn't put it in the computer, then, as far as this company is concerned, it doesn't exist and that's the end of that story. (*Pause*) Does that take care of your problem?

DENNIS. You're saying that, as far as you know, I got nothing to worry about.

LINDA. I am saying that you are not being transferred to St. Louis.

DENNIS. Well, good. That's good. Only, where's the new guy going to sit?

LINDA. What new guy?

DENNIS. A new guy starts work next Monday. In Assembly.

LINDA. Oh sure. Alex Blickem. I know about that. That is in the computer.

DENNIS. Right. And we only got sixteen Burton-Hughes office modules. Sixteen Burton-Hughes office modules for sixteen assemblers. Come Monday we're going to have seventeen assemblers but only sixteen Burton-Hughes office modules. The way I figure it, that makes us one short.

LINDA. Burton-Hughes ... what?

DENNIS. Office modules. Haven't you seen them? Oh, they're great. Really. Come in a carton about so by so. (*Indicating with outstretched arms*) But real flat. And with a screwdriver and a pair of pliers, you can snap one of those puppies together in about ten minutes. Bingo: Instant office. All the assemblers got one. We all get a little computer console. Like our own little toy offices. Only right now there are sixteen modules and seventeen assemblers. So I say to myself, something is not right here. Looks to me like somebody's got to go to St. Louis in order to make room for this new guy. Doesn't it look that way to you?

LINDA. (*Thrown for a moment*) You know, you should really bring this up with your supervisor.

DENNIS. Right. Right. I agree. A thousand percent. And that's what I was going to do. Only, I don't know who he is.

LINDA. (*Thrown for a longer moment*) What?

DENNIS. Actually, none of us know who he is. Well, we know who he is. He's Doug Cockrum. But no one in Assembly has ever seen him.

LINDA. What?

DENNIS. NOT THAT WE'RE COMPLAINING! I don't wanna get the guy in trouble.

LINDA. No one in Assembly has ever seen Mr. Cockrum?

DENNIS. Not as far as anyone remembers. Let me take that back. Old Rocky, he thinks he might have seen him once a few years ago, but Rocky sees Jimmy Hoffa sometimes so ...

LINDA. Then where do you get your instructions from?

DENNIS. Drafting. They send us the schematics and we hook the wires together. No big deal. Red to red. Yellow to yellow. Puce to puce. A monkey could do it.

LINDA. Who makes sure that the stuff you make is put together right?

DENNIS. Engineering. They let us know right away if we goofed something up. Say a yellow wire hooked up to a green one. Boy, does THAT throw a monkey wrench into the works!

LINDA. Who makes sure that everybody is working?

DENNIS. No one. Why would anybody have to? It's not like there's a lot of other things we could be doing down there. I mean, it's an assembly area, not a recreation room. NOT THAT I'M COMPLAINING! Although, a ping-pong table might be kinda nice. But that's not why I came up here.

LINDA. Mr. Post ...

DENNIS. Boy, I liked it better when you were calling me Dennis.

LINDA. ... are you telling me that there is no one supervising the assembly area?

DENNIS. Aw, now see, this is what I wanted to avoid. You're mad at Cockrum now, right? Listen, the department is running fine. We get the work done and we're usually on time and under budget. That's the mark of a good supervisor, isn't it? I don't know that we should be making a big deal out of the fact that nobody has seen or heard this guy in three years.

LINDA. Three years?! Mr. Post—Dennis—do you have any idea what you're suggesting here?

DENNIS. I'm just suggesting that I would be a happier guy if somebody other than me got shipped to St. Louis.

LINDA. You're suggesting that we have a thirty-four-thousand-dollar-a-year middle manager who hasn't come to work in three years.

DENNIS. Thirty-four thousand dollars a year? That position pays thirty-four thousand dollars a year? Listen, do you think I could apply for that job? Maybe Cockrum would like to go to St. Louis. I really think I could handle it. Really. I could even come to work if you want.

LINDA. Dennis, no one is going to St. Louis. But I gotta tell you, what you've told me about Mr. Cockrum is really disturbing. Don't you find it disturbing?

DENNIS. Look, I'm sure Cockrum is around. Somewhere. We just don't know where.

LINDA. (*Mostly talking to herself; mostly ignoring Dennis*) Well, he must be in the computer. (*Entering into her computer*) Cockrum comma Douglas. Hmm. (*Reading from her screen*) "Cockrum comma Douglas." There he is.

DENNIS. Well, then, I guess everything's okay.

LINDA. (*Reading from her screen*) "Paid biweekly at the rate of one thousand three hundred seven dollars and sixty-nine cents." But if he never comes to work, how does he pick up his check?

DENNIS. No one is saying that Cockrum doesn't deserve every cent he's paid.

LINDA. (*Reading from a different part of the file*) "Direct deposit to Madison National Bank." Of course! Direct deposit!

DENNIS. An option for which we are all grateful, although personally I have never taken advantage of it. But I'll suffocate if I have to live in St. Louis. Really. It'll kill me.

LINDA. Will you stop saying that? You're not going to St. Louis! Nobody is going to St. Louis!

DENNIS. (*Quietly, after a pause*) But what about the sixteen office modules? What are they going to do about having seventeen assemblers and only sixteen office modules?

LINDA. HOW DO I KNOW?!

DENNIS. (*Sulking now*) Well, don't yell at me.

LINDA. (*To David and Kimberly, who have risen from their desks and are staring disapprovingly at Linda*) I'm sorry I yelled. (*David and Kimberly sit back down again. Linda speaks to Dennis*) I'm sorry I yelled. Look, Dennis, I think you're being a little paranoid about this. I can think of a lot of ways they might take care of that problem, you know?

DENNIS. What do you mean? Have you heard something?

LINDA. All I'm saying is that sending someone to St. Louis is not the only way of taking care of an overcrowded assembly area. Now can you just sit quietly for a sec? I'm trying to find out what the story is with this Cockrum guy.

DENNIS. I just want to steer clear of St. Louis.

LINDA. You're not going to St. Louis! You're not going to St. Louis! YOU'RE NOT GOING TO ST. LOUIS! GOODNESS!

DENNIS. (*Thinks about that for a minute*) Well, that takes care of me. Listen, thanks. I'll be going to back to work now —

LINDA. No! Stay here! I want you to stay here for just a sec. Until I figure out where Cockrum is. (*She begins entering commands into her PC. Dennis mutters to himself*)

DENNIS. "Sending someone to St. Louis is not the only way of taking care an overcrowded assembly area." Sure. There are other ways. (*He thinks*) Like what?

LINDA. Hmm. Ah, here he is. (*Reading from her screen*) Started working five years ago. M.S. from the University of Michigan. B.S. from Ohio University. Married. Two kids.

DENNIS. (*Suddenly*) MY GOD, THEY'RE GOING TO FIRE ME!

LINDA. Will you give me two seconds to figure out what is going on?

DENNIS. That's it, isn't it? They're going to fire me. You don't want to tell me because you don't want to hurt my feelings. But you're reading that on you're terminal right now: "Post comma Dennis colon Terminate."

DENNIS. Oh, Dennis, please, just shut up a second, will you?

DENNIS. Yes m'am. (*Under his breath*) Oh God, oh God, oh God, oh God …

LINDA. Well this is stupid. I'll just call him. (*Reading from the screen*) Cockrum comma Douglas should be at extension two-seven-four. (*Linda picks up her phone and punches two-seven-four. The phone on Kimberley's desk starts ringing. Kimberly picks up her receiver*)

KIMBERLY. Hello, Kimberly Miles.

LINDA. (*Surprised, looking at Kimberley*) Kim?

KIMBERLY. Linda?

LINDA. Um, uh …

KIMBERLY. Linda, why are you playing with the telephone?

LINDA. Uh, I'll call you back. (*She hangs up quickly. Kimberly pushes her monitor aside and gives Linda a peculiar look*) Dennis,

would you mind telling Miss Miles the same thing you just
told me?

DENNIS. I just wanna keep my job.

LINDA. Look, Dennis, you have pointed out a sort of ... well,
a bug in our system. This is very upsetting, really. For all
of us. You included. For example, you're worried that
you're going to be shipped to St. Louis. But the only one
who can transfer you is Mr. Cockrum. And we don't know
where he is. Now, I just want you to talk with Miss Miles
about the same things that you just told me. So we
can confirm that you're not going to be transferred to
St. Louis—WHICH YOU'RE NOT—only it would be nice if
we could confirm that with somebody in the real world. So
will you talk with Miss Miles?

DENNIS. Sure. Anything. Just don't fire me.

LINDA. Nobody is firing anybody. Just wait here. Just ... wait
here. (*Linda crosses to Kimberly's desk*) Kim, can you talk to
this guy for a second?

KIMBERLY. I'm on lunch.

LINDA. I know. I know. Only ... (*She is not sure how to approach
this*)

KIMBERLY. (*Pushing her monitor aside*) Linda, what's the matter?
You look sick.

LINDA. I'm, uh ... do you know Douglas Cockrum?

KIMBERLY. Sure. He's the supervisor in Assembly.

LINDA. No. I mean, have you ever met him?

KIMBERLY. Oh no. I don't go down to Assembly. It's pretty
gross down there.

LINDA. I really think you ought to talk to this guy. I don't
know what's going on, but something's not right.

KIMBERLY. Is that Douglas Cockrum?

LINDA. No. His name is Dennis Post. Could you just talk to
him? Please.

KIMBERLY. I'm on lunch.

LINDA. Pleeeze.

KIMBERLY. (*Giving in, she addresses Dennis*) Uh, Mr. Post?

DENNIS. (*Rising quickly, he crosses to the edge of the carpet*) Yo!
Here! (*Kimberly gestures with a curled first finger that Dennis
should come to her desk*) Oh. Uh, but the carpet. I'm not

supposed to walk on the carpet. (*Kimberly gestures again*) Right. On my way. (*He begins to cross toward Kimberly's desk. But he cuts the corner too closely when rounding Linda's desk and knocks the large stack of papers on the floor. Instantly, he falls to his knees and becomes a machine that rapidly picks the papers up, one at a time, and replaces them on the desk*) I'm sorry. I'm sorry. It was an accident. (*Linda crosses to Dennis*)

LINDA. Stop that. Just leave them. I'll get them later. (*Dennis does not even look up. He continues to shovel papers back onto Linda's desk*)

DENNIS. I'm so sorry. Really. It was an accident.

LINDA. Stop it. Just leave them alone. (*Linda steps between Dennis and her desk. This turns out to be a mistake. Dennis does not notice her and his next attempt at placing a paper on her desk causes him to plunge his hand up her skirt. Linda screams*)

DENNIS. I'M SORRY! I'M SORRY!

LINDA. GET IT OUT! GET IT OUT!

DENNIS. I CAN'T! MY RING'S CAUGHT!

LINDA. (*In a panic, slapping the hand that is still up her skirt*) OUT! OUT!

DENNIS. I'M TRYING! DON'T HIT ME! (*Kimberly and David are both staring at this scene, unsure of what they should be doing. Linda starts swatting at Dennis's head*)

LINDA. GET OUT! OUT!

DENNIS. (*Suddenly free*) THERE! I'M OUT. DON'T HIT ME! (*Turning to David and Kimberly*) No problem! Everything's okay! Just a little accident. Everything's cool now. (*There is a long moment during which no one moves. Linda is breathing deeply, recovering from her ordeal*)

KIMBERLY. Linda?

DAVID. Are you all right?

LINDA. It's fine. Everything is fine.

DAVID. Do I have to call Security?

LINDA AND DENNIS. No!

LINDA. It was … uh … I guess it was just an accident.

DENNIS. Yeah! An accident. I knocked over her papers and then got my hand stuck up her dress. Nothing. An accident.

LINDA. (*To Kimberly and David*) I'm fine. Really. (*David gathers some papers from his desk and crosses to Kimberly's desk*)

DAVID. Handle it. (*David exits through the front door*)

DENNIS. Maybe I ought to leave, huh?

LINDA. NO! I want you to talk to Miss Miles.

DENNIS. Okay. But, listen, I am so sorry about this.

LINDA. Let's just not discuss it.

DENNIS. Well, okay, only . . .

LINDA. No! I don't want to talk about it.

DENNIS. Fine. We won't talk about it. Only . . .

LINDA. YOU'RE GOING TO TALK ABOUT IT! I DON'T WANT TO TALK ABOUT IT.

DENNIS. IT'S NOT ABOUT THAT. IT'S ABOUT SOMETHING ELSE.

LINDA. WHAT!?

DENNIS. (*Pause*) You've still got my ring.

LINDA. What?

DENNIS. You've still got my ring.

LINDA. Where?

DENNIS. I don't know. I just know I had to take it off to get my hand out. It was caught on something.

LINDA. Caught on what?

DENNIS. I don't know. One of those things girls wear. (*Linda turns her back and adjusts her clothing. Then she turns around and hands Dennis back his ring*)

LINDA. Here.

DENNIS. Thank you.

LINDA. Sit over by Miss Miles now, please.

DENNIS. It's my class ring. Otherwise I wouldn't make such a big fuss about it.

LINDA. Please, sit over by Miss Miles now.

DENNIS. Okay. (*He crosses to Kimberly's desk and sits at one side. Linda seats herself on the other side. Kimberly sits in the middle. No one says anything for a moment*)

KIMBERLY. Now then, what is the problem? (*No response*)

LINDA. (*Slightly threatening*) Tell her.

DENNIS. Nothing. No problem.

LINDA. (*Very threatening*) Tell her what you told me!

DENNIS. Hi, my name is Dennis Post and your name is . . . (*Reading her name plate*) . . . Kimberly! Nice name. Listen, Kimberly, the thing is, I thought you were going to ship me to St. Louis but I guess I was wrong about that 'cause

Linda here says it's just not in the computer, only now it looks to me like maybe they're planning to fire me and I really can't afford to lose this job right now. I mean, you can only go to the First National Bank of Mom so many times for a loan before your credit rating goes flat. So listen, if keeping my job means moving to St. Louis, well, meet me in St. Louie! Only, don't fire me. Please don't fire me. God, please don't fire me.

KIMBERLY. (*To Linda*) Why am I talking to this man?

LINDA. Tell her what you told me about Douglas Cockrum!

DENNIS. Nice man! Heck of a guy! We all like him a lot!

LINDA. TELL HER!

DENNIS. Honestly, I didn't expect everybody to make such a big deal out of this. I'll go to St. Louis. Really. I WANT to go to St. Louis.

LINDA. He told me that no one in Assembly has ever seen Douglas Cockrum.

DENNIS. Oh boy. Now I'm in it. I'd really rather we just let the whole thing drop.

KIMBERLY. (*Incredulous, to Dennis*) What are you saying? (*He isn't saying anything, in fact*) Are you saying that Mr. Cockrum has been taking unauthorized days off?

LINDA. YEARS! He said no one has seen him in THREE YEARS!

DENNIS. There's probably a darn good explanation for this.

KIMBERLY. That's ridiculous. How could a man be on the payroll for three years without ever coming to work?

DENNIS. You know, she's right. It's ridiculous. I probably just made the whole thing up. So, I'll be in bright and early Monday morning. Just tell me what city I should report to.

LINDA. His paycheck is direct deposited. When you dial his extension it rings your phone. Now I don't know what's going on, but I'm sure that something about this is not right.

DENNIS. And I'm sure you guys can straighten it out without any more help from me. In fact, could you just sort of forget I ever came up here? I don't want to get a reputation for being the pipeline to the top.

KIMBERLY. Well, obviously, somebody must have seen the man

in three years. Who do you get your instructions from, Mr. Post?

LINDA. Drafting.

KIMBERLY. Who inspects your work?

LINDA. Engineering.

KIMBERLY. I was asking him.

DENNIS. Oh no. She's doing fine.

KIMBERLY. Well, I'll just call Cockrum's manager. (*After punching some numbers on her phone*) Kristi Kerr, please ... Mrs. Kerr? ... This is Kimberly Miles in Administration ... I'm having a little trouble locating an employee of yours ... Mr. Douglas Cockrum in Assembly ... But he works for you ... I see, and how long has it been since you last saw Mr. Cockrum? ... Well, how long have you been working for us? ... And in all that time it never occurred to you that someone else might be interested in knowing that there was an employee missing? ... How does Assembly operate without a supervisor? ... I see. Well, thank you, Mrs. Kerr. (*She hangs up the phone*) Mrs. Kerr tells me that you fellows in Assembly seem to do pretty well on your own.

DENNIS. Well, we try. So, guess I better get back to work ...

KIMBERLY. Mr. Post?

DENNIS. Yes?

KIMBERLY. If you have no supervisor, who did you think was going to fire you?

LINDA. (*To Dennis*) For that matter, who hired you?

DENNIS. Personnel.

KIMBERLY. Oh, I am sick of these responses. You can't talk to "Personnel." Personnel isn't a person, it's a department. You don't get your instructions from a department. You don't get hired by a department. A person—a living, discrete, individual organism—has to hire you. You were interviewed before you were hired, weren't you?

DENNIS. Grilled, actually.

KIMBERLY. But by a person. Not a department, but a person. Right?

DENNIS. Right!

KIMBERLY. So who was it that interviewed you?

DENNIS. Some gal in personnel.

KIMBERLY. Mr. Post, do you recall this "gal's" name?

DENNIS. I sure don't. I just remember she really put me through it. "What makes you think you're Jericho material?" "Do you think you can fit in with the Jericho system?" "What special qualities do you have that make you suitable for the Jericho team?" I mean, who are we kidding? What is the "Jericho team"? Are we going to have a little inter-corporate basketball?

KIMBERLY. What did she look like?

DENNIS. This was a long time ago, you know. But she had kinda short hair, pretty, wore glasses, few freckles ... (*He trails off and, for the first time, takes a good look at Kimberly*) As a matter of fact, she looked like you.

KIMBERLY. ME?

DENNIS. She looked exactly like you.

LINDA. Well, Kim, you used to work in personnel, didn't you?

DENNIS. My God, it was you, wasn't it?

KIMBERLY. Ah, um, uh ... it may have been ...

DENNIS. Listen, that interview wasn't really so bad. I exaggerate. You were just doing your job. I wasn't really mad or anything. And I am proud to be a part of the Jericho team!

KIMBERLY. Mr. Post, how did you come to apply for a job with Jericho in the first place?

DENNIS. I wanted to be a part of the Jericho team.

KIMBERLY. No. This is not an interview. I merely want to find out what brought you to Jericho. How did you hear about us?

DENNIS. There was an ad in the Trib: "Send your résumé to ..." some post office box or other "... for an opportunity to join the nation's fastest growing and most exciting industry: Factory Automation." So I did. Then I got a letter from Personnel requesting that I come in for an interview. That's when you and I first met. I have always remembered that day fondly.

KIMBERLY. But you just sent your résumé to a post office box? There was no one's name that you sent it to?

DENNIS. Oh, no. There was a name. Douglas Cockrum. I sent

it to Douglas Cockrum.

LINDA. He sends a résumé to Douglas Cockrum, Cockrum sends a written request to Personnel, Personnel conducts a screening interview and judges him to be acceptable and I get the notice to put him on payroll. He gets hired and never meets the man who hired him. That could happen. That could work.

DENNIS. It does work. It works great. No complaints here. So probably we can just forget I ever brought this silly thing up, right? So what if you can't find Cockrum? I really think we're making a big deal out of nothing much.

KIMBERLY. Well, who hired Cockrum? Whoever hired Cockrum must have seen him.

LINDA. Sure. That should be on file. Open up personnel. (*Kimberly punches a few keys on her computer keyboard*) Okay, now Cockrum comma Douglas. (*Kimberly types Cockrum, Douglas*) And there we have his file. First communication, résumé submitted, résumé approved by K. T. M. Who's K. T. M.?

KIMBERLY. I am.

LINDA. YOU hired him?

KIMBERLY. Well, I guess I checked his references and credentials. He checked out okay. So I approved him. Someone else must have interviewed him.

LINDA. Sure. Interview conducted by M. K. Who's M. K.? (*Both Kimberly and Linda look at the words* MARK KROPP *which are painted on the door behind them*) Why would Mr. Kropp be interviewing a low-level supervisor?

DENNIS. Well, I don't know, but I'm sure he must know what he's doing. So, glad I could help to clarify all this. Probably time I got back to work.

KIMBERLY. (*She does not want to have to repeat this*) Stay!

DENNIS. Yes m'am. (*Muttering to himself*) Get off the carpet. Sit. Stay. Roll over. Play dead. (*Kimberly glares at Dennis*) Sorry.

LINDA. Okay, what would you have done in order to check his credentials?

KIMBERLY. I would have called the University of Michigan to see if they had a record of a Douglas Cockrum.

LINDA. At this number? (*She is pointing at the computer screen*)

KIMBERLY. Yes. (*They look at each other for a moment, then Linda begins to dial the phone*)

LINDA. May I speak with, uh ... What did you say? ... Holiday? You mean like Holiday Inn? Is this area code three one three, five five five eight seven nine five? ... Ann Arbor, Michigan? ... Thank you. (*She hangs up*) Kimberly, this phone number is for the Holiday Inn in Ann Arbor.

KIMBERLY. The Holiday Inn?

LINDA. The one on the east side. She says there are two in Ann Arbor.

KIMBERLY. But I called that number. I talked to Records. I must have.

LINDA. You know what probably happened? Probably you called that number, they answered, "Holiday," — which you didn't even hear because nobody listens to receptionists — and so you asked for extension two-four-seven. She connected you with room two-four-seven, which could have been occupied by anybody. Maybe even Mr. Cockrum himself. So Cockrum picks up the phone, says, "Records," and you proceed to ask for information about Douglas Cockrum and he tells you that Douglas Cockrum is a great guy and we ought to hire him. And so you approve him and we hire him. Now that could happen. That could work.

DENNIS. And, really, where's the harm?

LINDA. In a way, it's kinda funny.

KIMBERLY. (*She has become surprisingly harsh*) I don't think it's funny.

LINDA. I just meant, in a way ...

KIMBERLY. I think it's sick. I think it's appalling. I think it's disgusting. I think it's perverse.

DENNIS. Perverse? Are we talking about the same thing?

KIMBERLY. Mr. Post, didn't it ever occur to you that you had a responsibility to the company to report the fact that your supervisor was neglecting his duties?

DENNIS. How do I know what his duties are?

KIMBERLY. Well, you could assume that one of his responsibilities was showing up to work.

DENNIS. How do I know that? I'm not management. You wanna know the truth? There's more than a couple things you guys do that don't make a whole lot of sense to me. If I went around reporting it every time you guys made a decision I thought was dumb I wouldn't have any time left for hooking wires together and that's a fact.

KIMBERLY. But don't you think it's the responsibility of every employee of this company to come to work?

DENNIS. That sounds like a good arrangement to me. But like I say, I ain't management and nobody's asked me. I mean, just what did you expect me to do about it? Was I supposed to file a formal complaint?

KIMBERLY. An Employee Report. We do have Employee Report forms available. (*Abruptly turning on Linda*) Thank you, Linda, I can handle this from here.

LINDA. Oh, uh . . .

KIMBERLY. We'll let you know if we need any more help.

LINDA. (*Hurt that Kimberly has apparently turned on her*) Yes, Kim. (*Linda returns to her desk*)

KIMBERLY. Uh, Linda?

LINDA. Yes?

KIMBERLY. Go down to Assembly and see if you can find Mr. Cockrum.

DENNIS and LINDA. Oh, he's not there.

KIMBERLY. Just the same, why don't you check that out.

LINDA. (*Curtly*) Yes, Miss Miles. (*She exits through the front door*)

KIMBERLY. Do you have any idea how embarrassing this is for me?

DENNIS. No, actually. What is it that you find embarrassing?

KIMBERLY. I approved a man's résumé based on a recommendation from the Holiday Inn!

DENNIS. Wow! Can you imagine that! (*Beat*) Uh, should that surprise me? I want to make sure I'm responding appropriately.

KIMBERLY. And YOU! You should have reported him your first day of work.

DENNIS. Me?! What about all those other guys that haven't seen him in three years?

KIMBERLY. They should have reported it too.

DENNIS. And what about you guys? Don't you ever check on your employees?

KIMBERLY. Of course we do. We get evaluations on every single employee from — (*An epiphany!*) WAIT A MINUTE! Employee Evaluations! Cockrum is responsible for sending us Employee Evaluations every six months. I should have a record ... (*Kimberly begins punching her keyboard again*) Assembly. There it is. Employee Evaluations. Uh-huh. (*She looks oddly at her screen*) Here they are. How is it possible? Every six months, Employee Evaluations for sixteen employees, all filed by Douglas Cockrum.

DENNIS. And you thought he was neglecting his duties.

KIMBERLY. (*A mean idea has entered her head*) Mr. Post, would you like to hear what he has to say about you?

DENNIS. (*Afraid of this*) Well, that's against company policy, isn't it? I'm not supposed to hear my own ...

KIMBERLY. (*Reading*) "Mr. Post's work is generally acceptable although well short of outstanding."

DENNIS. Well, acceptable is pretty good, isn't it. Is that like a "C"?

KIMBERLY. "He has a tendency to be insubordinate, although his lack of initiative makes it unlikely that he would ever be a serious threat."

DENNIS. What kind of a crack is that? I can be as much of a threat as anybody.

KIMBERLY. "For the most part he is reliable and valuable to the company."

DENNIS. There. See?

KIMBERLY. "He is congenial and well liked."

DENNIS. Yeah. Everybody likes me.

KIMBERLY. "However, his grooming and his peculiar taste in clothing make it impossible to consider him for any field assignments."

DENNIS. (*Shocked into silence for a moment*) What's wrong with my taste in clothing?

KIMBERLY. He says it's peculiar.

DENNIS. Well, for crying out loud, I work in Assembly, not fashion. Am I supposed to wear a tux to work? It's not the cleanest place in the world down there you know.

KIMBERLY. I'm just reading you what Mr. Cockrum wrote.

DENNIS. Well, that lousy rat ... (*He catches himself before he says anything too insubordinate*) ... uh, probably had a darn good reason for saying that. Listen, there wasn't anything in there about firing me or shipping me to St. Louis was there?

KIMBERLY. (*Angered and amazed*) DON'T YOU UNDERSTAND? HE JUST MADE ALL THIS UP! He doesn't know if you're insubordinate or reliable or well liked or anything else. He just made up a bunch of meaningless details so as not to attract any attention to himself. He's never seen you. He says you're reliable but insubordinate. Who isn't at times? He says you're well liked. Well, who's going to say you aren't. He says you have peculiar taste in clothing ... (*Kimberly interrupts herself as she sees how Dennis is dressed*) ... which could easily be a lucky guess on his part. What Mr. Cockrum is doing is a threat to this company and he needs to be stopped.

DENNIS. What are you yelling at me for? I'm not the one who hired him. (*Suddenly aware*) I didn't mean it that way. Look, that was an innocent mistake. No one can blame you for that.

KIMBERLY. (*Coldly*)Mr. Post, why have you come up here?

DENNIS. I was afraid I was going to lose my job.

KIMBERLY. (*With a vague, implicit threat*) And do you wish to keep your job?

DENNIS. Yes! Yes! I wanna keep my job!

KIMBERLY. I see. And do you also wish to file a report about your supervisor?

DENNIS. File a report? You mean, do I want to make a complaint?

KIMBERLY. They are not complaints. We do not "complain" at Jericho. They are reports. Do you wish to file a report?

DENNIS. Is that how it is? In order to keep my job I have to turn Cockrum in?

KIMBERLY. Mr. Post, you came up here for help. Now, as it turns out, it is my job to review Employee Reports. But unless you wish to file an Employee Report, I do not know how I can help you.

DENNIS. (*Rising from his chair, he begins to pace around the room*) What kind of a position is that to put me in? How can I betray my supervisor, the man who hired me in the first place? (*He seems about to kick the filing cabinet*)

KIMBERLY. Don't kick the filing cabinet. (*He kicks the filing cabinet then continues to pace*)

DENNIS. It's the McCarthy hearings all over again. Never mind who gets hurt. Never mind what lives you destroy. Turn friend against friend, brother against brother, employee against employer. You're going to put me on the stand and I'm going to spill my guts. Because I'm a spineless, self-interested sycophant, that's what I am! I'll do anything to keep my job and you know it.

KIMBERLY. Don't kick the wall. (*He kicks the wall*)

DENNIS. How can I do this to a man who called me congenial and well liked? A man who said that my work was generally acceptable?

KIMBERLY. A man who said you had peculiar taste in clothing, don't forget.

DENNIS. (*That freezes Dennis in his tracks*) All right. I'll do it. God forgive me, I'll do it.

KIMBERLY. Really, you're making much too much out of this. "McCarthy hearings": honestly! We don't go on witch hunts. This is just a report. As such, it will be evaluated along with other reports. That way a fair decision can be reached. We are not interested in culling out communists. We are merely interested in evaluating our staff. Do you understand the difference?

DENNIS. Is it real important that I understand?

KIMBERLY. Yes.

DENNIS. Okay then. I understand.

KIMBERLY. Fine. Please sit down over here.

DENNIS. What?

KIMBERLY. (*Pointing at the chair next to her desk*) Sit.

DENNIS. Woof. (*Kimberly ignores the bark. Dennis sits*)

KIMBERLY. All right, then. Your name?

DENNIS. What?

KIMBERLY. I said, Your name?

DENNIS. You know my name.

KIMBERLY. Mr. Post, if you are going to file a report then I need to have you tell me your name. An efficient operation does not take shortcuts. Now, will you please tell me your full, formal name?

DENNIS. Whitaker Chambers.

KIMBERLY. (*Pause*) Would you like to forget the whole thing?

DENNIS. Why does my name gotta be on this thing? Can't I file this anonymously? (*Kimberly is glaring disapprovingly*) Dennis Post.

KIMBERLY. What department do you work in?

DENNIS. Aw, for pete's sake, we just went over this. (*Kimberly glares again*) Assembly.

KIMBERLY. The name of the employee you wish to report on?

DENNIS. Douglas Cockrum.

KIMBERLY. His department?

DENNIS. When you go by the numbers, you go by the numbers, don't you? Assembly.

KIMBERLY. The nature of your complaint?

DENNIS. Report. We don't make complaints at Jericho. We report.

KIMBERLY. (*Only slightly stung*) Very well. The nature of your report?

DENNIS. Yeah. I wanna report that Cockrum hasn't been to work in three years. Okay? You happy? Probably ruined this man's life. His wife'll probably leave him and then he'll commit suicide. His kids will grow up without a father figure and become unemployable substance abusers. Feel good about that?

KIMBERLY. Is that all?

DENNIS. All? We just killed the guy. What more do you want?

KIMBERLY. I am merely asking if there is anything else you would like to report.

DENNIS. Yeah. Sure. He's a communist too. And his work is generally acceptable. Only he dresses funny. He mixes plaids and wears white in the winter. He buys penny loafers and punches holes in 'em so that people will think he's wearing wing tips. I say we fire the bum.

KIMBERLY. Mr. Post, when you make whimsical statements like that, it casts doubt on everything you say. We don't know when to trust you. Is that what you want? Do you want to cast doubt on everything you have told us? (*Dennis does not respond*) I said, do you want to cast doubt on every —

DENNIS. (*Snapping back*) I'm thinking!

KIMBERLY. Mr. Post, is there any truth to anything you have told us?

DENNIS. Yes! Absolutely. I really don't want to go to St. Louis! That's the God's honest truth.

KIMBERLY. (*After a considered pause*) Do you like your job here?

DENNIS. What?

KIMBERLY. Do you like your job here?

DENNIS. Look, I know you're someone who likes to go by the numbers, so would you mind telling me: what number are you on?

KIMBERLY. It will be my job to evaluate this report you have just given me. Part of my evaluation will be to consider the credibility of the man who made the report. Sometimes people make reports because they have an axe to grind. Sometimes there is a personal problem. (*Pointedly*) SOME-TIMES employees are just destructive by nature. They intentionally put bugs in the system. They are not team players. I'm wondering about you now, Mr. Post. Are you a team player? Or one of those people who puts bugs in the system? And so, the question is: Do you like your job here at Jericho?

DENNIS. Do you have any idea what my job is? I look at diagrams that show me where there are supposed to be wires. Then I put the wires where they're supposed to be. And that's about all there is to it. It amazes me, in fact, that a company that specializes in factory automation hasn't figured out a way to automate my job. So, what's the question? Do I like my job? What's not to like? On the other hand, what's to like? It's okay, you know? I can't think of any other job I'd really want. Except one, maybe.

KIMBERLY. Oh? And what's that?

DENNIS. I think I'd like Cockrum's job. Will you let me know if that opens up?

KIMBERLY. I cannot imagine why you seem to envy a man who has not come to work in three years. It seems to me that what he has done to Jericho amounts to fraud. Do you admire fraud?

DENNIS. I don't know how you can say that. No one even noticed he wasn't here for three years. Seems to me that what he did to Jericho amounts to automation.

KIMBERLY. (*Choosing to ignore this*) I will pass on your report.

DENNIS. Do I keep my job?

KIMBERLY. I will pass on your report.

DENNIS. Do I keep my job?!

KIMBERLY. All I can do is pass on your report. I guess I know of no reason why you can't keep your job. But I have to tell you, I am appalled by the general lack of ethical standards that seems to run rampant in our Assembly area.

DENNIS. WHAT?! You're going to talk to me about ethical standards? An office that keeps a four hundred thousand dollar slush fund has the gall to talk to me about ethical standards?

KIMBERLY. (*That got her attention*) What?

DENNIS. (*Wishing he had not said that*) Nothing.

KIMBERLY. What?!

DENNIS. Nothing.

KIMBERLY. What did you say?

DENNIS. It was nothing. I was babbling. Garbage comes out of my mouth. What do you expect from a guy with peculiar taste in clothing and no ethical standards?

KIMBERLY. You said "slush fund."

DENNIS. Four hundred thousand dollar slush fund. But how would I know about that? It's probably just another one of my paranoid delusions.

KIMBERLY. I insist upon knowing why you implied that we are keeping a four hundred thousand dollar slush fund.

DENNIS. Oh God. I've done it now. Listen, I haven't told anybody. And I won't. What do I care what you guys do with your money. Bahama vacations, new sports cars, condominiums in Punta Gorda — whatever you guys think is best.

KIMBERLY. TELL ME WHAT IT IS YOU THINK YOU KNOW!

DENNIS. I just accidentally one day ran across file number

three-one-three-five-three a few months ago. But I never told anybody about it. Honest.

KIMBERLY. What is file number three-one-three-five-three?

DENNIS. Are you pulling my leg? You really don't know? Or are you playing dumb? (*Kimberly is glaring angrily. She is not going to ask one more time. Dennis walks behind her chair so that he can see her monitor*) All right, get back to the main menu. (*Kimberly hits some commands on her keyboard*) Now enter four to get us over to Administration. (*Kimberly does so*) Now from here we got only two choices. We can punch one for POLICY or two for ACCOUNTS.

KIMBERLY. Yes.

DENNIS. What happens if you punch three?

KIMBERLY. Three does not exist.

DENNIS. I know. But try it. What does the computer say if you punch three?

KIMBERLY. (*After punching three, she reads from her screen*) "THREE DOES NOT EXIST."

DENNIS. Ah. But now, enter three-one-three-five-three. (*Kimberly enters 31353. She is then stunned by the result*) How about that!

KIMBERLY. There's a file.

DENNIS. Sure is.

KIMBERLY. How did you find this?

DENNIS. By accident. I was just playing around and that's what I found.

KIMBERLY. BY ACCIDENT?!

DENNIS. Yeah. By accident.

KIMBERLY. Do you know what the odds are against your finding a five number code by accident?!

DENNIS. Sure. One in a hundred thousand. IF you only guess once. On the other hand, if you guess a hundred thousand times, the odds are much better.

KIMBERLY. When would you have time to try a hundred thousand different entries?

DENNIS. I get two fifteen minute breaks and a half hour for lunch.

KIMBERLY. And you have nothing better to do with your time than to check to see if we have any secret files in the computer?

DENNIS. You know, that came up earlier today. It would be real nice if we could get a ping-pong table down there. I mean, we're men, not machines, right?

KIMBERLY. No one wants you to be machines. Mr. Post, how do you know this is a slush fund?

DENNIS. Probably it isn't. Probably I just made that part up. Probably this is just an arbitrary list of numbers which all have little dollar signs in front of 'em.

KIMBERLY. Well, I'll admit that this is odd, but it does seem to be something of a quantum leap to decide that this is a slush fund.

DENNIS. Right! I'm famous for making quantum leaps. It isn't labled "Slush Fund." It's probably nothing.

KIMBERLY. If they wanted to keep a slush fund, why would they enter it into the main computer at all? That doesn't make any sense. If this was supposed to be a secret, why wouldn't they keep their records on paper, locked away somewhere?

DENNIS. Another good point! Boy, you sure shot my theory full of holes. This is probably left over from the Christmas party when the execs got together to play monopoly. Totally meaningless. And I'm very sorry if I questioned the ethics of your office. Can I go back to work now?

KIMBERLY. No.

DENNIS. Are you going to fire me?

KIMBERLY. What?

DENNIS. I'm going to be fired, aren't I? It's inevitable now, isn't it?

KIMBERLY. Why is it inevitable now?

DENNIS. Because I know too much. They're going to have to fire me in order to silence me.

KIMBERLY. Good grief! And they say women are illogical.

DENNIS. They do?

KIMBERLY. Nobody's going to fire you in order to silence you. That's stupid. If there really is a slush fund — and I don't believe there is — by firing you they'd be admitting guilt. They'd be inviting you to go to the *Sun-Times*. Don't you ever think things through before you start flying off the handle?

DENNIS. Not generally, no.

KIMBERLY. Well, I'm going to talk with Mr. Rajeski. I'm going to see if he knows about this file number three-one-three-five-three. And I want you to stay here in case he has any questions. Okay? Just stay here. Don't move.

DENNIS. Right. (*Kimberly exits through the front door to talk with David*) Boy, I wish I'd never started this. (*He kicks Linda's desk*) But at least I know they aren't going to fire me. Big deal. They aren't going to fire me from the world's most boring job. (*He kicks the filing cabinet*) Because if they fired me it wouldn't silence me. I could just call up Mike Royko and spill my guts. They don't want me to do that. (*He pulls his foot back as if he is about to kick Kimberly's desk. His foot remains frozen in mid air as a horrible thought occurs to him*) OH MY GOD, THEY'RE GOING TO HAVE ME KILLED! (*Dennis kicks Kimberly's desk hard enough to knock out the legs on one side. The desk top is now raked at a steep angle and, despite Dennis's best efforts, everything that was on the desk crashes to the floor. Dennis is left standing in a pile of rubble, holding the paperweight he managed to catch. David, Linda and Kimberly come running into the office*) AN ACCIDENT! IT WAS AN ACCIDENT! DON'T KILL ME! PLEASE DON'T KILL ME. I'LL KEEP MY MOUTH SHUT. I'LL GO TO ST. LOUIS. I'LL GO TO MOOSEJAW, SASKATCHEWAN! NO ONE IN MOOSEJAW WILL CARE IF I TALK. DON'T KILL ME.

DAVID. (*He speaks very quietly but very sternly. He is all three-piece business. He never laughs or smiles*) Put the paperweight down. (*Dennis immediately drops the paperweight*) Come over here. (*Dennis obeys*) Stop. Sit down here. (*David indicates the chair next to his desk. Dennis sits in it*) You've made quite a mess of things in here.

DENNIS. Yes sir. I seem to have.

DAVID. Yes, well, there's a reason we don't allow just anyone onto the carpet.

DENNIS. Would you like me to leave?

DAVID. Soon. Yes. I would like that very much.

DENNIS. I could leave now. Just tell me how far you want me to go.

DAVID. For the moment I want you to stay where you are.

DENNIS. Yes sir. (*Pause*)

DAVID. Ms. Miles tells me that you have found something of a
bug in our system.

DENNIS. Yes. Well, no. Well, listen, it's no big deal, really. See
what happened was, my name is Dennis Post, and — (*David
slams his hand on his desk. Dennis is shocked into silence*)

DAVID. Mr. Post, I am going to ask you some questions. I
want you to answer them. That's all you have to do.
Please, do not extemporize. It annoys me.

DENNIS. Yes sir.

DAVID. And, Mr. Post, before you begin, let me warn you
about one thing: I do not have a sense of humor.

DENNIS. I see.

DAVID. I take my work very seriously. I don't joke around the
way Ms. Taylor and Ms. Miles do.

DENNIS. You don't?

DAVID. No. I don't.

DENNIS. I see.

DAVID. I hope you do.

DENNIS. That's a shame, really.

DAVID. Perhaps. Now please start from the beginning and tell
me everything. Do you understand?

DENNIS. Yes.

DAVID. I mean, do you understand what I mean by
"everything"?

DENNIS. Yes. I think so.

DAVID. Then go ahead.

DENNIS. My father was a member of the communist party. For
that matter, so was my mother. And an uncle on my
father's side except he was only a half-uncle. That is, he
was my dad's half-brother. Am I going too fast?

DAVID. Hmm. Mr. Post, perhaps I spoke too broadly when I
used the word "everything."

DENNIS. You're not really interested in hearing about my folks,
are you.

DAVID. No. I'm not. I want to hear about you.

DENNIS. Fine. That's fine. I can do that.

DAVID. Then go ahead, please.

DENNIS. I was born on the lower floor of an apartment building
my parents owned on Taylor. The upper floor was rented

out to an old guy who didn't wash very often but he had a lot of young girlfriends that came to visit him … (*David is drumming his fingers*) … and this isn't what you wanted to hear either, is it? (*David shakes his head no*)

DAVID. No, it's not. Mr. Post, I am going to give you one more chance. But before you open your mouth again. I want you to think very, very carefully. (*Dennis faces front. He is thinking very, very carefully as the lights fade to black*)

act 2

It is only a little later in the day. David and Dennis are still at David's desk; Dennis is wrapping up his life story. Kimberly is back to reading her computer output. Her desk has been propped up on a couple manuals so that the top is nearly level again. Linda is inputting data.

DENNIS. … so, I don't know, maybe I kicked too hard or maybe the legs were weak but, anyway, the desk toppled and all the stuff on top started sliding toward me. I tried to catch as much as I could—honest—but the only thing I came up with was the paperweight, which probably wouldn't have broken anyway. Then you came in and told me to drop the paperweight and you told me the thing about how you don't kid around the way Linda and Kim do and … well, you pretty well know the rest, right? (*David seems to be listening to this, but he does not respond to the question*) Is that pretty much everything you wanted to know?

DAVID. Hmm. Well, no.

DENNIS. No?

DAVID. What you have told me is both more and less than I want to know.

DENNIS. Sorry.

DAVID. All right.

DENNIS. (*He is trying to pull something out of the sole of his shoe*) I'm trying to be cooperative. Really.

DAVID. I understand.

DENNIS. Sometimes, though, I get rolling and—

DAVID. DON'T!

DENNIS. Don't what?

DAVID. Don't "get rolling." Please.

DENNIS. Oh. Okay.

DAVID. You respond poorly to commands. Did you know that?

DENNIS. Oh, no I don't. Not really. I'm a little slow sometimes, maybe. But I'm only human.

DAVID. I see.

DENNIS. We're all only human, right?

DAVID. Right.

DENNIS. God knows we can't be machines.

DAVID. We can only aspire.

DENNIS. What?

DAVID. What are you doing to your shoe?

DENNIS. Oh, there's something stuck in the sole. I think it's a tack.

DAVID. A tack?

DENNIS. There! I got it out.

DAVID. Why would there be a tack in this office? We don't use tacks.

DENNIS. I think it's an upholstery tack.

DAVID. Oh. Mr. Post—

DENNIS. In fact, I think it came out of your chair.

DAVID. Perhaps. Mr. Post—

DENNIS. (*Getting on all fours and crawling behind David*) I can probably put it back.

DAVID. No. Don't do that.

DENNIS. Probably from the seat.

DAVID. (*Wriggling slightly as Dennis, out of sight, gropes for the proper place to put the tack*) Stop. Stop that.

DENNIS. Sometimes they just work their way loose—

DAVID. (*Without rising*) STOP THAT!

DENNIS. (*Quickly returning to his seat*) Yes sir.

DAVID. (*Opening his desk drawer*) Give me the tack.

DENNIS. I don't have it anymore.

DAVID. Where is it?

DENNIS. I put it back in your chair. I found where it went.

DAVID. Oh.

DENNIS. You're welcome. (*David closes the drawer*) Wait a minute. What was that in your drawer?

DAVID. I don't know what you mean.

DENNIS. Was that a gun?

DAVID. Oh. Perhaps. Mr. Post—

DENNIS. A real gun?

DAVID. Probably. Mr. Post—

DENNIS. You keep a gun in your desk?

DAVID. Yes. Mr. Post—(*Dennis leaps from his chair and dives for cover behind Kimberly*)

DENNIS. LOOKOUT! HE'S GOT A GUN!

DAVID. Mr. Post! Stop it. Come back here at once. (*Dennis stands up; his hands raised over his head*) Stop that. Put your hands down! (*Dennis does so*)

DENNIS. (*To Kimberly*) He's got a gun in his desk. Did you know that?

DAVID. Come back here and sit down.

DENNIS. (*To Linda*) Did you know he has a gun in his desk?

DAVID. Stop making such a fuss. It is just a gun. I am quite certain that it comes as no great surprise to either Ms. Taylor or Ms. Miles that I have a gun in my desk. (*In fact, it is quite apparent, by the expression on their faces, that this news came as a considerable surprise to both Linda and Kimberly*) Mr. Post, there are going to be some rules from now on.

DENNIS. There are?

DAVID. Rule number one is that you are going to remain in that chair until I tell you to get out of it. Do you understand?

DENNIS. Not really. I mean, I just saw a gun and I panicked a little, but I don't see why ... (*He becomes aware of David's growing ire*) ... uh, that is, sure, I understand. You bet! Stay in the chair. No problem. If you want me in the chair—

DAVID. Rule number two is that you will only speak when responding to a direct question and then you will answer that question quickly and with the fewest possible words. I don't want you to second-guess why I am asking these questions. I just want you to answer. Do you understand rule number two?

DENNIS. (*Immediately*) Yes.

DAVID. (*Impressed*) Very good.

DENNIS. (*Immediately*) Thank you.

DAVID. Yes. Then ... (*He spits the words out abruptly*) ... WHAT IS YOUR NAME!

DENNIS. (*Spitting back*) DENNIS POST.

DAVID. WHERE DO YOU LIVE?

DENNIS. THIRTY-THREE FIFTY-EIGHT NORTH SOUTHPORT APARTMENT TWO-B!

DAVID. WHERE DO YOU WORK?

DENNIS. JERICHO INCORPORATED.

DAVID. WHAT DO YOU DO THERE?

DENNIS. I'M PART OF THE JERICHO TEAM! (*There is a moment of silence. A rather long moment. Kimberly and Linda have looked up from their work to see what all the yelling is about. David glares at them and they return to their chores. A second burst of questions erupts*)

DAVID. HOW MANY AMPS IS TWELVE-GUAGE WIRE RATED FOR?

DENNIS. TWENTY.

DAVID. WHAT DO WE USE RED INSULATED WIRE FOR?

DENNIS. A HUNDRED AND TEN VOLTS A.C.

DAVID. WHEN DO WE USE BLUE WIRE?

DENNIS. TWELVE VOLTS D.C.

DAVID. WHEN DO WE USE GREEN?

DENNIS. FOR GROUNDING.

DAVID. WHEN DO WE USE PUCE?

DENNIS. WHEN WE'RE OUT OF EVERYTHING ELSE. (*Another long silence while David regroups*)

DAVID. WHO IS DOUGLAS COCKRUM?

DENNIS. NO ONE KNOWS, SIR.

DAVID. WHAT IS FILE NUMBER THREE-ONE-THREE-FIVE-THREE?

DENNIS. I DON'T KNOW.

DAVID. WHAT DO YOU THINK IT IS?

DENNIS. THE RECORD OF A SLUSH FUND.

DAVID. WHY DO YOU THINK IT'S A SLUSH FUND?

DENNIS. BECAUSE I'M A PARANOID AND I ALWAYS MAKE UP MINDLESS CONSPIRACY THEORIES BASED ON VIRTUALLY NO EVIDENCE. (*David begins what is, for him, an almost friendly approach*)

DAVID. Dennis, Dennis, Dennis. Why would Jericho want a slush fund?

DENNIS. I don't know. Probably they wouldn't.

DAVID. Why do you THINK Jericho might want a slush fund?

DENNIS. Oh, I don't know. To buy a senator?

DAVID. Really! For four hundred thousand dollars? Senators cost more than that.

DENNIS. Maybe an alderman.

DAVID. Alderman don't cost that much.

DENNIS. Or maybe they'd use the money to topple a government in a South American country that won't allow them to remove their capital without paying a huge amount in taxes.

DAVID. (*Suddenly quiet*) What?

DENNIS. (*Very uneasy*) Did I say something?

DAVID. What would make you say that?

DENNIS. I don't know. I don't think I did say it. What was it I said? See? I've forgotten already. Probably just more mindless paranoia —

DAVID. Why would you specifically mention South America?

DENNIS. I don't know. Don't we have some offices in South America?

DAVID. We have offices in a lot of places. St. Louis, for example, as you are so fond of reminding us.

DENNIS. It just didn't seem real likely to me that anyone would spend four hundred thousand dollars to topple the government in Missouri.

DAVID. Mr. Post, you have an annoying habit of seeming to know more than you are saying. Do you know more than you are saying?

DENNIS. No! No! Less! I swear, I didn't know.

DAVID. Didn't know what?

DENNIS. About the assassination plot in South America.

DAVID. What assassination plot?

DENNIS. THERE'S MORE THAN ONE?

DAVID. I DIDN'T KNOW THERE WERE ANY!

DENNIS. THEN WHAT ARE YOU GETTING PARANOID ABOUT?!

DAVID. I'M NOT PARANOID! YOU'RE PARANOID!

DENNIS. WELL, IF I'M PARANOID, WHY DO YOU LISTEN TO ME?!!

(*Another long moment of silence passes while David collects his thoughts once more*)

DAVID. (*Calmly*) You know, you very nearly caused me to lose my cool just now.

DENNIS. Sorry.

DAVID. All right. Of course, the whole notion of assassins in South America is ridiculous.

DENNIS. That's what I think.

DAVID. You get carried away with your fantasies and, because you do have a certain amount of charm about you, others tend to get caught up with you.

DENNIS. Thank you. I think you are charming also.

DAVID. Still, can't really deny that something about this whole thing isn't quite right.

DENNIS. I guess.

DAVID. There does seem to a bit of a bug in the system. (*He gets carried away by his own description*) A rather large bug, it would seem. A large, multilegged, venomous insect with huge mandibles and a stinger on its backside that LEAKS A TRAIL OF SLIME ON EVERYTHING IT CRAWLS OVER!!

DENNIS. I just don't want to go to St. Louis.

DAVID. (*Snapping back to the real world*) Yes. You mentioned that. Well, I imagine it's time we brought Mr. Kropp into this. Excuse me a moment. (*David rises from his chair. In so doing his suit coat tears up the back*)

DENNIS. Oh my. (*David is glaring at Dennis*) It looks like I tacked your coat to your chair. Listen, I am really sorry. (*Dennis goes to the chair in order to free David's coat*) I was in a hurry. I didn't know your coat was in the way. Honest. (*Dennis has freed the coat. David is gazing at the rend. He is near tears*) It looks to me like it took it out at the seam. Really, any tailor ought to be able to ... (*David glares sufficiently to shut Dennis up*) Sorry. (*David hangs his coat up with the tenderness of a man burying his mother*)

DAVID. (*Forcing his composure*) Do not move from that chair again.

DENNIS. I won't.

DAVID. Ever.

DENNIS. I won't.

DAVID. I am going to inform Mr. Kropp about our illustrious Mr. Cockrum. We will talk about my coat later. (*David crosses to Kropp's door*)

DENNIS. (*Muttering to himself*) Yeah. Great idea. Ask him why he hired Cockrum in the first place.

DAVID. (*Stopping in his tracks*) What did you say?

DENNIS. Uh, well, I said, "Yeah. Great idea. Ask him why he hired Cockrum in the first place." No big deal, you know.

DAVID. Mr. Kropp hired Cockrum?

DENNIS. Oh. Yeah. Did I leave that part out? I'm sorry.

DAVID. So what are you suggesting?

DENNIS. Nothing.

DAVID. Are you suggesting that Mr. Kropp is a part of this conspiracy of yours?

DENNIS. No. I'm sure he has a perfectly wonderful explanation for the whole thing.

DAVID. Are you suggesting that Mr. Kropp has something to hide?

DENNIS. Not at all. He probably wants this whole thing out in the open. He's probably dying to talk about why he hired a guy who, as far as anyone can tell, doesn't exist. (*David thinks a long moment about this. Suddenly, he turns to Kimberly*)

DAVID. Ms. Miles, who hired Douglas Cockrum?

KIMBERLY. Apparently, Mr. Kropp did.

DAVID. Hmmm. Mmmmhmmm. I see. Hmmm. (*Kimberly and Dennis both are now watching David pace*) Yes, well, hmmm. That doesn't mean there's any hanky-panky going on.

DENNIS. You got me convinced. If I were you, I'd go blow the whistle on Cockrum.

DAVID. (*Continuing to pace*) Hmmm. Yes. Hmmm. Mmmhmm. Mr. Post?

DENNIS. Sir?

DAVID. The mere fact that Mr. Kropp hired Mr. Cockrum does not in any way suggest that Mr. Kropp is involved in any misbehavior.

DENNIS. I agree.

DAVID. Indeed, Mr. Kropp has doubtless hired scores of people in his tenure as president as I am sure Ms. Miles can attest.

KIMBERLY. This is the only one I know of.

DAVID. The only one? Are you sure? The ONLY one?

KIMBERLY. Maybe not the ONLY one, but it is unusual.

DAVID. Unusual, perhaps. But, as I am sure Ms. Taylor can attest, not unheard of.

LINDA. I never heard of it.

DAVID. Indeed. Ms. Taylor has never heard of it. But, as I am sure Ms. Taylor will be the first to admit, she does not hear everything.

LINDA. Almost everything.

DAVID. Perhaps. But I can attest to the man's character. No man, in all of business, has more character than Mark Kropp. And I am sure that if something is not right with Jericho Incorporated, Mr. Kropp is no part of it and will wish to be informed. Immediately.

DENNIS. Great! That's what I was hoping for. Listen, while you're in there, could you ask him about St. Louis?

DAVID. People who are themselves of low character tend to believe the worst about other people. They project their own greed and cowardice and lack of moral fiber on men whose character is unassailable. This does not speak poorly of the accused; it is an indictment of the accuser!

DENNIS. Right on! Are you going to talk to him sometime today? (*David continues to pace the room. Everyone is watching him. There is an uncomfortable silence. He paces over to his computer, enters a few commands and frowns at the response on the C.R.T. He walks to Kropp's door and stands there for a while with his back to the audience. His hands remain at his side. He stands there for a long time*)

DAVID. Hmm. (*He crosses back to his own desk and seats himself*) Very well, Mr. Post, thank you for bringing this matter to our attention. I promise you that we will look into it with deliberate speed and in a thorough manner.

DENNIS. That's it?

DAVID. Yes. That's it. Thank you. You may get out of the chair now.

DENNIS. You're not going to talk to Mr. Kropp?

DAVID. Mr. Kropp is a very busy man. I don't wish to bother him with this.

DENNIS. How would it be if I went to talk to him? Just about St. Louis. I won't even mention the other stuff.

DAVID. Out of the question, I'm afraid.

DENNIS. Can I assume that I'm not going to be sent to St. Louis?

DAVID. I don't know that.

DENNIS. Don't know?! Can you tell me if they're going to fire me?

DAVID. I just don't have anything to say on that topic. I can't promise you anything.

DENNIS. Can you at least promise me that I'm not going to be hit by one of your assassination squads?

DAVID. Mr. Post, I am not going to dignify that question with a response.

DENNIS. That's it, isn't it? You're going to have me killed, aren't you?

DAVID. Now, Mr. Post, you don't really believe ...

DENNIS. Who doesn't believe? I believe it. I think that's what you were doing on the computer just now. I think you just sent out a secret order to have me killed. I think that I won't last two seconds in that hallway. I think they're lined up with machine guns ready to nail the first poor slob who steps out that door.

DAVID. Well, I'm not even going to discuss anything as ridiculous as that.

DENNIS. Yeah? Well, I'm not walking through that door!

DAVID. Oh yes you are. You are going to leave this office at once. Go back to Assembly where you belong.

DENNIS. You want me to go back to Assembly?

DAVID. Fervently.

DENNIS. Then you walk through that door first.

DAVID. Oh for heaven's sake.

DENNIS. I dare you.

DAVID. If it will make you feel better, Ms. Taylor will be glad to go out in the hall and let you know that the coast is clear.

KIMBERLY. You guys? Cut it out, okay? This stuff really scares me. (*Linda starts to walk toward the door*)

DENNIS. (*To Linda*) DON'T DO IT! IT'S A TRAP! (*Dennis's scream *startles Linda. Kimberly is cowering deeply and murmuring. "Oh God, oh God, oh God")*

DAVID. Kimberly, please, stop whimpering. (*To Dennis*) Ms. Taylor does not share your deluded view of this world, Mr. Post. She isn't afraid that overzealous maniacs with machine guns are going to cut her down as soon as she steps out into the hall. Ms. Taylor, would you please just step outside and reassure Mr. Post that there are no hit squads out there?

LINDA. (*Very hesitant*) Do I have to?

DAVID. (*Hurt*) Linda!

LINDA. Yes?

DAVID. What are you implying?

LINDA. Nothing! Only, if I don't have to go out in the hall, I'd rather not.

DAVID. Do you really think there are armed, private soldiers out there?

LINDA. Well, no.

DAVID. Do you believe that I could be responsible for an assassination plot?

LINDA. Well ... no. (*Linda walks slowly toward the door again*)

KIMBERLY. Linda, be careful. Oh God, oh God, oh God. (*Dennis suddenly pulls the gun from David's drawer and races to block Linda's way*)

DENNIS. GET BACK! EVERYBODY GET BACK! (*Everybody does. He addresses David*) What kind of man are you? You would allow this woman to walk into an ambush just to avoid losing an argument with me?

KIMBERLY. Oh God, oh God, oh God.

DAVID. Put the gun down.

DENNIS. Oh, you'd like that wouldn't you?

DAVID. (*Bravely walking toward Dennis*) Give me the gun.

LINDA. Dennis, don't do this.

DENNIS. Stay back! I'll shoot!

DAVID. No, I don't think you will, Dennis. (*He continues to move in on him*)

DENNIS. (*Backed up to the door*) No. I will. Honest.

LINDA. David?

DAVID. I just don't believe you anymore, Dennis.

DENNIS. What are you, mental? A crazy paranoid like me says he's going to shoot you and you don't believe him? What's wrong with your head?

DAVID. I just don't think you're going to shoot me.

DENNIS. Oh you don't, huh? Well, what are you going to do if you're wrong?

DAVID. Just give me the gun. (*He is toe to toe with Dennis now, the gun pointed at his heart*)

DENNIS. (*After a long moment*) Boy! Are you ever cocky.

KIMBERLY. My God. My God. My God.

DAVID. Give me the gun.

DENNIS. I hate people like you. It'd serve you right if I did shoot you.

DAVID. GIVE ME THE GUN!

KIMBERLY. (*Startled*) Oh my God!

DENNIS. Oh, that's real smart. Yell at a guy who's pointing a gun at you. Why don't you try shouting, "BOO!"

DAVID. GIVE ME THE GUN!

DENNIS. Not until we straighten a couple things out.

DAVID. We are not going to straighten anything out until you give me that gun. I make it a rule not to negotiate with people who point guns at me.

DENNIS. Has that rule come up a lot?

DAVID. If you want to talk, we can talk. But first you will give me that gun.

DENNIS. Well, I'm not giving you the gun. You think I'm stupid? We've already established that you've hired a hit squad to off me; you think I'm going to just give you a gun?

DAVID. If you wish to talk with me you will simply have to give me that gun. That's all there is to it.

DENNIS. Oh yeah? (*Dennis suddenly races across the room and holds the gun to the C.R.T. on Linda's desk*) NOW NOBODY MOVES OR I'LL BLOW ITS HEAD OFF!

DAVID. (*Regarding this situation very differently*) STAND BACK EVERYBODY. I DON'T THINK HE'S BLUFFING THIS TIME!

KIMBERLY. My God. My God. My-y-y-y uh, oooooooh . . . (*She passes out*)

DAVID. What is it you want?

DENNIS. (*Concerned about Kimberly*) Is she all right?

DAVID. Tell us what you want.

LINDA. Yes. Tell us what you want, Dennis. Don't shoot the computer.

DENNIS. Don't you think you ought to make sure she's okay?

DAVID. TELL US WHAT YOU WANT!

DENNIS. OKAY! Boy! This guy loves to yell.

LINDA. He doesn't mean to yell. But there's no point in shooting the computer, Dennis. Really.

DENNIS. Oh, I won't really shoot it.

LINDA. You hear, Mr. Rajeski? He won't really shoot it.

DAVID. And you believe him?

DENNIS. All right, Rajeski, here it is. I want you to promise me that I won't be shipped to St. Louis.

DAVID. Fine. I promise. You won't be shipped to St. Louis.

DENNIS. And I'm not going to be fired.

DAVID. I promise. You won't be fired.

DENNIS. And promise me that you won't have me killed.

DAVID. I promise. I won't have you killed.

DENNIS. Yeah?

DAVID. Yeah.

DENNIS. Well, what good is a promise from somebody who would hire a hit squad in the first place?

DAVID. (*Trying an entirely new tack as he edges his way toward the hall door*) No good, Mr. Post. Absolutely no good at all. So what are you going to do about it?

DENNIS. Huh?

DAVID. Sooner or later you're going to have to go out that door. Sooner or later you will have to face seven mindless assassins who are poised and waiting for you to step through that door. (*Linda gives a frightened look to David and begins to edge away from him*) There's no other way out.

LINDA. David?

DENNIS. Stay away from the door!

DAVID. You can shoot the computer, but then what can you do? Sooner or later my boys — I like to think of them as my boys — are going to get you. They are just waiting for my command. And there's nothing you can do about it.

DENNIS. Oh, this is clever of you. Feed my fantasy; that'll calm me down.

DAVID. There's nothing to be calm about; you are a goner already.

LINDA. (*Really scared now*) David?

DENNIS. All right. That's enough.

DAVID. In fact ... (*Abruptly, David points to the window behind Dennis and shouts*) THERE'S ONE OF MY BOYS NOW! (*Dennis screams and whirls toward the imaginary invader. Linda screams and dives behind a desk. Dennis fires a shot at something. Who knows what. The computer monitor next to him explodes. This apparently sets off some sort of chain reaction because the computer monitor on Kimberly's desk also explodes. And all the lights in the room go out. The room is filled with smoke. A smoke detector goes off. David lunges for Dennis. Emergency lights come on creating odd shafts of light in the smoke. These emergency lights seem to be aimed arbitrarily*) GIVE ME MY GUN. YOU WANT A GUN? BUY YOUR OWN GUN.

DENNIS. I LIKE THIS GUN.

DAVID. BUT THIS IS MY GUN. MY GUN!

DENNIS. Hey. Careful. Don't squeeze my hand. (*The next shot knocks out the alarm. It moans for a while, gasps, then dies*) SEE WHAT YOU MADE ME DO? (*David and Dennis continue to grapple. They are locked in some impossible intertwinement*)

DAVID. GIVE ME THAT GUN!

DENNIS. YOU'RE CRAZY! YOU KNOW THAT? YOU'RE REALLY CRAZY (*From somewhere a voice is heard. It is quiet at first, then it grows louder. However, there is no urgency or panic in this voice. Mostly it is friendly and inquisitive. It is also Mr. Kropp*)

KROPP'S VOICE. Hello? Hello? Anybody out there? (*David and Dennis stop fighting. They stare at the little box on Linda's desk from which the voice is emanating. It is a nice voice — almost like that of an F.M. disc jockey. But it is odd. When it responds to questions it is just a tad late*) Hello? Hello?

DAVID. (*Into the intercom*) Hello.

KROPP'S VOICE. David?

DAVID. Yes, sir?

KROPP'S VOICE. This is Mr. Kropp.

DAVID. Yes, sir. I know.

KROPP'S VOICE. (*Jovially*) Say, what's going on out there?

DAVID. Well, we're being held at gunpoint, sir.

KROPP'S VOICE. (*Pause*) I see. (*Pause*) Anyone hurt?

DAVID. (*Looking at Kimberly who is reviving*) Uh, I don't think so, sir.

KROPP'S VOICE. (*Pause*) Good! Glad to hear it. (*Pause*) Say, what does this fellow with the gun want?

DAVID. Well, sir, he says he doesn't want to go to St. Louis.

KROPP'S VOICE. (*Long pause*) I see. Can't blame him for that! (*He laughs at his little joke*) Ever been to St. Louis, David?

DAVID. No sir.

KROPP'S VOICE. That's probably why you didn't laugh.

DAVID. Perhaps, sir.

KROPP'S VOICE. Why did this fellow with the gun come up here?

DAVID. Well it's complicated, sir. I think he wants to talk to you.

KROPP'S VOICE. To me?

DAVID. Yes, sir.

KROPP'S VOICE. Well, send him in.

DAVID. (*Stunned*) WHAT?

KROPP'S VOICE. I said, send him in.

DAVID. (*What alternative is there?*) Yes sir. (*He stands for a moment in disbelief. Linda and Kimberly are somewhat surprised also. Finally, David turns to Dennis and says*) Mr. Kropp will see you now.

DENNIS. Great! I'm sure we can straighten this thing out in no time. (*Combing his hair with his fingers*) How do I look?

DAVID. Fine.

DENNIS. Linda?

LINDA. You do. You look fine.

KIMBERLY. My God. My God.

DENNIS. Well, here goes. (*He starts to walk toward the door. Abruptly he turns and runs back to David*) Here. Take the gun, will you? I don't want the boss to think I'm nuts. (*David takes the gun. Dennis then runs to Linda and kisses her full on the mouth*) For luck! (*Dennis opens the door to Mr. Kropp's office. Blinding light pours out. It almost appears that Dennis has stepped into heaven. Or hell. He closes the door behind him. The room is silent for quite some time*)

DAVID. Hmm. (*Then, for want of anything else to do, all three return to their desks and to their work. This is a pretentious effort, however, since there is only a small amount of light in the room and their desks have essentially exploded. Still, they pretend—going through the motions of what used to be their jobs*)

LINDA. (*After a time, speaking mostly to herself*) Maybe he *will* be sent to St. Louis. Maybe that would be best. I don't think he's happy here. Not really.

KIMBERLY. I hate him. (*Pause*)

LINDA. I don't hate him. I feel sorry for him. He seems sort of . . . lonely.

DAVID. Like a little lost tarantula. (*Pause*)

LINDA. Actually, I hope they do transfer him. For his sake.

KIMBERLY. I hope they fire him.

DAVID. I hope they kill him. (*Kimberly and Linda turn and stare at David. David looks embarrassed*) I don't mean that literally, of course. Metaphorically, I hope they kill him. Symbolically. Figuratively. I hope they figuratively kill him. For his sake. You know?

KIMBERLY. I wish I knew what was going on in there.

LINDA. (*To Kimberly*) My computer exploded. Can you look up something on yours?

KIMBERLY. Mine exploded too.

DAVID. Mine still works.

LINDA. Try calling up account file three-one-three-five-three. (*David enters the appropriate commands*)

DAVID. (*Reading from the screen*) "THREE-ONE-THREE-FIVE-THREE DOES NOT EXIST."

KIMBERLY. Are you sure those are the right numbers?

LINDA. Pretty sure. (*To David*) And there's nothing there?

DAVID. (*Busily poking keys*) I'm not finding it.

LINDA. Try calling up Douglas Cockrum's personnel file. (*David again enters the appropriate commands*)

DAVID. (*Reading from the screen*) "DOUGLAS COCKRUM DOES NOT EXIST." (*After a few more attempts*) It's all been purged.

KIMBERLY. Maybe it got purged when the computers exploded.

LINDA. Or maybe somebody purged 'em.

DAVID. Really, Linda. More conspiracy theories? He's only been in there a minute.

LINDA. (*Moving behind David so that she can read his screen*) Okay, look up Dennis Post's personnel file. See if that's still there.

DAVID. (*He punches keys until he has the file on screen. A horrified look comes over their faces*) Oh dear God.

KIMBERLY. David?

LINDA. Oh my.

KIMBERLY. Did they transfer him? (*Linda shakes her head no*) They fired him, didn't they?

DAVID. Worse.

KIMBERLY. (*Afraid to say it*) You mean they've had him . . .

LINDA. . . . promoted.

KIMBERLY. Promoted?!

DAVID. He's in charge of Assembly. He's got Cockrum's old job. (*Kimberly moves behind David in order to see for herself. There is a rattling at the doorknob*) Here he comes!

LINDA. Already?

KIMBERLY. Shhh! (*Dennis reenters. He is a new man. His hair is lying flat. His shirt is tucked in. He is probably on his way to Marshall Field's in order to upgrade his wardrobe. He seems quite calm now — almost suave. The lights come back on as he reenters*)

DENNIS. Hello.

KIMBERLY, DAVID AND LINDA. Hello.

DENNIS. Listen, I hope I didn't upset everybody. There was never anything to get upset about. (*To Linda*) It was pretty much what you figured it was.

LINDA. Oh? What was that?

DENNIS. I'm sorry. What?

LINDA. What did I figure it was?

DENNIS. Well, I'm not sure, exactly. Didn't you figure it was something?

LINDA. I said it was probably nothing.

DENNIS. Yes. That's it! And you were right, too. That's exactly what it was. So just forget I ever mentioned anything, all right? And don't worry about anything I said. Just forget I was ever here, okay? I was never here. (*Dennis exits. Everyone is silent for a moment, waiting for the sound of machine-gun bullets. There is no such sound*)

DAVID. What happened in there?

LINDA: David, when's the last time you actually saw Mr. Kropp?

DAVID. What do you mean?

LINDA. I mean, I've never seen him. I talk to him on this little box, but I've never actually seen him. And, Kim, you don't go in there, do you?

KIMBERLY. No.

LINDA. David, you are the only one that actually goes into his office. So what I'm asking is: when you go in there, do you actually see him? When's the last time you actually saw Mr. Kropp? When's the last time ANYBODY actually saw Mr. Kropp?

DAVID. (*He thinks very, very carefully before he opens his mouth*) When I go into that office —

KROPP'S VOICE. David?

DAVID. Yes, sir?

KROPP'S VOICE Is there anything else I need to take care of?

DAVID, KIMBERLY AND LINDA. (*After a moment of consideration*) No.

KROPP'S VOICE. Well, then, can we get back to work, please? (*All three face front. Their hands are glued to their keyboards*)

KIMBERLY. (*Very quietly*) Oh God, oh God, oh God. (*The lights fade to black*)

doug wright
interrogating
the
NUDE

In 1913, Americans caught their first glimpse of Modern European Art at the Armory Show in New York City. Picasso, Braque, and Brancusi were all represented in the exhibition. The unqualified "hit" of the show, however, was a painting by a little-known French artist named Marcel Duchamp. Its title was *Nude Descending a Staircase*, and it showed a cubist nude set in motion down a series of steps. Reaction to the painting ranged from ridicule to outright hostility. The public had never before seen the most sacred of art's subjects — the human form — treated with such irreverence. The show was picketed, riots broke out, and Theodore Roosevelt took a loud stance against the "immoral" painting. Consequently, it sold for a handsome price. Duchamp became an instant celebrity in this country, and later was credited as founder of the New York Dada movement. His reputation as dandy, philosopher, and "enfant terrible" of the art world almost eclipsed his reputation as an artist.

In exploring the genesis of Duchamp's notorious painting, this play disregards the biographical aspects of Duchamp's life in favor of his body of work: the art itself. Biographical data has been reordered to serve the plot, and many events are purely fictive, including the play's central metaphor, the murder of Rose Selavy. I hope the play captures in spirit the mystery, the morbid whimsy, and the sinister wit of Duchamp's world.

I further hope it examines art's function in a repressive culture. This issue is as topical today as it was almost a century ago. In fact the House and Senate have recently floundered dramatically in their attempts to elucidate the distinctions between art and pornography, innovation and affrontery, decoration and revolt. In Duchamp's day, this debate led to explosive innovations in the art world. It raised voices instead of silencing them. Unfortunately, in our era, the debate has elicited criminal prosecution, and threatened the existence of many of our nation's premier art institutions as well as the freedom of artists to explore certain realms of the human experience. The late Robert Mapplethorpe has assumed the mantle of provocateur once worn by the inimitable Duchamp, and Senator Jesse Helms has adopted the role of Police Inspector. Hopefully, the play resonates with their voices as well as the voices of its historical subjects, reinforcing its concerns as immediate and relevant, not the stodgy stuff of rarified aesthetic theory.

Interrogating the Nude was workshopped at the National Playwrights Conference of the Eugene O'Neill Theater Center, and was subsequently produced by the Yale Repertory Theater and the Actor's Theater of St. Paul. People who have contributed generously to the play's development include Lloyd Richards, Gitta Honegger, Ernest Schier, Michael Miner, Robert Cole, and Christopher Ashley. My warmest thanks to them all.

characters

THE DISTINGUISHED GENTLEMAN: A renowned art historian. He wears thick glasses and is prone to overlong pauses when lecturing, which he does with droll pomposity.

MARCEL DUCHAMP: A slender man with delicate features, a dangerous wit, and a pronounced European flair. A cool exterior, with an impish glint in his eyes.

THE INSPECTOR: A hard-boiled gumshoe. Devoted to Truth, the New York Police Department, and his three little girls.

CONSTABLE PUBLICK: An overworked, underpaid rookie. More fond of gambling in the back room than he is of police work. The "Greek messenger" of the play.

MAN RAY: Swarthy and intense, with all the temperament that comes with artistry. Most vulnerable when it comes to booze and sex.

ROSE SELAVY: A dark, wily creature of formidable passion. Fond of disguise, mystery and deception. Pale skin and a black soul.

NOTES FOR CASTING: *The same actor may double in the roles of* THE DISTINGUISHED GENTLEMAN *and* CONSTABLE PUBLICK. *In addition, the role of* ROSE SELAVY *should be undertaken by a male actor, similar in build and appearance to the actor cast as* MARCEL DUCHAMP.

time

1913. The year of the Armory Show, the first major exhibition of Modern European Art in the New World. A time caught between the lumbering grind of the Industrial Age and the permissiveness of the Roaring Twenties.

setting

The majority of the play occurs in a police precinct on the West Side of Manhattan. The station occupies an isolated space downstage. It may be illustrated by a few well-chosen properties: a large, rough-hewn desk, a low hanging interrogation bulb, and a few stiff chairs. Amber hues spill across the floor, and the air is thick with cigarette smoke. A ceiling fan might turn ominously, casting shadows across the furniture.

During the play's first act, Duchamp may transform the areas surrounding the precinct office into other locales by simply opening traps, drawing curtains, and magically introducing selective objects into the space. Like a ringmaster, he guides the action and worlds of the murder story. He may re-create Man Ray's apartment by snapping his fingers, thereby producing a clothesline dripping photographs, a camera atop a tripod, and a cot. His own studio might be suggested by an easel, a bottle rack, and a bicycle wheel mounted on a stool. Large movie lights placed strategically about the stage allow him to focus action as he chooses, in pools of directed light.

In the second act, the prison cell may be indicated by bars, or a gridlike pattern of yellow light. The locales should flow effortlessly from one to the next, and the actors should move about the space with fluidity.

Far upstage, looming above the precinct office, is a large artist's canvas, rippling with the image of a reclining, classical nude. An imposing staircase rips through the canvas, and winds downward to meet the floor. Its steps are large and splintered, jutting out at uneven angles. It's clear that this climb is a perilous journey. The stairs broaden at the base, opening out to form the stage.

prologue

Silence. Blackness. Lights fade up on the Distinguished Gentleman, who speaks with an authoritative voice from behind a podium.

DISTINGUISHED GENTLEMAN: Like the pilgrims who settled at Plymouth Rock and the Gold Miners who braved the untamed West, so too has the history of American Art enjoyed its pioneers. Just as our forefathers washed upon the shore, Europe's dispossessed, eager to forge cities in the uncharted landscape, foreign artists came to challenge our aesthetic terrain. One such artist was Marcel Duchamp. Although he grew up outside Paris, in a town as picturesque as any found in Monet, at the fledgling age of twenty-eight, Duchamp packed his palette and sailed aboard the S. S. Rochambeau, arriving in New York on June 15, 1915. A reticent intellectual who scorned undue attention, the genteel painter was as content playing chess in quiet repose or enjoying a well-blended tobacco in his signature pipe as he was unleashing new designs upon canvas. He was hardly prepared for his reception in the New World. His painting *Nude Descending a Staircase*, with its curiously disjointed form, its angular composition and altogether strikingly original portrayal of a nude caught in the act of descension, captured the whimsy of connoisseurs and the public alike, and established the young Duchamp as a major force in a country eager to make its own bold strides into art's future. Duchamp spent the majority of his life in New York, eventually abandoning painting for philosophy until his death in 1968. (*Duchamp enters on a bicycle. He stops, parks, and approaches the podium. From his pocket, he pulls a small tin of black paint and a brush. As the lecture continues, he paints a goatee on the Distinguished Gentleman's face. When he completes his work, Duchamp returns to his bicycle, mounts it, and pedals offstage*) After his death, his work was bequeathed to the Philadelphia Museum, where a special gallery now pays tribute to his invaluable contributions to a country forever bent on broadening her horizons. (*Blackout*)

act 1

Lights rise to reveal Duchamp standing at the top of the stairs. To the strains of "La Vie En Rose," he lights his pipe, and slowly descends. At the base of the stairs, he regards the audience for a moment, smiling. Next, he steps forward to confront the Inspector, who sits behind his desk. Lights rise to a full glow in the precinct office.

DUCHAMP. Pardon, Monsieur, I wish to report a crime.

INSPECTOR. Who doesn't? Have you filed a form?

DUCHAMP. A form?

INSPECTOR. Look, pal, it's a big city. Men get their pockets picked. Women get their purses snitched. Kids get their ice cream licked clean off the cone. So don't waltz in here boasting you've got some crime to report. You fill out a proper form, then you make an appointment, like the rest of 'em.

DUCHAMP. I'm afraid it's urgent.

INSPECTOR. Of course it is. They always are. What happened? Somebody lift your timepiece? Somebody spit on your shoes?

DUCHAMP. A woman's been dismembered.

INSPECTOR. What?

DUCHAMP. A nude woman, torn apart limb by limb, the pieces hurled down a staircase.

INSPECTOR. (*Blanching*) My God ...

DUCHAMP. Perhaps you have an appointment available this afternoon?

INSPECTOR. Don't get fresh with me, Mister. If some poor girl's been butchered, that's serious business. Only how do I know you're on the up-and-up?

DUCHAMP. There's a leg on the landing.

INSPECTOR. Hm. Yes. What say I file a report ... (*The Inspector pulls a thick stack of forms from his desk*) You discover the body?

DUCHAMP. I did.

INSPECTOR. Your name.

DUCHAMP. Duchamp. Marcel Duchamp.

INSPECTOR. Come again?

DUCHAMP. D-U-C-H-A-M-P.

INSPECTOR. A foreigner, eh?

DUCHAMP. A Frenchman.

INSPECTOR. And what do you do for a living, er ... ah ... (*The Inspector slips on Duchamp's name*) ... Mr. Doo-Champ? Don't tell me. Let me guess. Import, export. Wines, perfumes, ladies undergarments and the like. I know you Frenchmen.

DUCHAMP. I am an artist, Inspector. (*The Inspector makes a note*)

INSPECTOR. Unemployed. Any idea when the violence occurred?

DUCHAMP. Early morning. Half past one.

INSPECTOR. That's very good. Very exact. An eye for detail, eh, Mr. Doo-Champ?

DUCHAMP. The eye of an artist, Inspector.

INSPECTOR. We'll have our man in no time, won't we?

DUCHAMP. I expect we shall.

INSPECTOR. The scene of the crime.

DUCHAMP. Thirty-three West Sixty-seventh Street.

INSPECTOR. A residence?

DUCHAMP. Mine.

INSPECTOR. Is that so? (*Pause*) I want to send a patrol man around to your place. You won't mind if he does a little poking around? Chalk on the floor, some dusting. Standard procedure. (*The Inspector calls for Constable Publick*) Constable Publick, inside my office, pronto! (*No answer. The Inspector questions Duchamp further*) Your apartment? Burglarized?

DUCHAMP. Nothing to take, Monsieur.

INSPECTOR. Any telltale clues lying about the room?

DUCHAMP. All about. Arms, legs, feet, ribs, somersaulting down the steps ...

INSPECTOR. No, goddammit, I mean the weapon! The machete. The scythe. The hacksaw.

DUCHAMP. A palette knife and two paintbrushes. Camel hair. (*Duchamp presents a small bundle to the Inspector*)

INSPECTOR. Nothing else? A hatchet, perhaps? Not even a lousy breadknife?

DUCHAMP. Wedged beneath the sofa, crumpled in a heap, I

found these (*Duchamp holds forth another bundle*) A feathered hat and some old opera gloves. (*The Inspector takes the bundle and inspects the clothes. The gloves are black and beaded, and the hat is an explosion of dark feathers*)

INSPECTOR. Hm ... expensive fabric. Possibly imported. Goddammit, where is he? CONSTABLE! GET IN HERE! NOW!

PUBLICK. (*From the wings*) Aw, Chief, I got a helluva hand here!

INSPECTOR. YOU HEARD ME! (*Publick enters, cards in hand*)

PUBLICK. Chief, look! A full house. And I'm in hock up to my elbows! Only thing I got left as collateral is my goddamn badge!

INSPECTOR. Remember your post, Constable. You're on assignment. This is Mr. Doo-Champ. Claims he witnessed a homicide around one-thirty in the A.M. I want you to verify his story. Round up the boys and visit this address. Inspect the premises for any disarray. Furniture topsyturvy. Broken windows. Appendages.

PUBLICK. Ah-penda-what?

INSPECTOR. Who told you police work was pretty, Publick? You want a dainty job, paint pictures. Right, Mr. Doo-Champ?

DUCHAMP. Ooh, quite right.

INSPECTOR. Report back to me with your findings. If necessary, notify the coroner.

PUBLICK. Dead dogs on trolley tracks. Squabbles in butcher shops. Explosions in orphanages. I get the dregs, you know that?

INSPECTOR. Take a bucket, just in case.

PUBLICK. I could've played the saxophone. I had the talent. (*Publick exits. He can be heard on his way out*) Cash in your chips, boys, we're on duty!

INSPECTOR. If there's a weapon to be found, he'll smell it out. Kid's got a nose like a bloodhound.

DUCHAMP. The killer used brute force.

INSPECTOR. Bare hands?

DUCHAMP. Without question.

INSPECTOR. You said the body was hacked in pieces ...

DUCHAMP. It was ... fragmented.

INSPECTOR. What are you telling me, that a human being had the strength to tear limbs like drumsticks? Impossible.

DUCHAMP. I was there, Inspector.

INSPECTOR. You saw the assailant?

DUCHAMP. Oh, yes. Indeed.

INSPECTOR. With his bare hands, eh? Well now. My, my. He must've been a mighty big thug. A giant, subhuman son-of-a-bitch. Fire in his eyes, blood on his breath, and fists like cannonballs.

DUCHAMP. He was a slender man with a dapper profile and a pronounced European flair. Adored by a few bosom friends, and a well-kept mystery to the public at large.

INSPECTOR. That's our man?

DUCHAMP. That, Inspector, is he.

INSPECTOR. Doesn't sound like a homicidal mangler if you ask me.

DUCHAMP. It's always the quiet ones in the end. The men you least suspect.

INSPECTOR. The eye of an artist, you say. Let's put that to the test, shall we? You say you saw the man. What was he wearing? His shoes, did they lace or buckle? Come on now! Tell me. Were his fingernails clean?

DUCHAMP. Cordovans, tightly laced. Flecks of paint wedged beneath his nails. Slight, ethereal and fond of good tobacco. (*Duchamp pulls a pipe from his breast pocket and begins filling it from a pouch*)

INSPECTOR. That so? (*The Inspector stares at Duchamp a moment, then begins circling him slowly*) How tall would you say he was?

DUCHAMP. My height, I should say.

INSPECTOR. Is that right?

DUCHAMP. In these shoes.

INSPECTOR. Catch wind of the fella's voice? An accent, perhaps?

DUCHAMP. Decidedly Francaise.

INSPECTOR. That's downright chilling, isn't it?

DUCHAMP. Chilling. (*Duchamp lights his pipe and begins to puff*)

INSPECTOR. You're an artist, eh?

DUCHAMP. I confess. I am.

INSPECTOR. The tools of the trade, that would include ...

DUCHAMP. A palette knife and some camel brushes . . .

INSPECTOR. Let me see your fingernails. (*Duchamp thrusts out his hands*) I think, Mr. Doo-Champ, that we've found our man.

DUCHAMP. Yes, Inspector, I believe we have. Will you be notifying the papers, or should I? (*With amazing speed, the Inspector pushes Duchamp into a chair. There is an abrupt change of lighting; the interrogation bulb glows white-hot, and illuminates the two men while the surrounding stage is plunged into darkness. The Inspector is hunched and sweaty; Duchamp shifts in his seat. It's as if the interrogation has been going on for hours*)

INSPECTOR. I'll teach you to play games with the N.Y.P.D! So you're a killer, are you?

DUCHAMP. Only when provoked, Monsieur.

INSPECTOR. Let's start from the beginning. The night of the crime, you and the victim were alone together in your apartment. Correct?

DUCHAMP. Very much alone.

INSPECTOR. At approximately half past one you slit the victim's throat with the palette knife from beneath your easel, and then you proceeded to subdivide her.

DUCHAMP. Precisely.

INSPECTOR. With your bare hands.

DUCHAMP. Indeed.

INSPECTOR. That's hard to believe. You're a slight man.

DUCHAMP. Perhaps she was a slight woman, Inspector.

INSPECTOR. Who was she?

DUCHAMP. Ooh, a dangerous question . . .

INSPECTOR. Maybe you didn't know her name. Won't be the first time I've seen it happen. Rosy, nameless farm girl comes into the Big City. She's got stars in her eyes, you've got bloodlust in yours. Poor girl winds up buried in a hat box. Wouldn't surprise me at all if you never even thought to ask after her name . . .

DUCHAMP. Eros is eros is a Rose.

INSPECTOR. Huh?

DUCHAMP. Rose. Her name was Rose.

INSPECTOR. She got a last name?

DUCHAMP. Selavy. Rose Selavy. Eros C'est la Vie!

INSPECTOR. French, was she?

DUCHAMP. Of course!

INSPECTOR. One of your own, eh? My God, buddy, you're a bona fide cannibal, aren't you? Now what may I ask was the little lady's profession?

DUCHAMP. My muse. My Mama Dada.

INSPECTOR. Come again?

DUCHAMP. An artist's model. She posed for me in my studio.

INSPECTOR. I've heard that one before. Model. Actress. Chanteuse. All means the same in the end. Five dollars, and a cheap hotel. Just how did she pose, Mr. Doo-Champ?

DUCHAMP. With composure.

INSPECTOR. No, I mean ... how? What did she wear ... when she posed ...

DUCHAMP. She was nude.

INSPECTOR. Of course. You're a healthy man, eh, Mr. Doo-Champ? And this Rose. She's a hearty woman ...

DUCHAMP. What are you suggesting?

INSPECTOR. Let me see if I got this down. She would stand at one end of the room, in the buff, à la naturale, naked under the eyes of God, and you would stand at the other, all by your lonesome, hidden behind an easel, twiddling your brush. Well?

DUCHAMP. I have a small apartment, Inspector. The easel and the bed, they are side by side.

INSPECTOR. Aha. Good. Thank you. So it is, in fact, fair to suggest that your relationship with Miss ... er ... (*Again, the Inspector trips on the name*) ... Sellavie extended beyond professional.

DUCHAMP. I suppose so.

INSPECTOR. Way beyond.

DUCHAMP. Perhaps.

INSPECTOR. That you were, in fact, party to certain acts, private acts, possibly even perversions.

DUCHAMP. Please, Inspector.

INSPECTOR. Painting's not your only pleasure, is it, Mr. Doo-Champ? (*Duchamp is silent*) Come now. I'm a man's man. No need to be shy.

DUCHAMP. We fucked, Inspector, like machines. Together, grinding, pounding with the relentless tenacity of steam engines. The mice beneath the mattress would scurry for their very lives. Afterwards, we would sleep for days, our bones gelatinous and our skins chafed so great was our exhaustion. We would forget to eat for weeks at a time, until we noticed our ribs arching outward beneath our naked skin. Then we would refuel, only to continue our recklessness. Sometimes I would abandon my canvas and paint Rose, her lips a fiery slash and her nipples sunbursts. I would create landscapes on her belly, and portraits on each cheek of her great white ass. Now are you satisfied, Inspector?

INSPECTOR. (*Scribbling madly*) Great ... white ... ass ... (*The Inspector pauses a moment, and rereads what he has written*) I can't put this filth in my report! I'd be discharged! ... Sunbursts, eh?

DUCHAMP. Ablaze.

INSPECTOR. Those paintbrushes of yours should be burned. Profaning human flesh like that (*The Inspector makes a few more hasty notes*) What about her family, eh? I've got to polish my brass and stand tall, and tell some poor parents that they're sweet baby's been pulverized. Any of her people living in this country?

DUCHAMP. Only me.

INSPECTOR. Blood relatives, Mr. Doo-Champ.

DUCHAMP. Rose was my twin.

INSPECTOR. WHAT?

DUCHAMP. We shared the same umbilical cord, Rose and I. For a while, it was feared we shared the same heart.

INSPECTOR. You and this Rose, this tart with the fire on her titties and the faces on her ass, you had the same father? The same mother?

DUCHAMP. We were joined at birth.

INSPECTOR. Sure, sure. Like dogs in jars at Coney Island.

DUCHAMP. Even in the womb, we cuddled. It was predestined, before we entered the world. What could be done, Inspector? Try and resist Fate.

INSPECTOR. I shouldn't be listening to this pornography. I've got a wife and three little girls at home. Brother and sister; it's a fact?

DUCHAMP. Fact or fiction; that's your department, not mine.

INSPECTOR. This Rose. Did she pose for other artists, too?

DUCHAMP. I flattered myself that Rose and I were inseparable.

INSPECTOR. Were you?

DUCHAMP. Apparently not.

INSPECTOR. She doublecrossed you, did she?

DUCHAMP. Rose would lick my eyelashes with the tip of her tongue and promise in a low voice to pose only for me. Only I was privy to every curve, every follicle. Only I could breathe her breath, taste her hollows, reproduce her form . . .

INSPECTOR. Answer the question.

DUCHAMP. Yes. She doublecrossed me.

INSPECTOR. So there were other men.

DUCHAMP. One. Another artist. If she'd betrayed me with countless others, it would have been easier. Better her heart be splintered in a thousand shards than two equal halves.

INSPECTOR. Now this, ah, third party, was he . . .

DUCHAMP. No relation.

INSPECTOR. Thank God! But you knew him . . .

DUCHAMP. He's a photographer. Nudes are his specialty. "Nudescapes," he calls them.

INSPECTOR. "Skintypes," I call them. He took nudie pictures of your twin sister?

DUCHAMP. Made me a cuckold. A clown.

INSPECTOR. And just what does this photographer do with these skintypes of his?

DUCHAMP. Many sell at fashionable galleries at fashionable prices.

INSPECTOR. And the shots of your sister. He sold them to strangers?

DUCHAMP. The pictures of Rose are his private stock. He hoards them like a greedy child stashes sweetmeats. I've heard he keeps them locked in a birdcage, beneath his bed.

INSPECTOR. So tell me. This pornographer. Does he have a name?

DUCHAMP. He calls himself Man Ray.

INSPECTOR. An alias if ever I heard one. We'll need a description to track the son-of-a-bitch down for testimony.

DUCHAMP. By day, he's a man's Man, swilling beer, wine and whiskey in a single glass, spouting dirty stories in the middle of an arm-wrestle.

INSPECTOR. But by night . . .

DUCHAMP. He fancies himself a ladies' Man, going through models the way most artists go through paint, teasing them with his lens, then throwing them away like torn celluloid or spent cigarettes.

INSPECTOR. Or faded Roses, eh, Mr. Doo-Champ?

DUCHAMP. Some have a weakness for bonbons. Others for gadgets and automobiles. But Man Ray, impulsive and heedless, Man Ray had a penchant pour la femme. (*Duchamp stands, steps away from the precinct office, and pulls open a trap door. A red light glows from beneath, suggesting a darkroom*) He once told me: (*Man Ray emerges from below*)

MAN RAY. Christ, Duchamp, you've got me pegged all wrong. It's got nothing to do with lust. It's technique! To get a girl on film, I've got to know her body firsthand. Hell, Cezanne squeezed pears before sketching them, didn't he? It's symmetry. It's proportion. You understand. I use sex to compensate for a bad eye.

DUCHAMP. (*To the Inspector*) I'll never forget the night he confessed the hope that Rose might join his celluloid harem. It was well after midnight; we'd emptied a bottle of pirated booze and took turns sucking on it for flavor. He broached his scheme with due caution; his boorishness had driven all other prospects away . . . (*Lights rise on Man Ray's apartment. Duchamp enters the space. While Man Ray hangs fresh photos on the line, Duchamp fiddles with the pieces on a nearby chessboard*)

MAN RAY. I've had it, Duchamp. The last straw.

DUCHAMP. What now?

MAN RAY. Look at me. Am I such an almighty, everloving PIG?

DUCHAMP. Another model, flown?

MAN RAY. Bernice, the barmaid, works at the Pepper Pot. Two beers and a lobster dinner. I take her back to my place, pull out my camera, and you know what she says to me? "Portraits only from the neck up!"

DUCHAMP. So?

MAN RAY. So if I want headshots, I'll snap my own! But I butter her up. "In a photograph," I tell you, "you can live forever. No wrinkles. No liver spots. Let me stitch you forever in the fabric of time ..."

DUCHAMP. (*Aside, to the Inspector*) Under duress, the photographer turns poet!

MAN RAY. Pearls before swine! "Listen here, Ace"—the tart starts screaming—"When I said I'd come back with you, I never promised a souvenir program!" I offer money; that really lights her fuse. "Oh, hooray! Mr. Vanderbilt! Quick, I'm gonna book myself a cruise!" She heads for the door. "In Paris," I say, "even aristocratic women are dying to pose. On their knees, they beg men like me."

DUCHAMP. And did she?

MAN RAY. "Vive le France!" she says, and slams the door.

DUCHAMP. You've been chasing nudes for months. Try something new.

MAN RAY. Like what? Bowls of fruit?

DUCHAMP. An apple or a melon might weather your insults better than a woman.

MAN RAY. I should photograph Rose.

DUCHAMP. Who?

MAN RAY. Your sister. Rose. She's been kicking around inside my head for weeks. You say she's exotic ... that she bristles with mystery ...

DUCHAMP. Rose—my Rose—in your apartment, on your couch, pinned beneath your camera? No. Why, it's absurd.

MAN RAY. Photographs. That's all I want from her.

DUCHAMP. I know you better than that.

MAN RAY. She's your sister! Private property. Look, if you'd feel safer. I'll tie my hands behind my back and pull the birdie with my teeth, eh?

DUCHAMP. You've never even seen her. She photographs poorly, I guarantee.

MAN RAY. She's your twin, isn't she? People give you the eye; I've seen it. Women, sure, but men, too. Your sister must be—how do you say it?—a "femme fatale." So at least ask her. A little favor between friends. What's to lose?

DUCHAMP. Impossible. Even the suggestion is shocking ... beyond remarkable ...

MAN RAY. Let her speak for herself. Who knows? She might like me. Some women have.

DUCHAMP. Rose has little in common with your downtown girls.

MAN RAY. I'm through with tarts, once and for all. All those big, lazy bodies dripping off stools. I want a woman with a brain to expose as well as a chassis! Push past the flesh to capture the subconscious! Let the camera penetrate the mysteries of the mind. Shoot what's inside a woman's head. What beats in her chest.

DUCHAMP. And Rose is your first candidate ...

MAN RAY. Yes!

DUCHAMP. Pity.

MAN RAY. What do you mean?

DUCHAMP. She'll refuse, of course.

MAN RAY. How do you know?

DUCHAMP. She's private by nature. Rose would never put her dreams on exhibition.

MAN RAY. A thought passes across her forehead. A look. A gesture. SNAP! I've got it on film. She'll never know what hit her.

DUCHAMP. Rose will know. She may turn the camera on you instead.

MAN RAY. Trust me. I can handle her.

DUCHAMP. You say you want to peel her apart ...

MAN RAY. In a photograph ...

DUCHAMP. To expose her core ...

MAN RAY. Landscapes of the mind ...

DUCHAMP. Hm ... Fascinating! (*Pause*) No. Absolutely not. Never.

MAN RAY. WHY THE HELL NOT?

DUCHAMP. You'll thank me in the future.

MAN RAY. DON'T BE AN ASS! JUST ASK HER! WHAT HARM COULD COME OF IT?

DUCHAMP. Harm? What harm indeed ... (*Duchamp breaks free*

from the scene and returns to the Inspector. The lights in Man Ray's apartment fade)

INSPECTOR. This Man Ray fellow. Went behind your back, did he? Lead your sister down the wayward path ...

DUCHAMP. No, Inspector! It was she who approached him. A born strumpet, Rose. The secret trysts. The midnight assignations. She orchestrated them all.

INSPECTOR. All the while, pulling the wool over your eyes.

DUCHAMP. Oh, I knew, Inspector, I knew. In his apartment, in his studio, on backstreets. I was never far behind.

INSPECTOR. Hot on their trail, were you? An amateur detective? A Peeping Tom. Learned more than you bargained for. I'll hazard.

DUCHAMP. My suspicions were confirmed. My darkest fears made palpable.

INSPECTOR. Just what went on behind closed doors?

DUCHAMP. Why, Inspector. I'm surprised. Your wife and your three little girls ...

INSPECTOR. I'm not here to tickle my jollies, Mr. Doo-Champ. I mean business.

DUCHAMP. Then prepare yourself. I'll spare no details.

INSPECTOR. By all means.

DUCHAMP. What follows may unnerve the faint of heart.

INSPECTOR. My heart's granite, Mr. Doo-Champ. Stone. (*As Duchamp launches deeper into his confession, his voice rises in and out of fever pitch, his story a blend of farce and grand guignol. He draws a red silk curtain behind the Inspector's desk. Translucent, behind the curtain, Rose appears, alternating in the light between nudity and silhouette. Duchamp begins his litany, and Rose follows instructions. The inspector watches with all the salacious enthusiasm of a peepshow devotee. "La Vie En Rose" wafts into the room)*

DUCHAMP. I remember the night of their first meeting. I watched from the bed, feigning sleep, while Rose enacted her ritual. Composing herself before the mirror. The soft, pink palette of Fragonard. Her Botticellian hips. Pivoting before the glass, tripling her reflection, like Raphael's Graces in a hedonistic dance. She peeled off her nightdress, and the air caressed her shape. She powdered her body till the skin shone like bone, parched and smooth. (*Rose powders herself with an oversized puff*) She painted her lips violet. Violent violet (*Rose applies lipstick*) Silk stockings like second skins ... (*Rose slips on stockings*) She stepped into shoes with sloping heels and beady-eyed buttons. (*Rose steps into a pair of high-button black shoes*) Gloves to cover the hands which would tousle his hair and plow the furrows of his back. (*Duchamp gingerly unfolds the gloves which lie atop the Inspector's desk. He fondles them gently as Rose pulls on an identical pair which extend to her shoulders*) And then, a crown of magnificent plumage. (*Duchamp considers the hat, while Rose places the same hat on her head*) Ostrich and peacock feathers sprouted from her temples, swooping down in the back to bob at her waist. Finally, she slid into a cloak as black as her soul. (*Rose pulls on a stunning black cloak, dripping beads and bursts of vulture plumes. Rose admires herself, posing for the glass*) At last, the masking was complete. "Where are you going, ma cherie?" I called from beneath the covers. (*Rose pulls the red curtain aside, and steps into full view*)

ROSE. Out.

DUCHAMP. — she replied. With that, she crept from the apartment, confident she'd left me behind. I hid in her shadow; our footfall synchronized. (*Rose slips from the precinct office: Duchamp follows her. Together, they slip in and out of darkness. Rose casts furtive glances over her shoulder, and Duchamp quickly conceals himself in response. They play cat and mouse. The Inspector watches every move*) Together, we dodged the abandoned streets. Finally, she knocked on his door. (*They arrive at Man's Ray's apartment. Man Ray is asleep, tangled in sheets. Rose pounds madly. Duchamp slinks into the shadows to observe*) I lodged myself beneath an open window, out of sight but not of sound. (*Man Ray tosses and turns*)

MAN RAY. Oh God ... Oh, shit ... HEY, WHOA, SHUT-UP! NOBODY'S HOME! GET BACK ON THE STREETS WHERE YOU BELONG! (*Rose pounds harder*) I'M TOO DRUNK, BABY, AND BESIDES, I'M BROKE! FINIS! KAPUT! TRY THE RUSSIAN DOWNSTAIRS! (*Man Ray wraps stray bedding around his waist, then goes to the door. When he swings it open, Rose wafts into the room*)

ROSE. A gracious welcome, Monsieur.

MAN RAY. Christ, I thought you were someone else. Who are you?

ROSE. Close the door.

MAN RAY. Are you lost? Big night on the town, too much juice, now you're all turned backwards? You remember the name of the bellhop, but not the hotel?

ROSE. You American men are all the same. Every woman you meet is a potential prostitute.

MAN RAY. Optimists, all of us. Look, ah, lady. Strangers don't usually drop by in the middle of the night.

ROSE. No? It sounds as though you are quite accustomed to strange ladies banging down your door. Turn out the lights.

MAN RAY. Do I know you? Have we met before? (*Rose turns out the lights. The moon spills across them*) Wait a goddamn minute! With all due respect, this is my apartment! You can't barge in here like a fucking locomotive!

ROSE. Shh! We'd better speak softly. I thought I heard some-one behind me in the dark. They'll be trouble for us both if he discovers my whereabouts.

MAN RAY. Maybe you've got the wrong address.

ROSE. Don't toy with me, please. (*Man Ray opens the door and sticks his head outside. Duchamp, lurking in the shadows, skirts out of sight*)

MAN RAY. HELLO? ANYBODY THERE? YOO-HOO! HEY, ANYBODY LOSE A PRETTY LADY WITH A BIG BLACK HAT —

ROSE. Don't shout! Your mustn't!

MAN RAY. All's clear. Street's empty.

ROSE. Vive Dieu! Perhaps it was the echo of my own footsteps. (*Rose seductively tugs at her garter*)

MAN RAY. Miss, look at me, eh? I'm tired. I'm tanked. Hell, I'm wearing nothing but laundry. How 'bout we meet for breakfast instead ...

ROSE. But you are Man Ray, no?

MAN RAY. How do you know my name?

ROSE. I know much more than your name. Monsieur.

MAN RAY. Oh my God. It's you, isn't it? He said you'd never come! He said it was impossible, you'd be insulted ...

ROSE. Marcel pretends to know who I am and what I want.

That pesky little man is always putting words into my mouth.

MAN RAY. God knows what I expected, but I didn't expect ...

ROSE. Rose disappoints you?

MAN RAY. I didn't say that. (*Rose heads for the door, ready to depart*)

ROSE. Perhaps I am not the woman you hoped for. Perhaps your bottle is better company. (*Man Ray intercepts her*)

MAN RAY. Don't go. Not yet.

DUCHAMP. (*Turns to the Inspector, and remarks*) They were attracted to each other with the pungency of alleycats.

MAN RAY. You came to pose?

ROSE. That depends, Monsieur. If I consent to pose, what will I receive in return? Surely you don't expect me to sneak out of the apartment at absurd hours, incognito, and come all the way here in blinding cold only to shiver naked in front of machinery?

MAN RAY. Ah ... what did you have in mind?

ROSE. Equitable treatment. The same attention you grant your other models.

MAN RAY. My other models all come from the Bowery. I could never treat a lady the way I treat a whore.

ROSE. Why not, if the lady prefers it?

MAN RAY. Then she's no lady.

DUCHAMP. (*Again, makes an aside to the Inspector*) Bravo, Man Ray! He'd hit the nail on the head!

MAN RAY. You've been here two minutes and already we're in hot water. Hell, Duchamp's my best friend. I swore up and down ... I couldn't possibly.

ROSE. Ah! I see now. You're afraid of me.

MAN RAY. Don't be stupid.

ROSE. You've never been afraid of a woman before. They've always been afraid of you, yes?

MAN RAY. Nothing personal, but you move faster than sparks through wire.

ROSE. All I ask is to be kept warm.

MAN RAY. You understand, of course, that in my line of work, indiscretion is an occupational hazard. It's not easy doing what I do. Arranging the model. Assessing every curve.

It's true, I'm an artist, but I'm also a man. Every photograph I take is a triumph of mind over body. Of, ah ... art over urge.

ROSE. It's what renders them provocative, Monsieur.

MAN RAY. Just so I don't alarm you.

ROSE. C'est impossible. (*Man Ray ushers Rose to the bed*)

MAN RAY. Your charm's downright dangerous. It may melt the lens clean off my camera. (*Rose primps on the bed*) We'll begin with a simple portrait. Nothing racy, nothing rude. Now if you'd be so kind — (*Man Ray adjusts his camera, then flips on a lamp to illuminate Rose's face. He stares at her a second, then recoils*) Oh fuck ...

ROSE. My brother and I are bookends, are we not. Monsieur?

MAN RAY. Bookends! I might as well seduce Duchamp ...

ROSE. Prints from the same negative. I've been known to hide in my brother's profile.

MAN RAY. Let's forget the whole thing. Tonight never happened. Understood?

ROSE. Do you know what I risked coming to see you this way? You're not tossing me back onto the street!

MAN RAY. Think of Duchamp. He'd hate us both. We can't do that to him, can we?

ROSE. I'm not his property. I do as I please.

MAN RAY. It's no use! I look at you, but I see him!

ROSE. Perhaps you'd prefer his company. I've never seen two men so enamored of one another. Together at all hours, boozing, carousing. God knows how you pass the time ...

MAN RAY. It's late. I'm warning you. Run along home.

ROSE. You're blushing! (*Rose swivels the camera to capture Man Ray's crimson expression, then dissolves into giggles*)

MAN RAY. You're shameless!

ROSE. I'd envisioned you to be so many things. A coward wasn't one of them.

MAN RAY. Is that a challenge?

ROSE. Perhaps you're only capable of shooting with your camera.

MAN RAY. Who else do you tease behind his back? The milkman in the morning? The postman in the afternoon?

ROSE. Tell me, does this pass for wit on the Bowery?

MAN RAY. How about the policeman on the corner when Duchamp ducks out for the evening paper? Or the dogs who come up the back stoop begging for soup bones?

ROSE. Tu es un homme deguelasse!

MAN RAY. I won't be the first to pluck you, Rose! (*Man Ray climbs atop the mattress, and plants a passionate kiss on Rose's lips. He loosens the sheet around his waist, and, with a flourish, covers them both. Duchamp gasps, and puts his head in his hands. The Inspector bursts forth to halt the action*)

INSPECTOR. That'll do! Yes. Thank you. That's sufficient. The gist of the matter, it's very clear. (*Lights fade on Man Ray's apartment*)

DUCHAMP. He violated every inch. He blackened every orifice. Then he photographed her for hours. Each fragment, each limb. Her backbone, her throat, her belly—a positively encyclopedic array. And he didn't stop there, Inspector. Oh, no. He photographed the two of them together, suspending his camera to immortalize their coupling. She never protested once.

INSPECTOR. Does this room seem warm to you? Look at me. I'm sweating like a pig. (*The Inspector offers Duchamp water from a pitcher on his desk*) Water?

DUCHAMP. Merci. (*They drink*)

INSPECTOR. So how long did the two of them continue to meet?

DUCHAMP. Days. Weeks. On into months.

INSPECTOR. And you knew all along?

DUCHAMP. Rose knew she could never deceive me. We shared the same breath the same heartbeat. She did it to torture me, to prove her independence.

INSPECTOR. Why didn't you call the little lady's bluff?

DUCHAMP. I thought I could torture her by feigning indifference! I proved a poor actor.

INSPECTOR. Months of pentup rage, disrupting the ebb and flow of the body's humors. Building to explosive levels. A walking time bomb, eh, Doo-Champ? Describe the moments which preceded her murder. (*Duchamp stares at the Inspector for a moment. The Inspector coughs, then barks*) Accuracy and detail, sir! Those are my interests!

DUCHAMP. It was late, almost midnight. I sat in one corner of the room, hunchbacked over my easel. Rose stood across from me. The moon spilled through the window and glazed us both. It was pagan, Inspector, in the extreme. (*Duchamp swivels a nearby light to reveal Rose, posing in a loose dressing gown. She stands astride a chaise lounge, decked in pillows. An easel stands nearby. Duchamp enters the scene. Together, they play the following sequence with melodramatic furor, occasionally glancing over shamelessly to gauge the Inspector's response*) I dabbed, dipped, scraped, and stroked. I noticed how with each passing minute, she grew restless, until at last she erupted, a full-blown symphony of nerves. Her toes tapped, her fists contracted, and her eyes darted back and forth like anxious little fish in big glass bowls. I could no longer paint her. She was flickering like a Vita-Graph. (*Duchamp turns on Rose*) Still, goddammit! Aha! See there! You're twitching! Why so fretful? Am I keeping you from something, Rose?

ROSE. At this hour? Yes, Marcel. From bed.

DUCHAMP. Whose?

ROSE. What are you suggesting?

DUCHAMP. I hear you unlatch the door in the middle of the night. I watch from the window as you skulk down the alley. Seems I'm tending a nocturnal Rose.

ROSE. Yes, Marcel, you've found me out! Every night at this hour I go down to the shipyards to visit the sailors. Goodness, is it after midnight? The crew will be frisky. They'll be eager to dock their vessels. Joe carries a heavy cargo, and Freddy is quite the rear admiral. That's what you want me to say, isn't it? Anything to justify your suspicions, to make your anger rightful. (*Rose adjusts the pillows on her chaise, then reclines. She tosses open her dressing gown, revealing her backside, à la Ingres's "Odalisque"*)

DUCHAMP. I added a touch of bitumen to her joints, and smeared her belly in pale ochre. My own body was primed, every fiber pulled taut. I could feel the veins encircling my heart like coiled wire. I contemplated Rose from the rear; the way her hair met her shoulders in tendrils, the small scoop of her back, the pink undersides of her kneecaps. I hated the very bones that slid up and down beneath her skin. (*Duchamp reclines beside Rose, and spits the following accusation in her ear*) You've been posing for him, haven't you?

ROSE. For who? Who are you talking about?

DUCHAMP. He's captured every wrinkle, every pore on film, hasn't he? Those photos hanging in his darkroom are flaps of your hide!

ROSE. Listen to yourself. It's revolting.

DUCHAMP. He never captures the whole, does he? No. Oh, no. He only photographs the pieces. A sloping neck. An ass. Arms that float. He chops you up with that canvas of his, doesn't he?

ROSE. Paint fumes have melted your brain.

DUCHAMP. Is the butcher waiting for you now? Is he blowing hot air on his lenses, polishing then with your discarded drawers?

ROSE. Tell your stories to the mirror. Don't waste your breath on me.

DUCHAMP. Are you too late? Have I kept you too long? Is he all alone with his birdie and nothing to shoot?

ROSE. STOP IT!

DUCHAMP. HOW COULD YOU?

ROSE. GOD, YES, MARCEL! THAT'S ALL I AM! YOUR EMPTY-HEADED PUPPET, YOUR PORCELAIN ROSE! AND NOW MAN RAY HAS STOLEN THE STRINGS!

DUCHAMP. So it's true ...

ROSE. I ran to him in the middle of the night and gave him every curve, every follicle. Da Vinci smile. Botticellian hips. With every flash of his camera, he locked me in time.

DUCHAMP. You're over there now, aren't you? Caged in his little black box. Scorched onto his film! He's got you dangling in his darkroom, staring at him from a thousand tiny frames —

ROSE. Yes! I've spawned myself a hundred times! Man Ray taught me how! Thanks to him, my soul has been squared! NOW, MARCEL, AM I PAINTING THE PROPER PICTURE?

DUCHAMP. He touched you, didn't he?

ROSE. YES! YES, HE DID! Look, Marcel! Here's where he kissed me! And oh — here is where his nails dug into my back! What else can I show you, hm? (*Duchamp lunges toward Roses and attacks*)

DUCHAMP. I took her face in my palms, like wood in a vice waiting to be splintered. I circled her neck with my right arm, using my free hand to find the palette knife hidden in my smock. She let out a squeal, and in a spasm broke away and ran from the room. On the landing, I lunged after her, grabbing her ankle. She slid forward and together, we tumbled down the steps and then ... Oh God forgive me ... I was upon her ... (*Duchamp trembles a moment, then breaks free. Rose recedes into darkness*) I'm sorry. I can't go on.

INSPECTOR. Good Lord, don't stop now!

DUCHAMP. She ... I ... It ... No!

INSPECTOR. Goddammit, Frenchman, I need a full report! You can't stop short of the crime itself!

DUCHAMP. I've told you enough, Inspector. Deduce the rest!

INSPECTOR. What's the matter, Doo-Champ? Story frozen in your throat? The thought of your poor sister, all piecemeal, turning the carpet crimson ...

DUCHAMP. Don't, please!

INSPECTOR. She's gone forever, erased, finished, thanks to you. Takes the wind out of your sails, doesn't it? DOESN'T IT?

DUCHAMP. Stop. I beg you.

INSPECTOR. Pity we can't turn back the clock, eh, Doo-Champ? Pity we can't PICK UP THE PIECES?

DUCHAMP. LEAVE ME ALONE!

INSPECTOR. Can't finished what you started, can you? Last night, when you were tearing up the poor girl, it almost felt good didn't it? DIDN'T IT? Blood pumping. Muscles popping. Heat rising out of your pores. A new feeling, eh, Doo-Champ? Enough to turn a slight man into a giant?

DUCHAMP. Mon dieu!

INSPECTOR. But this morning, it hurts, doesn't it? This morning, you're all alone. No more Rose. No more cheeky portraits. No more sunbursts. No one to blame but yourself. Funny thing about regret. Always arrives too late. (*Duchamp picks up the feathered hat from the Inspector's desk. He strokes it gently. There is a long pause*) Sad son-of-a-bitch. Railroaded your way in here for a reason. Carrying an ugly secret around for hours, weighing you down, breaking your back, making you crazy. Do yourself a favor. Lift the load. Out with it.

DUCHAMP. Swim about in my nightmare, sir, and I guarantee it will soak through your skin. However, if you insist . . .

INSPECTOR. I insist.

DUCHAMP. (*Calmly*) Very well. Rose kept wriggling in an effort to crawl down the stair. Her skin turned to canvas beneath me, rough in texture and drawn tight, its surface crusted with ancient paint. With my palette knife, I carved out her da Vinci smile. A single quick motion ripping through cloth, and Lo and Behold, I'd severed her head. (*Duchamp drops the hat. It lands on the floor*) I disarmed my Venus. (*Duchamp takes the opera gloves from the inspector's desk, unfolds them, and lets them billow to the ground*) With a loud creak, I tore apart her frames at each jointure. (*Duchamp cracks a pencil in half for emphasis*)

INSPECTOR. My God . . .

DUCHAMP. Her legs jerked back and forth and back and forth, like pendulums in manic tempo. Her hips swivelled joyously like gears set free. Like a marionette cut loose from its wire, her limbs fell willy-nilly into blackness. And that, Inspector, was that. (*The Inspector pauses, staring at Duchamp for a long time. Finally*)

INSPECTOR. Monster.

DUCHAMP. You've heard the truth, Inspector. The mystery is solved. Now I suggest you notify the papers. I'll be happy to receive interested reporters in my cell. The whole story, uncensored. I'm prepared to repeat it all.

INSPECTOR. The hell you will.

DUCHAMP. Please, Inspector, there isn't much time! Tomorrow's edition must go to press. You'll be wanting recognition for your outstanding efforts in this case, I'm sure.

INSPECTOR. If I had my way, Frenchman, you'd hang without a word. (*Constable Publick enters. He carries a large, flat canvas*)

PUBLICK. Yo, chief. You positive you gave me the right address? Thirty-three West Sixty-seventh?

INSPECTOR. Quick. What did you find?

PUBLICK. That's just it, sir. Nothing.

INSPECTOR. What?

PUBLICK. A few things, sure. A bicycle wheel. A snow shovel. A bottle rack.

INSPECTOR. That's it?

PUBLICK. And this. It's a painting of some kind. Me and the boys, we couldn't quite figure out what it's supposed to be. (*Publick holds the canvas up for the Inspector. Until the close of the play, the painting is always held so it faces upstage, concealed from the audience's view*)

DUCHAMP. Constable, please! You have my life in your hands.

PUBLICK. Reilly said he thought it was a cello filled with dynamite. Magruder said it looked to him like a fire in a cardboard factory. Me, I just call it ugly.

INSPECTOR. Did you look for bloodstains, did you check under the floorboards, in the closets?

PUBLICK. I'm telling you, Chief, there was nothing. No appendages, not even a finger or a toenail. For this, I lost a full house.

INSPECTOR. Constable Publick, your job is riding on this case. Now are you absolutely sure the place was clean?

PUBLICK. Come on, Chief. If there'd been a human head on the doorstep, I think I would've noticed.

INSPECTOR. Goddamn you, Doo-Champ. What the hell are you trying to pull?

PUBLICK. Pardon me for saying it, Chief, but it looks like you've got another half-wit on your hands.

INSPECTOR. Nobody asked you, Publick.

PUBLICK. I mean it. Probably wandered in here from Bellevue, just aching to spill sick stories into somebody's ear.

INSPECTOR. And I'm the man idiot enough to listen, is that it?

PUBLICK. No offense meant, but it's happened before. Remember that crackpot from the pet shop on Park? Three victims, he said: Mabel, Mattie and Moe. Said he'd strung 'em up with fishing wire in the basement under the store. You book him on three counts of murder, find out later they was all Pekinese. Outside, all around, true blue crimes are being committed, and here we are busting our chops over some Joe who's knocking off pups in the cellar!

INSPECTOR. Do me a favor, Constable. Stick to your job, so I can do mine.

PUBLICK. But if the man's a loon —

DUCHAMP. What would I gain by telling lies? The motive for

murder, it's clear, but the motive for spinning idle stories?

PUBLICK. I'm telling you, Chief, he'll make us look like morons.

INSPECTOR. BUT GODDAMMIT, SUPPOSE HE'S TELLING THE TRUTH! Suppose the victim's here, somewhere in the city, buried in the park or stuffed in a suitcase? We sense a smirk at our expense, and we send him home, scott-free, the charges dropped. The man's confessed a crime, and we've said "No, thank you." Next week, her head arrives by post in Des Moines. The week after, her feet in Fort Lee. HOW WILL WE LOOK THEN, CONSTABLE? EH? I DON'T WANT HER BLOOD ON MY HANDS! This man is guilty until we prove him innocent! UNDERSTOOD?

PUBLICK. Yes, sir.

DUCHAMP. Who is more frightening, Inspector? The man who once in his lifetime commits a crime, or the man who dreams daily of committing a million?

INSPECTOR. Listen, you. I want some hard-boiled evidence, and I want it now? Unless you can back up your ten dollar boasts, I'm going to dismiss this case.

DUCHAMP. What would you like me to tell you, Inspector?

INSPECTOR. THE TRUTH, FOR CHRISSAKES!

DUCHAMP. My truth, or your truth?

INSPECTOR. All right, you spindly little charlatan. I won't be made to look like a dolt. I've spent thirty years here at the N.Y.P.D., and I'm not bending over backwards to satisfy the sordid fetishes of a foreign pervert! When I say hard-boiled, I mean hard-boiled!

DUCHAMP. The painting. I offer you my painting. Solid evidence, no? Canvas, a wooden frame ...

INSPECTOR. What's your painting got to do with anything?

DUCHAMP. You wish to see the body of the victim? There it is.

PUBLICK. Aw, Chief, here he goes! Don't swallow the same bad egg twice!

DUCHAMP. All that remains of my precious Rose is now on that canvas.

INSPECTOR. What the hell are you talking about?

DUCHAMP. After I killed her, her body became my palette. I dipped my brush into her veins to find the crimson hues. The black tones I owe to the vitreous liquid of her eyes, which I split open like plums. To achieve the lighter shades, the yellow and the beige, I crushed her bone with mortar and pestle and ground the powder with the grease from her fat.

INSPECTOR. You smeared the victim all over that slab?

DUCHAMP. Rose is now in my oeuvre forever! The painting was born of her spirit. Listen, and you'll hear it breathe . . .

PUBLICK. Chief, you're following him like a dog with a bone tied to the end of its nose! Don't you see, that's what he wants?

INSPECTOR. THE TRUTH, YOU SON-OF-A-BITCH, THE TRUTH!

DUCHAMP. Buried in the park. Stuffed in a suitcase. Lost in the post. That's what you'd like me to say, isn't it? That, you'd believe!

INSPECTOR. Go ahead. Make it difficult. Make it ugly. We're not leaving the room until the truth gets told. (*Silence. The Inspector stares at Duchamp. Duchamp looks straight ahead without flinching. Constable Publick rocks back and forth on his heels. Seconds tick by*)

PUBLICK. Yo, Chief.

INSPECTOR. Now what?

PUBLICK. One thing you should know. While I was there, in his apartment, Mr. Doo-Champ had a visitor. Fella nearly knocked me down he was pounding so hard.

DUCHAMP. Zut alors!

PUBLICK. I opens up the door and he starts shouting, "Where is he? Where the hell's Doo-Champ?" "Who wants to know?" I says back to him.

DUCHAMP. What did you tell him? Please . . .

PUBLICK. The truth, what else? I told him you were here, sipping tea with the New York Police Department. That's what I told him!

DUCHAMP. Pour quoi lui? Pour quoi maintenant?

INSPECTOR. QUIET, FRENCHMAN! Publick! Did you get the man's name?

PUBLICK. He was down the stairs and out the door before I had the chance. A real suspicious character, Chief. I'll wager he wanted more than a cup of sugar. (*Man Ray bursts into the Inspector's office. He spies Duchamp instantly*)

MAN RAY. There you are! I've been up and down the whole West Side. Hey, Sport, what the hell are you up to? (*Duchamp turns away from Man Ray*)

INSPECTOR. Just one minute there, Mister. You can't just bust in here! This is a highly confidential criminal interrogation. Make an appointment!

PUBLICK. Chief, it's him! He's the one!

INSPECTOR. Mr. Doo-Champ, do you know this man?

DUCHAMP. I've never seen him before in my life.

MAN RAY. WHAT?

INSPECTOR. All right, you. Your name. For official police records.

MAN RAY. Man Ray. What's it to you?

INSPECTOR. You're the pornographer?

MAN RAY. Photographer!

INSPECTOR. Whatever! You're him?

DUCHAMP. Constable Publick, show this man to the door.

INSPECTOR. Don't move, Publick! (*The Inspector towers over Duchamp and places his billy club over Duchamp's throat*) Maybe Mr. Ray here knows where you stashed the body. Maybe that's why you don't want him interrupting our little tete-a-tete. How about that, eh?

MAN RAY. Body? What body? Whose body? FOR THE LOVE OF CHRIST, WHAT THE FUCK IS GOING ON?

INSPECTOR. Your friend here is under arrest for the murder of Miss Rose Sellavie.

MAN RAY. WHAT?

DUCHAMP. It's true, Man Ray. Forgive me.

MAN RAY. That's rich! God, that's good. Tell me, Inspector. What was the weapon? Charcoal? A paintbrush?

INSPECTOR. Perhaps the pornographer knows too much!

MAN RAY. This is ludicrous!

INSPECTOR. Maybe. Maybe not. Husbands shoot their wives. Parents shoot their children. Twins shoot each other. Every night I go to bed sure I've seen it all. Every morning I rise to a world ripe with grisly possibilities.

MAN RAY. Christ, can't you feel your leg being pulled?

INSPECTOR. Murder is no laughing matter! He's already confessed to the charge. What the hell. We'll lock him up.

DUCHAMP. Man Ray, please. You had no business finding me here. Get out. Go home. Leave us alone.

MAN RAY. Duchamp, listen to me. A game's a game, but you're playing with fire. These bumblers swallow your story, they'll lock you away for life.

DUCHAMP. Go. Please. It's the last favor I'll ever ask of you.

INSPECTOR. Nobody leaves!

MAN RAY. I'm telling you, Inspector, it's all a hoax!

INSPECTOR. Look at them, Constable. They're both raving.

MAN RAY. THERE'S BEEN NO MURDER!

DUCHAMP. Don't, Man Ray! You mustn't! Please!

MAN RAY. ROSE SELAVY IS ALIVE AND WELL! (*Blackout, fast*)

act 2

At rise, seconds have elapsed since the close of Act 1. The Inspector, Constable Publick, Man Ray and Duchamp are all still assembled.

INSPECTOR. What? Rose Sellavie, still alive? How can that be?

MAN RAY. He's a milquetoast, a pussycat. He'd kill himself before he'd ever lay a finger on Rose.

DUCHAMP. Lies, all lies. She's dead and gone. Her body's exploded outward in a symphony of color. She's dancing in the clouds above us, Inspector, lilting with the music of shattered violins!

MAN RAY. I know him; he's all talk! A lot of gory stories, sure, but inside, he's gentle as a lamb. Just look at him, for Chrissakes! Look at those hands. They're soft. White. Hairless. They're designed to hold paintbrushes, not knives or pistols! And what about that face, I ask you! You call that a killer's mug? No! A dandy, maybe, but never a crook.

DUCHAMP. Who is more cunning? The criminal who kills with a knife, or the dandy who kills with a glance?

MAN RAY. What proof have you got of the crime? Any physical evidence? Anything at all?

DUCHAMP. They've confiscated my painting. What more do they need?

INSPECTOR. A victim, that's what we need!

PUBLICK. Apartment's clean. I'll stake a fiver on it.

MAN RAY. Don't believe a word he tells you. He makes a living off his fantasies. Never trust an artist, Inspector.

INSPECTOR. Just what do you call yourself?

MAN RAY. A photographer. I don't invent pictures, I capture the truth!

DUCHAMP. My God, Inspector! Is the world so corrupt that a man can't even confess his own crimes? Does the burden of proof now fall on the criminal? What must I do? Must I offer her remains on a plate? Her digits festooned?

INSPECTOR. An elbow or a kneecap might lend a little credibility to your story, Frenchman.

DUCHAMP. I'm warning you, I won't keep quiet. I'll go straight to the papers. Try withholding my story then, and see how the citizens turn against you. They'll storm the station. Men armed with baseball bats. Women brandishing rolling pins. People don't like being duped when they're in danger.

MAN RAY. By all means, Inspector. Host a party for the press. Announce a murder that never happened. Terrify the whole damn city. Then see how they thank you once they learn the truth.

INSPECTOR. Damn you, Mr. Ray. What makes you think you're any better than he is? Violating young ladies and recording it on film. The way I see it, you're both degenerates. You storm in her bellowing, "She's alive! Alive and well!" What brilliant piece of evidence have you put on the table, eh?

DUCHAMP. Bravo! Bravo, Inspector!

INSPECTOR. (*To Duchamp*) Another peep out of you, and I'll string you up in my own backyard. (*To Man Ray*) Answer me. What proof do you have that Rose Sellavie still breathes with the best of us?

MAN RAY. Let me speak to you in private.

DUCHAMP. It's a trick, Inspector!

INSPECTOR. SNUFF IT, FRENCHMAN!

DUCHAMP. But this is an official police interrogation! This man is lampooning it with his cheap theatrics!

MAN RAY. *My* cheap theatrics? That's the pot calling the kettle black!

INSPECTOR. ENOUGH! Constable Publick, I think we'd better give Mr. Doo-Champ here a chance to cool off. I'd like to speak to Mr. Ray alone.

PUBLICK. A pleasure, Chief. (*Constable Publick seizes Duchamp*)

DUCHAMP. Take your knobby little fists off me.

PUBLICK. Thataway, here we go. Upsie-daisy. (*The Constable pulls Duchamp toward the door. Man Ray rushes after him*)

MAN RAY. I'm warning you, sport. You've pushed the limit with this gag. I'm only here to save your skin. I'm not here to play along.

DUCHAMP. The moment before her death, she tried to call out your name, so I tore out her tongue.

MAN RAY. Why, you puny little savage —

INSPECTOR. ANOTHER WORD, AND I'LL SHOOT! (*Publick drags Duchamp away*) A man strolls in here with his confession on a silver platter. Offers up everything but the one piece of evidence we need most. The body! Why? Without it, his claims don't hold piss.

MAN RAY. I'm telling you, it's a FALSE ALARM! You've been had, Inspector! There's no body. There's nothing. It's one big joke! Sick, sure, but that's his humor. The man's a walking circus. As long as you keep jumping through hoops, he'll keep tossing them in your direction.

INSPECTOR. Ever been the victim of a crime, Mr. Ray?

MAN RAY. You're the victim here, not Rose!

INSPECTOR. Ever seen a body gunned down in the heat of passion? Ever been down to the county morgue and peered under the sheets?

MAN RAY. Of course not!

INSPECTOR. Well I have, and it keeps me awake nights, believe me. Clinging to the bedposts, listening to my heart beat. Crime's not the stuff of comedy!

MAN RAY. Hell no. Crime's food on your table. It's a roof over your head. But to Duchamp, it's a good guffaw.

INSPECTOR. Nobody here is laughing, Mr. Ray. That man is hiding something. Something big.

MAN RAY. It's a publicity stunt, that's all. When it comes to the tabloids, he'd stand on his head and paint with his prick, I guarantee.

INSPECTOR. But would he falsify murder?

MAN RAY. Why not? Men test the limits of the law every day to forward their careers. Lawyers, bankers, politicians. Why should an artist behave differently?

INSPECTOR. One thing's clear. He'll never get famous off his painting. I'd sooner let a monkey paint my portrait. A blind monkey with four broken hands.

MAN RAY. You're a policeman. You don't know art from your ass.

INSPECTOR. Don't talk to me about asses and art. Just what do you photograph? Landmark architecture?

MAN RAY. What do you hang up on the wall, other than your hat?

INSPECTOR. I'd sooner hang my hat than that jigsaw nude!

MAN RAY. You couldn't tell a decent painting from a third rate billboard!

INSPECTOR. I don't know much about art, but I do know this: here, we like our models clothed and in one piece.

MAN RAY. Fat ladies and fruit bowls. Weather-beaten barns, standing in wheat. I can guess your taste, Inspector.

INSPECTOR. I'll take an artist who knows the difference between anatomy and geometry, Mr. Ray!

MAN RAY. What's a painting to you, eh? Something to fill up a wall without windows?

INSPECTOR. Me, I got paintings all over the house! Daffodils and dogs and refined folks in velvet. You know why? BECAUSE THERE ARE CRACKS IN THE PLASTER, THAT'S WHY! I'd sooner look at flowers than at water spots. Now this work of his. This naked puppet. Why the hell would any God-fearing American hang one eyesore to cover up another? Eh? EH?

MAN RAY. You want the goods on Duchamp, or don't you?

INSPECTOR. That's what we're here for, isn't it?

MAN RAY. A ten-month show at a fancy Paris gallery, and he couldn't sell a single goddamn painting.

INSPECTOR. That's one helluva surprise. Can a grocer sell rotten fruit? Can a baker sell burned bread?

MAN RAY. YOU WANT THE DIRT, OR DON'T YOU?

INSPECTOR. Shoot.

MAN RAY. Overseas, competition's thick, and Duchamp was pitted against a tough crowd. This Spanish heavy named Pablo and his three henchmen: Brancusi, Braque, and Boccioni. Together, they'd glutted the market. People, pipes guitars — they'd all been shot through the prism. When revolution's in fashion, what's the point? Here in New York, he thought his luck might turn.

INSPECTOR. In America, it's open season? Asylum for every half-cracked looney with a paintbrush in his hand? I hate to disappoint the fella, but here we know the value of our dollar!

MAN RAY. But suppose his painting was connected to a headline crime. A portrait of the victim. Her only remains. Buy the painting, and you'd buy a chunk of history. Edge your way onto the front page.

INSPECTOR. This painting of his. It's gonna hang? In public?

MAN RAY. At the Armory Show, down on Twenty-sixth Street. This story hits the press, and it's as good as sold. Three, maybe four hundred bucks.

INSPECTOR. All this hoopla over a two-bit picture painted by a charlatan? An artsy-fartsy freak show? For this, he'd drag his sister through the mire?

MAN RAY. Worse. He'll drag you right along with her.

INSPECTOR. Not on your life.

MAN RAY. Just wait. Weeks pass, you can't deliver a corpse, you'll look like a buffoon. You'll be washed up. Not even fit for Dog Catcher. (*The Inspector's brow creases. He ponders this for a moment. Man Ray leans in and whispers in his ear, building an ugly scenario*) I can hear them now ... the Constable and his rookie buddies snickering in the back room, taking bets over your job. You married? (*The Inspector nods*) Your better half, crying every night into her pillow, tears of shame ... Children? (*The Inspector holds up three fingers*) Aw, Christ! I don't envy their time in the schoolyard. Their father, a laughing stock. Their little pinafores muddy with the dirt of your once-good name ... (*The Inspector can't take it any longer; his forehead streams sweat, and his bulging cheeks are about to explode. He bolts up and shouts in the direction of Duchamp's cell)*

INSPECTOR. WHY, THAT NO GOOD SKINNY LITTLE SHIT!

MAN RAY. Don't get mad, Inspector. Get even. Hold him here a week, maybe two, behind bars. That way, his story won't leak to the press. The whole affair will blow over without a word.

INSPECTOR. I'll teach him the high price of low pranks. Let him stew a few days, eh? Bread and water. Maybe a coupla hours in the ice house.

MAN RAY. Inspector, I misjudged you. Why, you're sharp as a razor. Make sure he learns his lesson. Now if you don't mind, I'm going home to bed. It's not even noon.

INSPECTOR. Oh, no you don't! You're not leaving this station! (*The Inspector pushes Man Ray into a chair, and the interrogation bulb burns once again*)

MAN RAY. What the hell—you can't—shit!

INSPECTOR. I'm placing you in police custody.

MAN RAY. I came to set the record straight! You almost made an ass out of yourself before the whole precinct!

INSPECTOR. Don't get in a conniption. One person holds the key to this case. I'd like her to confirm your story.

MAN RAY. You don't mean ... no ... no, that's impossible.

INSPECTOR. We'll let the victim speak for herself!

MAN RAY. Oh God ...

INSPECTOR. Getting hot and bothered, eh? What's the matter now?

MAN RAY. DON'T DRAG ROSE INTO THIS MESS. She's a fragile lady. She'll melt under the heat, I know it!

INSPECTOR. All she has to do is show herself, and you're home free.

MAN RAY. You'll never find her.

INSPECTOR. Why not?

MAN RAY. You don't know where to look.

INSPECTOR. She sounds recognizable enough. Don't play innocent with me. I know every lurid detail, from the first leer to the final thrust.

MAN RAY. Duchamp told you ... he said that Rose and I ...

Ha! He sure paints some bold pictures, doesn't he?

INSPECTOR. Come clean. Where is she?

MAN RAY. I haven't got a clue.

INSPECTOR. Bullshit.

MAN RAY. She's gone into hiding.

INSPECTOR. How do you know?

MAN RAY. A letter. This morning, Rose slipped a letter under my door.

INSPECTOR. Why didn't you say so before? Hand it over, quickly. Let's have a look.

MAN RAY. No! I mean, I can't. Shit. I don't have it.

INSPECTOR. That letter may be your ticket to freedom.

MAN RAY. Give me half an hour. I'll dash over to my place, and come back, letter in hand.

INSPECTOR. Don't insult me, Mr. Ray. You stay put, where you belong. I'll send the Constable. He'll rifle it down. Where'd you stash it? WELL? Speak up, Mr. Ray. I can't hear you. (*Man Ray pulls a letter from his jacket*)

MAN RAY. What luck! Right here, in my pocket. Christ, I feel like a fool.

INSPECTOR. How convenient. Give it here.

MAN RAY. No, I can't do that. This letter, it's highly personal. In fact, it's embarrassing. Rose would have my head.

INSPECTOR. I'll have you head if you don't give it here. (*The Inspector lunges for the letter*)

MAN RAY. NO! GODDAMMIT, INSPECTOR! Have some respect for a man's privacy. If you don't mind, I'll read it to you. (*Man Ray unfolds the letter. Lights rise on a landing halfway up the stair. Rose reads the following*)

ROSE. Mon Cher: We've been found out! The weasel accused me of an affair. Last night while I was posing for him, he attacked me with his palette knife. It's no longer safe for me here. I've decided to disappear until his temper cools. I cannot tell you where I am, or how long I will remain. Rest assured that I am safe. My poor Man Ray. My poor, poor Marcel. You loved one another like brothers, and now I've splintered you apart!

MAN RAY. I'd prefer to skip this next part.

INSPECTOR. Read!

ROSE. Goodbye, Man Ray. When I sleep, I'll crease my pillow, and in my dreams thrust my lips between your flanks. (*Rose smiles, inserts the letter in the envelope, and licks its edges. She kisses the outside of the note*) Rose (*Rose fades into darkness*)

INSPECTOR. Downright primal, isn't she?

MAN RAY. The fact is she's gone. It's pointless to go looking.

INSPECTOR. Hand over that note. It's hereby property of the N.Y.P.D.

MAN RAY. No go, Inspector! (*The Inspector lunges again. Man Ray shreds the paper and stuffs it into his mouth. The Inspector circles Man Ray's neck with his right arm, and twists Man Ray's left arm behind the back of the chair with his free hand. He holds him for a moment. Strips of paper protrude from Man Ray's mouth*)

INSPECTOR. Publick! Get in here! Now! (*Publick enters, cards in hand*)

PUBLICK. Here, sir!

INSPECTOR. If he so much as blinks, Constable. (*Publick aims his pistol at Man Ray. The Inspector loosens his grip and handcuffs the photographer. He pulls the tattered letter from Man Ray's mouth. He inspects the soggy remains*) I suspected as much. An overdue bill for photographic supplies. I suggest you pay it. (*He dumps the bill into Man Ray's lap*)

MAN RAY. I burned the letter.

INSPECTOR. There is no letter. There never was. A final, flimsy stab at concealing the true crime. She's dead all right, and you had a hand in her killing.

MAN RAY. WHAT?

INSPECTOR. Pieces all fit. Touching, really. Doo-Champ takes the rap to protect you. Comes in unbeknownst, spills his guts, claims he's killed her all by his lonesome. You protect Doo-Champ, screaming she's still alive, improvising phony letters.

MAN RAY. Why would the two of us want Rose on ice?

INSPECTOR. Colleagues. Soulmates. Bloodbrothers. You share the same crackpot notions, the same artistic mumbo jumbo. Maybe Rose had your number. Maybe she knew too much …

MAN RAY. About what?

INSPECTOR. Scoundrels able to scoff at murder must be guilty of greater crimes themselves.

MAN RAY. Rose isn't some tart, plucked off the Bowery! She's the man's sister!

INSPECTOR. Rape your sister, and I'll hazard to say you could kill her as well. Admit it. There's a stiff, blue body collecting dust in your apartment. You don't want the Constable rooting around for fear he'll find it. Well, the game's over. What's your address?

MAN RAY. None of your goddamn business.

INSPECTOR. Hear that, Publick! He knows he's cooked.

MAN RAY. Forty-second Street, across from the station.

PUBLICK. On my way, Chief.

INSPECTOR. Break down the door if you have to.

MAN RAY. Do me a favor, Constable. Keep the hell out of my darkroom. (*The Inspector and the Constable smile knowingly at one another*) Open the door, and you'll bleach all my prints! Photographs, that's all you'll find!

PUBLICK. Dirty pictures, Chief, whaddaya bet? Back in a jiff. (*Publick exits*)

MAN RAY. He's done it, goddamn him. Wrapped us all up in the palm of his hand. (*The Inspector frees Man Ray from the chair*)

INSPECTOR. Stand up. Hands over your head. Face front. Follow me, you little photophile. (*The Inspector escorts Man Ray across the stage and into the prison cell. Duchamp sits on a cot*) Meet your cellmate, Mr. Ray. (*Duchamp and Man Ray don't acknowledge one another in the Inspector's presence*) Now you two bastards behave yourselves. You aren't dealing with amateurs. Constable Publick and I are trained to contend with the blackest of hearts. Rapists, pimps, cardsharks, thieves. Even con artistes like yourselves. (*The Inspector grins and exits*)

MAN RAY. You're digging a grave deep enough for both of us. I hope you know that.

DUCHAMP. No one asked you to come. You blustered in here of your own accord.

MAN RAY. I hope this joke has one helluva punchline, 'cause so far, I don't get it.

DUCHAMP. "Joke," Man Ray?

MAN RAY. You've got that poor oaf out there tripping over his own gumshoes. And he's not laughing, Duchamp. He's got steam coming out his ears!

DUCHAMP. The law is the law, yes? And when you're a civilized person, and you have broken the law, what do you do? Confess, of course.

MAN RAY. The Constable's ransacking my apartment right now, certain he'll find a body!

DUCHAMP. He won't. He never will.

MAN RAY. It doesn't matter! The next time a landlord finds bones in his furnace, or a leg washes up in the East River, they'll pin it on us!

DUCHAMP. Quiet. You'll give him ideas.

MAN RAY. Art and Crime, they don't tango. Shit, I never thought I'd see the day when a mixed metaphor could land a man behind bars.

DUCHAMP. What did you tell the Inspector?

MAN RAY. That you're after a few headlines. You want your painting reproduced in the paper, so it sells. That's how you'll be remembered, sport. A con man who was short on cash.

DUCHAMP. What does it matter, eh? History reinvents us all.

MAN RAY. So what have you done with Rose?

DUCHAMP. Ah! Ma petite fleur! The little blossom, she has dropped off the vine ...

MAN RAY. Well, the "Little Blossom" is due at my studio at midnight tonight! In full bloom, right down to her skivvies. A deal is a deal.

DUCHAMP. I can't. She can't. *We* can't.

MAN RAY. But I bought her a present. I was hoping she'd wear it at tonight's sitting. It's a mink stole with a genuine diamond clasp.

DUCHAMP. You shouldn't have.

MAN RAY. I didn't. It's rabbit with rhinestones, but in a photograph, who can tell for sure?

DUCHAMP. Indeed. In a photograph, things aren't always what they seem.

MAN RAY. So whaddaya say? Can I expect her?

DUCHAMP. No.

MAN RAY. Come on. I know Rose. The witching hour strikes, and she'll be dying to take to the streets.

DUCHAMP. Her days of Hide-and-Seek are through.

MAN RAY. You wanna put money on that?

DUCHAMP. I can do many things, Man Ray, but I cannot raise the dead.

MAN RAY. Stop jerking me around, Duchamp!

DUCHAMP. It's best that it happened this way. Without warning, in a spasm of passion. It would be unbearable for you to see Rose and know it was for the last time. You'd be devastated. You'd smash your camera.

MAN RAY. You owe me!

DUCHAMP. (*Definitively*) I am not playing make-believe, Man Ray. The deed is done.

MAN RAY. You're . . . you're not bluffing?

DUCHAMP. Decidedly, no.

MAN RAY. But she's your muse. How will you keep painting?

DUCHAMP. I'll find a new subject. The time for sluggish nudes, rotting poultry and dormant pears has passed. I'll paint engines, glistening oil, their levers erect and their cogs red-hot.

MAN RAY. What about me, eh? I finally find the perfect model, a woman unlike any other, and what happens? My best friend offs the lady!

DUCHAMP. The time had come. She gave birth to your photographs and to my painting. That's enough, isn't it?

MAN RAY. But you should see these prints! They're phenomenal! They're more than just portraits. They're X rays of the soul. Her image leaps off the page and burns itself onto your eyes! I've captured shots of something private, something never before revealed on film. A fantasy. A piece of the mind! Beyond naked. Beyond nude. A secret, utterly and completely exposed. I can't ler her go. I won't let her go. Not now.

DUCHAMP. You have no choice.

MAN RAY. A parting shot, eh? At least give me that.

DUCHAMP. No.

MAN RAY. WHY NOT?

DUCHAMP. She's lived between us long enough. Alone in my

head, what was she? An amusing fancy. A whim. After I introduced her to you, what was she then? A shared secret, nothing more. It's time we let the world take her.

MAN RAY. How can it, if you've killed her?

DUCHAMP. Try creating one thing without killing something else. What are your photographs but thin memorials to moments long dead? When Rose was invisible, she was ripe with possibility. Once you trapped her in your camera, she was done for. Certain face, certain hair, certain hat ... certain death.

MAN RAY. So that's it. We've lost her.

DUCHAMP. No! Not at all. Not if her murder is headline fare! The whole world will remember her, experience her, read about her in the paper, overhear on the stoop ... "Rose Selavy, why yes, she passed her every morning!" or "I saw her that night, walking toward his apartment, toward certain death ..." If the world gives Rose a place in its memory, then what has she become?

MAN RAY. ... a work of art?

DUCHAMP. Precisely!

MAN RAY. BUT MOST ART IS KEPT IN FRAMES, PAL! ON THE WALL!

DUCHAMP. Art belongs in cages, Man Ray? Confined for our amusement, bolted to the wall like a prisoner shackled to his torture rack? God forbid it should yank itself free, step into the third dimension and start breathing! God forbid it should wander the sidewalks, stroll in and out of buildings, or worse still, swing open the heavy door of a police station, yes? (*Pause*)

MAN RAY. God, sport.

DUCHAMP. Hm?

MAN RAY. (*Smiling1*) I'll miss her. (*Duchamp puts an arm around Man Ray's shoulder in mock sympathy*)

DUCHAMP. C'est la vie! (*The lights fade on the prison cell, and rise on the precinct office. The Inspector sits at his desk. Publick enters. He is carrying a small, square birdcage made from wire. It is filled with photographs. Publick hurries to the Inspector's desk*)

INSPECTOR. Over here, Publick, on the double!

PUBLICK. Bad news, Chief. Place was clean.

INSPECTOR. Not again!

PUBLICK. A camera, a tripod, a bed, nothing else.

INSPECTOR. What about the darkroom?

PUBLICK. Geez, you wouldn't believe it! Gams, elbows, faces, bellies all hanging off a clothesline. Downright eerie, I call it.

INSPECTOR. But no body?

PUBLICK. Nah. Only pictures.

INSPECTOR. What the hell have they done with her? Is she clogging the plumbing, or nourishing plants?

PUBLICK. Did find this, though, under the bed. Looks like a birdcage. It's got her name carved in the base. Good for fingerprints at least.

INSPECTOR. Better than that, Constable! You've found his private stash. His little box of nasties.

PUBLICK. Shall I have a look-see?

INSPECTOR. Keep your pants on, Constable. Our interest in these photographs is purely professional. (*The Inspector takes the birdcage from the Constable and sets it on his desk. He opens the door and withdraws the photographs. The Constable peers over the Inspector's shoulder throughout. The Inspector stares at the first photograph*)

PUBLICK. Got to watch out with a girl like that, Chief. Too hot for her own good. I'll bet when she kisses, it blisters.

INSPECTOR. Small wonder she drove two men to murder. Haunting, eh, Publick? His twin all right, no question. Same lofty brow . . .

PUBLICK. Same smirk, only lipsticked . . .

INSPECTOR. Same rigid nose . . .

PUBLICK. Same eyes, too, like they was looking past your body all the way to your shadow . . .

INSPECTOR. Same hands, tapering at the tips . . .

PUBLICK. Selfsame bones in his cheeks . . .

INSPECTOR. Same chin . . . (*Publick blanches*)

PUBLICK. Yo, Chief! You don't suppose —

INSPECTOR. Hm? What?

PUBLICK. Nah, forget it. My wife, she's always telling me I got a dirty mind.

INSPECTOR. Say it, Publick! What's on your mind?

PUBLICK. Without the hat . . . without the gloves . . . take 'em away, Chief, and what are you left with? (*The Inspector considers this for a moment. He tears a photograph, removing the top portion, presumably the hat. He then tears along the bottom, presumably removing the gloves. He stares at the torn image in his hand*)

INSPECTOR. That's impossible. It's preposterous. Worse, it's obscene!

PUBLICK. Got to learn to keep my mouth shut, that's all.

INSPECTOR. IT'S THE ANSWER! BY GOD, PUBLICK, YOU'VE HIT ON IT!

PUBLICK. Nah, you're bluffing. You're making fun.

INSPECTOR. ROSE WITH HER SKIRTS HIKED IS NO ROSE AT ALL! (*The Inspector collapses backwards into his chair*) Constable, water! (*Publick pours a glass of water for the Inspector, who downs it in a singe gulp*)

PUBLICK. Jesus, Mary and Joseph! Spit on 'em, Chief! (*Publick spits on the photographs*)

INSPECTOR. Bring 'em here. Bring 'em now. The time has come at last, Publick. I want to see them both exposed. (*Lights rise on the prison cell. Publick approaches*)

PUBLICK. Follow me. Bring your dancing shoes. You've got some fancy footwork ahead of youse. (*Duchamp and Man Ray exchange a look. Publick escorts them into the precinct office*)

MAN RAY. You caught us red-handed, Inspector. Murderers, both of us. Duchamp's got his paintbrush, and I've got my lens.

DUCHAMP. New York is not safe.

MAN RAY. Not till we hang.

INSPECTOR. In galleries, boys, or in gallows? (*The Inspector chortles at his little joke*)

MAN RAY. You want a formal confession? Start writing. I'll dictate.

INSPECTOR. Not so fast, Mr. Ray. Not until I've heard testimony from Rose Sellavie.

MAN RAY. I've told you, that's impossible.

INSPECTOR. Not anymore. I've found her.

DUCHAMP. You've what?

INSPECTOR. Oh, it wasn't easy, gentlemen. She kept herself well camouflaged. An ingenious creation, your Rose.

Nevertheless, I've rooted her out. With his eagle eye, Publick here led me straight to her source.

PUBLICK. First time ever my dirty mind paid off.

MAN RAY. It's a trick. Duchamp. He's goading us, hoping we'll slip and say too much.

INSPECTOR. Care to comment, Mr. Doo-Champ?

MAN RAY. Don't say a word.

INSPECTOR. Go ahead. Don't be shy. Tell us her true whereabouts. (*Duchamp is silent*) Shall I jog your memory, Mr. Doo-Champ? How about a friendly hint? Constable, give Mr. Doo-Champ the opera gloves. (*Publick hands Duchamp the opera gloves from the Inspector's desk*)

MAN RAY. Oh, shit!

INSPECTOR. Now if you'd be so kind ... put them on. We're waiting. All eyes are on you, my friend.

MAN RAY. Don't do it, Duchamp!

INSPECTOR. PUT THEM ON! (*Duchamp slips on the gloves*) Nice. Very nice. How do they fit? The proper size? Now, Constable, give Mr Doo-Champ the piece de resistance. The crowning flourish. Pass him the plumes. (*Publick passes the feathered hat to Duchamp*) Go ahead. I'm eager to meet the lady. Slap on the feathers, and let's see her smile. Marcel Doo-Champ alias Rose Sellavie! Oh, my, my. What a vision. A sight for sore eyes. Look, Publick, we've got a guest. Rose Sellavie, right here in our midsts!

Duchamp takes the hat; he puts it on. He now stands in his well-tailored suit, the opera gloves, and the cascade of feathers. The effect is lodged somewhere between transvestism and the surreal.

Rose appears at the top of the stairs. She is dressed as Duchamp in a matching men's suit. She also dons opera gloves and her signature hat. In addition, she carries a pipe. Together, she and Duchamp create mirror images of one another. Duchamp climbs the stairs to join her, where they strike a tableau.

The Inspector is agog. Publick's eyes bulge in disbelief. They watch the following action with varying degrees of wonder and horror. Even Man Ray, accustomed to Duchamp's trickery, is astonished.

The actor who has portrayed Rose until this moment in the play will now be referred to as Duchamp II. Both actors will on occasion assume Rose's liquid identity in their retelling of the mystery.

DUCHAMP II. So, Inspector. You think you're clever enough to nip Rose in the bud?

DUCHAMP. (*As Rose*) Bon jour, Man Ray! Still shocking the ladies with your big flash bulb?

MAN RAY. (*Blushing*) Well hello, Rose!

INSPECTOR. I'll be goddamned ... Constable, mark every word said. NOW! I want it all down in writing. Each stutter. Each pause. (*Publick pulls out a pad and pencil and begins scribbling furiously while the twin Duchamps spill their story*)

DUCHAMP. (*As Rose*) Who can truly be contained by a single sex, Inspector?

DUCHAMP II. Rose was my masterpiece. (*The two Duchamps descend the stair, their limbs intertwining in a series of bizarre poses*)

DUCHAMP. (*As Rose*) He composed me piece by piece, joint by joint ...

DUCHAMP II. Limbs lifted from other notorious nudes.

DUCHAMP. Fragonard's flushed bathers dipping rosy thighs into brine. Boucher's supine Venus. Da Vinci's bulbous Leda and her ornithological Zeus. (*Duchamp slithers up to the Constable, who sweats nervously*) Ooh-la-la! Such a sweet baby-faced Constable. Perhaps after the interrogation we could get together for an apertif, oui?

PUBLICK. Aw, Jesus! (*Duchamp distracts him by stroking his hair, meanwhile slipping the gun from his holster*)

DUCHAMP II. She was born of a thousand paintbrushes and a thousand years ...

INSPECTOR. Dress it up any way you like, Doo-Champ. It's still perversion, pure and simple! (*Duchamp fires the gun into the air. There is a sudden, unexpected change in lighting. The stage goes black, except for the large film lights. For the remainder of the confession, Duchamp and Duchamp II manipulate the lights, alternately focusing on each other, Man Ray, the Inspector and the Constable to heighten the telling of their tale*)

DUCHAMP. (*As Rose*) Nightly in his dreams we would dance!

DUCHAMP II. Remember, ma cherie, among my friends, or sitting over chess, how I painted you with words ...

DUCHAMP. (*As Rose*) Often you dropped only my name like a musical note torn from a score ...

DUCHAMP II. "My sister Rose composes prose."

DUCHAMP. (*As Rose*) Or my favorite: "When Rose arose—

DUCHAMP II. (Completing the pun)—I rose, aroused!" (*They laugh, a sound that falls somewhere between infectious and maniacal*)

DUCHAMP. (*As Rose*) Soon I began leaving traces of myself about your studio.

DUCHAMP II. You wrote lewd limericks and slipped them beneath my pillow.

DUCHAMP. (*As Rose*) "A question, mon cher, of intimate hygiene, yes? Should one put the hilt of the foil in the quilt of the goil?"

DUCHAMP II. Pornographic puns taped on the mirror ...

DUCHAMP. (*As Rose*) "An incesticide must sleep with his mother before killing her, oui?"

DUCHAMP II. It wasn't long before Man Rays curiosity was piqued! (*Duchamp hurls the spotlight on the Inspector. Duchamp II aims his spotlight at Man Ray*)

INSPECTOR. When you first requested to photograph Miss Sellavie, were you aware of her true identity?

MAN RAY. Duchamp said he had a twin sister. Is that so strange? (*Duchamp and Duchamp II quickly turn the lights back on one another*)

DUCHAMP II. Rose knew how he treated his Bowery models.

DUCHAMP. (*As Rose*) I'll teach him to tangle in my bed of thorns.

DUCHAMP II. I had to give her shape so she might carry out her plan. My own body was the canvas.

DUCHAMP. (*As Rose*) Gloves, gowns, a magnificent hat rimmed with ostrich plumes!

DUCHAMP II. Manners to befit a femme fatale.

DUCHAMP. (*As Rose*) You textured me with erotic appetites and a decadent heart.

DUCHAMP II. A saunter.

DUCHAMP. (*As Rose*) A pout.

DUCHAMP II. Soft eyes.

DUCHAMP. (*As Rose*) And a sneer.

DUCHAMP II. I poured my breath into you and—

DUCHAMP. (*As Rose*)—Voila!—

DUCHAMP II. You were complete. I followed my own footsteps out the door and into the darkness. (*Duchamp II keeps his spot aimed at Duchamp, and Duchamp shines his at Man Ray*)

DUCHAMP. (*As Rose*) Man Ray, please! Your turn. Don't be coy . . .

MAN RAY. It was late. I'd been slurping down vodka faster than it would pour. He . . . She . . . Rose showed up at my door.

DUCHAMP II. As I opened my mouth to speak, it was her voice which poured forth, not mine.

DUCHAMP. (*As Rose*) "It sounds as though you're quite accustomed to strange ladies banging down your door."

MAN RAY. He shut out the lights so I wouldn't see his face. You gotta believe me. I had no idea!

DUCHAMP. (*As Rose*) He lifted my chin and we kissed!

DUCHAMP II. I felt his whiskers push against mine.

DUCHAMP. (*As Rose*) Trembling, he peeled off my gloves!

DUCHAMP II. I felt his tongue nibbling on the tips of my fingers.

DUCHAMP. (*As Rose*) Finally, he heaved my skirt above my head, plucking the garters with his teeth!

PUBLICK. Aw, cripes!

MAN RAY. I've ducked under a thousand skirts, but this was a first! The floor slid clean out from under me! Rose was gone, and there was Duchamp, pinned down on the mattress, his eyes gleaming as if to say—

DUCHAMP. (*As himself*) Aha! I caught you.

DUCHAMP II. As quickly as Rose had consumed me, she disappeared. Man Ray had sought his psyche and found me hiding there. (*Duchamp II swivels his light away from Duchamp, and focuses it on the Inspector. Both the Inspector and Man Ray are illuminated for the following exchange*)

INSPECTOR. And still you took pictures. Even after you'd learned the truth.

MAN RAY. I was in a slump! I needed a change.

INSPECTOR. Pity you only had one other sex from which to choose.

MAN RAY. You bet your bottom dollar he posed for me. I made

him promise a whole series, right there on the spot! The phantom Rose, torn out of his subconscious and captured on film!

INSPECTOR. Flesh-peddlers, both of you.

MAN RAY. You don't understand one whit, do you? (*Duchamp II focuses on Duchamp, and Duchamp moves his spot to catch Man Ray*)

DUCHAMP. (*As Rose*) Man Ray flatters himself, Inspector. He pretends to know the whole story when he only knows a fraction.

MAN RAY. There's more?

DUCHAMP. (*As Rose*) Why, the painting, of course!

DUCHAMP II. Our confession's complete, Rose. It's time to stop.

DUCHAMP. (*As Rose*) Why, Marcel. It's the best part. (*Duchamp moves his spot from Man Ray to the Inspector*)

DUCHAMP II. But the Inspector has a pristine mind and a Christian soul. He has no interest in your lecherous tales.

DUCHAMP. (*As Rose*) No interest in our debauchery? No interest in our final, ruthless night of orgiastic frenzy? None at all?

INSPECTOR. Now hold on a minute, Doo-Champ. I'd like to hear what the little lady's got to say.

DUCHAMP II. Ah, mon dieu! I am crimson with shame, Inspector.

DUCHAMP. (*As Rose*) Late one night, Marcel came home to find me waiting at the top of the stair. (*From opposite sides of the stage the Duchamps focus their lights on the staircase. The beams crisscross, causing shadows to multiply. Duchamp races to the top of the stairs. Duchamp II stands at the base. In countless shadows, their figures dance across the rear of the stage. The two men shoot their lines back and forth at one another in a tense, staccato rhythm. While the language of the scene is playful, the intensity with which they spar suggests that the stakes of this game are deadly*) Psst! Mon Choux!

DUCHAMP II. Who is it? Who's there?

DUCHAMP. (*As Rose*) I'm ready to pose.

DUCHAMP II. No, ma cherie. Not tonight.

DUCHAMP. (*As Rose*) It was "no" yesterday.

DUCHAMP II. And it will be "no" tomorrow.

DUCHAMP. (*As Rose*) I won't move a muscle. You can capture every inch.

DUCHAMP II. There's no light.

DUCHAMP. (*As Rose*) We'll burn candles.

DUCHAMP II. There's no paint.

DUCHAMP. (*As Rose*) Your box is full.

DUCHAMP II. My palette knife is dull.

DUCHAMP. (*As Rose*) Newly sharpened.

DUCHAMP II. You devil, Rose. You'd let me hang by a noose to hang by a nail.

DUCHAMP. (*As Rose*) You've let me live inside your head, you've let me walk the streets, and still you won't commit me to canvas.

DUCHAMP II. You've been photographed? Isn't that enough?

DUCHAMP. (*As Rose*) I'm lodged in your brain, and a few camera flashes won't burn me away.

DUCHAMP II. Let Man Ray execute you. He's a better shot.

DUCHAMP. (*As Rose*) Don't you have the courage to execute your own creations?

DUCHAMP II. You're a hollow pose. An erotic fancy. Eros C'est la Vie! Your whole life is built on nothing more than a pun.

DUCHAMP. (*As Rose*) So what's the risk? Start sketching.

DUCHAMP II. I'm sorry, ma cherie, but you're not worth the paint.

DUCHAMP. (*As Rose*) Then model for me.

DUCHAMP II. What?

DUCHAMP. (*As Rose*) Go ahead. Slip into my skin.

DUCHAMP II. Don't be foolish. What for?

DUCHAMP. (*As Rose*) You won't paint my picture, so what can I do? Paint my own, yes? A self-portrait. You'll be my mirror.

DUCHAMP II. You'll trap me into painting your portrait, eh, Rose?

DUCHAMP. (*As Rose*) Oui, Marcel. Frame you into framing me.

DUCHAMP II. Duping oneself can be dangerous.

DUCHAMP. (*As Rose*) You were never one to refuse a good game.

DUCHAMP II. Ah, Mon Dieu! If my reputation's at peril, I accept!

DUCHAMP. (*As Rose*) So pass me your pipe. (*Duchamp II passes his pipe to Duchamp. Duchamp puffs on it, dropping Rose's demeanor. Duchamp II now adopts the role of Rose)*

DUCHAMP II. (*As Rose*) "A Rose pose, oui? A femme fatale? A camp vamp? Pass me on the street, and your prick'll prickle! Ooh-la-la!"

DUCHAMP. "A Recipe for Rose" by M. Duchamp. "Wrench her thighs from Rubens/And her bottom from Boucher/Deck her crotch in Delacroix/And her mind in Yves Tanguy!"

DUCHAMP II. (*As Rose*) "C'est magnifique! Bravo, Marcel! Bravo!

DUCHAMP. "Madames and Monsieurs, for my next feat—a poem in paint! Rose deflowered! Petal by petal and piece by piece!"

DUCHAMP II. (*As Rose*) "No! Boo! Hiss!"

DUCHAMP. "Quiet in the Gallery!"

DUCHAMP II. (*As Rose*) "But we've seen it before! Every carnival huckster! Every medicine show! The magician! The coffin! The lady! The saw!"

DUCHAMP. "But in my trick, we don't put back the pieces!" (*Darkly*) The game is over, Rose. (*Duchamp II drops the role of Rose immediately. Now the two men are virtually indistinguishable. They stalk one another, up and down the stairs*)

DUCHAMP II. What's this? You can't change the rules midstream.

DUCHAMP. Life from a new angle, yes?

DUCHAMP II. But I created you. I'm flesh and blood. You're just an idea!

DUCHAMP. The shoes have been switched.

DUCHAMP II. No. This is absurd.

DUCHAMP. The table's turned.

DUCHAMP II. Don't come any closer.

DUCHAMP. Your mind's in a somersault, ma cherie!

DUCHAMP II. I never wanted to pose for you!

DUCHAMP. Your shadow has stolen your soul, yes?

DUCHAMP II. You're mad! Your eyes are both prisms! Your head's jammed with puzzles!

DUCHAMP. And it is scrambling the pieces ...

DUCHAMP II. Loopy Leonardo! Raving Rembrandt!

DUCHAMP. I joined your limbs together; I can unjoin them, too!

DUCHAMP II. You'll make my breasts obelisks and my bottom

cubes! (*Duchamp pulls a palette knife from his pocket and raises it in the air. It glistens. Simultaneously, Duchamp II withdraws his palette knife. They circle one another dangerously*)

DUCHAMP. GET AWAY FROM ME!

DUCHAMP II. YOU THINK I'M WEAK, DON'T YOU? I'M MUCH STRONGER THAN YOU! I'VE WEATHERED THE ANCIENTS, AND I'LL WEATHER THE MODERNS, TOO!

DUCHAMP. GO AHEAD!

DUCHAMP II. CUT INTO ME!

DUCHAMP. WE'LL BLEED TOGETHER!

DUCHAMP II. A FINAL PORTRAIT — ROSE! (*Each raises his knife, ready to strike*)

Lights play across the large upstage canvas. With a loud creak, accompanied by the deafening sound of machinery, the canvas collapses. The two Duchamps disappear, and an enormous rendering of Duchamp's painting "Nude Descending a Staircase" is revealed. The staircase itself seems to jut forth from the painting's composition. The image of the fragmented nude consumes the stage.

Blackout. In the darkness, an eerie, almost muted voice whistles the song heard earlier, "La Vie En Rose." Lights slowly rise on the precinct office. The Inspector is all but collapsed at his desk. Publick stands with his mouth open. Man Ray breaks into slow, loud applause. Duchamp II stands at the base of the huge painting, smiling ever so slightly. He has removed the gloves and the hat, and now stands dressed in his customary suit. The original Duchamp is nowhere to be seen.

INSPECTOR. (*Slowly, then gaining momentum*) Riddle me this, Mr. Artiste. Mr. Painter. Why didn't you stay at home today and read the paper over coffee, or have a nice mid-morning nap? Why didn't you go for a stroll in the park? Why didn't you throw yourself under a fucking train? WHY THE HELL DID YOU WALK IN HERE AND DESTROY MY DAY? THIS MORNING I KNEW RIGHT FROM LEFT, BUT THIS AFTERNOON I CAN'T BE SURE! MEN TURNING INTO WOMEN AND BACK AGAIN AT THE DROP OF A HAT! ARMS AND LEGS AKIMBO IN THE AIR! I DON'T LIKE IT! IT'S NOT THE WAY THE WORLD SHOULD BE!

DUCHAMP II. (*Gently*) Then perhaps you can paint a different picture for us, yes?

INSPECTOR. Get out. GET THE HELL AWAY FROM HERE. I don't want the two of you crowding decent prisons, rabble-rousing and spreading ideas. Constable, throw them out.

DUCHAMP II. Inspector, please. You should sit down, put your feet up, have a smoke, (*Duchamp II gently steers the Inspector into his chair*) Thank you so much for your hospitality. (*Publick gestures toward the scale rendition of the painting which he confiscated earlier from Duchamp's apartment*)

PUBLICK. What should we do with the evidence, Chief?

INSPECTOR. Fuel for the boiler room!

DUCHAMP II. Let me keep it, Inspector.

INSPECTOR. Go ahead, Doo-Champ. Keep hacking yourself up and calling the pieces art. Where will it get you? You'll be a laughing stock.

MAN RAY. Spoken like a seasoned critic, Inspector!

PUBLICK. And the skintypes, Chief? (*Man Ray makes a quick grab for the birdcage*)

INSPECTOR. I've no use for them, Mr. Ray. I shudder to think of their value to you. (*Man Ray reaches into the birdcage and pulls out a single photograph of Rose, which he offers to Publick*)

MAN RAY. Souvenir? (*Publick hesitates, then grabs the photo and stuffs it in his jacket. Man Ray smiles*) Sometime I'd like to take a picture of what lurks in your head, Constable. I bet we could blow the roof off this joint.

INSPECTOR. OUT, I SAID! OUT, OUT, OUT!

DUCHAMP II. Au revoir, Inspector. Constable. May your days be filled with more manageable crimes! (*Duchamp II picks up his painting, and heads for the door. Man Ray follows with the birdcage. On his way out, Duchamp II gestures toward the coat rack standing idly by the exit. Under his breath, he whispers to Man Ray*) Psst! Coat rack! (*Slyly, Man Ray scoops up the coat rack. The two men slip out the door and into darkness*)

INSPECTOR. Lock the door. Bolt the window. I don't want them coming back. (*Publick follows orders*)

PUBLICK. Helluva day, Chief.

INSPECTOR. What say we keep today's adventures to ourselves.

PUBLICK. You kidding? Who'd believe it?

INSPECTOR. We'll file no report. We'll keep mum before the Commissioner. Agreed?

PUBLICK. Me, I been playing cards all day. I ain't heard a peep, or seen nothing.

INSPECTOR. Thatta boy, Publick.

PUBLICK. Just another routine day.

INSPECTOR. Ordinary. Uneventful.

PUBLICK. Downright dull. (*Both men attempt to sit calmly. Instead, they form a cacophony of fidgets and ticks. A long pause. Finally, the silence becomes unbearable. Publick clears his throat, and wipes the sweat off his brow*) Yo, Chief. Don't say I told you, but there's whiskey hidden in the lockup. You could use a glass. We could both use a glass. Back in a jiff. (*Publick exits. The Inspector sighs*)

INSPECTOR. My screws must be loose. I must be losing my mind. I got my own nightmares. I don't need his. (*He shakes his head a moment, sighs again, then shudders in an imaginary breeze. After shaking off the chill, he opens the day's newspaper. The door of the precinct office opens. Rose Selavy — this time, portrayed by Duchamp — enters, in full regalia. The gloves. The hat. The magnificent wrap. She pauses to speak*)

ROSE SELAVY. Pardon, Monsieur. (*The Inspector lowers his paper. Rose smiles*) I wish to report a crime ... (*The Inspector stares, transfixed*)

ANNE COMMIRE has also written *Shay* (published by Samuel French, Inc.), first performed at the O'Neill Theatre Center's National Playwrights Conference. Subsequent productions of *Shay* include the University of North Carolina (with Beverly Bentley), A.C.T. in San Francisco and Westport Country Playhouse (with Sada Thompson), Playwrights Horizons (with Marge Redmond), King's Head, London and Little Lyceum, Edinburgh (with Libby Morris), and the Los Angeles Public Theatre (with Karen Morrow). *Put Them All Together* (cited in *Best Plays of 1978–79* and published by Samuel French, Inc.) was first performed at the O'Neill Theatre Center's National Playwrights Conference. Subsequent productions include the McCarter Theatre, Princeton, New Jersey and the Los Angeles Public Theatre (both with Mariette Hartley), Loretto-Hilton Theatre, the Westchester Theatre and the WPA, New York (both with Alma Cuervo). *Melody Sisters* was first performed at the O'Neill Playwrights Conference with a subsequent production at Yale Repertory, 1989. The play is now in rehearsal at WPA in New York. In 1987, she co-wrote and directed *The NOW Show* at the Dorothy Chandler Pavilion, a two-hour variety show featuring over 100 "stars" celebrating the 20th Anniversary of the National Organization for Women. She is the recipient of a CAPS grant and a Rockefeller grant (fulfilled by being playwright-in-residence, Yale University, 1980–81); has written for television and film; and has written a biography with Mariette Hartley for G. P. Putnam's.

She was commissioned by Paramount to write the screenplay for *I'm Dancing as Fast as I Can.* Edgar Scherick and Michael Eisner were delighted with the results. Not so Jill Clayburgh. Her script is still considered the "one" that should have been filmed.

She was commissioned by CBS to write the teleplay *Rebel for God* (preferred title *My Sister Arlene* or *About the Nun Who Sued the Bishop*). She has also written for Dick

Cavett, Washington D.C.'s *Spread Eagle Review*, and Mariette Hartley's one-woman show.

PHILIP KAN GOTANDA is a third-generation Japanese American playwright and screenwriter. He holds degrees in Japanese Art from the University of California and in law from Hastings College of Law. Mr. Gotanda spent eighteen months studying pottery in Japan and performed extensively as a songwriter-singer early in his career.

Among Mr. Gotanda's awards and honors are a 1990 Guggenheim Fellowship, the NEA Playwriting Fellowship, four Rockefeller Awards, the New York Drama League Award, the McKnight Fellowship, a TCG/NEA Directing Fellowship, and numerous others.

Over the past ten years Mr. Gotanda has been one of the seminal forces in bringing Asian American stories to the public. Whether it be in the feature film *The Wash*, based on his own play and screenplay adaptation, or in his plays *Yankee Dawg You Die*, *A Song for a Nisei Fisherman*, *The Dream of Kitamura*, and *Fish Head Soup*, Mr. Gotanda has introduced to the American public a better understanding of the historical richness and emotional complexity of Asians living in America.

His play *The Wash* opened at New York's Manhattan Theatre Club in October 1990, directed by Sharon Ott. The production then moved to the main stage at the Mark Taper Forum in Los Angeles in January 1991. His newest work, *Fish Head Soup*, received it's world premiere at Berkeley Repertory Theatre in March 1991, co-directed by Oskar Eustis and Sharon Ott. He also has an upcoming Japanese-language version of his play *A Song for a Nisei Fisherman* tentatively scheduled for the 1991 season at the Bunkaza Gekikjo in Tokyo. Mr. Gotanda is presently writing commissioned works for South Coast Repertory Theatre, the Mark Taper Forum, and the Manhattan Theatre Club.

In addition to playwriting, Mr. Gotanda is actively involved in screenwriting. *The Wash* received a successful theatrical release and was seen most recently on American

Playhouse. He is presently writing a three-part dramatic miniseries for PBS's Great Performance Series about a Japanese family coming to live in America. Mr. Gotanda plans to be directing his own works in the near future.

Mr. Gotanda resides in San Francisco with his wife, actress Diane Takei.

RICHARD STRAND wrote his first play in 1976, a one-act entitled *Harry and Sylvia*. That play won two national awards, was published by Hunter Press, and premiered at the Theatre Arts Corporation of Santa Fe, New Mexico, in 1977. *Clown*, a full-length version of *Harry and Sylvia*, was premiered by Chicago's Victory Gardens Theater in 1981. Dennis Zacek directed.

Other plays include *Pigeons* which was presented by Circle Repertory Theatre's Directors Lab and *Can You Hear Me, Mr. Szczepanski?* which has been performed by Chicago New Plays Company in Chicago, Cab Theatre in New York, and Circle Repertory Theatre's Directors Lab.

Mr. Strand's script *The Bug* was premiered at the 1989 Thirteenth Annual Humana Festival at Actors Theatre of Louisville. It has been translated into German and, under the title *Fehler im System*, has been broadcast on German public radio. There have been several other productions in this country, including Theatre in the Square (Marietta, Georgia), Mill Mountain Playhouse (Roanoake, Virginia), Live Arts Theatre (Los Angeles), and The Z Collective (San Francisco).

Mr. Strand's most recent script, *The Death of Zukasky*, premiered at the 1991 Humana Festival at Actors Theatre of Louisville.

Mr. Strand also works extensively in technical theatre. He served for six seasons as the technical director for Thunder Bay Theatre in Michigan, he is the author of several published articles on technical theatre, and currently serves as the production manager for Skokie Centre East. He is a member of the Dramatists Guild and The American Blues Theatre.

DOUG WRIGHT's plays include *The Stonewater Rapture, Interrogating the Nude, Dinosaurs, The Rorschach Child, Lot 13: The Bone Violin*, and a musical, *Buzzsaw Berkeley*, written with Christopher Ashley and Michael John LaChiusa. Productions of Mr. Wright's work have appeared at the Yale Repertory Theatre, the WPA Theatre, and Lincoln Center Theater, among others. Television credits include pilots for producer Norman Lear. He received a bachelor's degree in art history from Yale University in 1985 and an MFA in playwriting from NYU in 1987, and is a member of the Dramatists Guild. Originally from Texas, he currently resides in New York City.